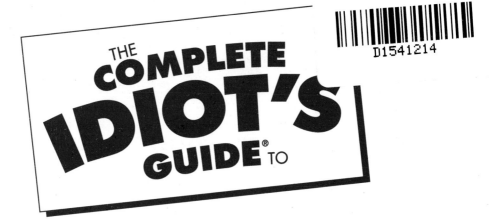

THE COMPLETE IDIOT'S GUIDE® TO

The Supreme Court

by Lita Epstein

ALPHA

A member of Penguin Group (USA) Inc.

Publisher: *Marie Butler-Knight*
Product Manager: *Phil Kitchel*
Senior Managing Editor: *Jennifer Chisholm*
Development Editor: *Nancy D. Lewis*
Production Editor: *Janette Lynn*
Copy Editor: *Drew Patty*
Illustrator: *Jody Schaeffer*
Cover/Book Designer: *Trina Wurst*
Indexer: *Aamir Burki*
Layout/Proofreading: *Angela Calvert, Cynthia Fields, Mary Hunt*

Contents at a Glance

Contents

Foreword

Even among Beltway insiders, the Supreme Court is often referred to as the "Secret Branch" of our government. While the Executive and Legislative branches thrive on (and their elected officials therein live or die by) publicity, the Supreme Court remains relatively private, holed up behind the walls of their "Marble Palace." Much of the general public knows something about the White House and the Legislature, yet few know anything more than superficial facts about our judicial branch.

But while the idea of a "secret" branch of government might have some conspiracy theorists salivating, the Court is anything but clandestine. The building is open to the public (and I urge anyone traveling to Washington, D.C., to be sure to put it on their sightseeing list), the cases are posted on-line, and their decisions and opinions are publicly available and often reported in the media.

The Supreme Court's reputation as a *Secret Branch* actually stems from much more noble factors. In this age of intense scrutiny of public officials, *messaging* by spin doctors tuned to focus groups and polling data, and a tsunami of real-time data, facts, and sound-bites, the Supreme Court and its justices quietly, assiduously, almost monk-like, pursue their judicial aims with at best only a modicum of praise and little glory. They are the interpreters of our Constitution, defenders of the ideals and vision of our founding fathers and the legal traditions of our nation. And for the justices and their staff, having the honor of upholding the highest legal standards for our nation is fanfare enough.

I had the privilege of seeing this first-hand when I worked in the Court's Marshall's Office. While many of my day-to-day duties were mundane tasks, the position allowed me the opportunity to get to know the building, its history, its processes, and its close-knit, almost familial staff. I was honored to work briefly in Justice O'Connor's chambers and those of retired Justice Brennan, sit behind the justices on the bench during oral arguments, and even once shot baskets with Justice Thomas on the basketball court located in the Court's attic, a facility that we called "The Highest Court in the Land."

The book you now hold in your hands is a guide for inquisitive people with a real desire to know more about the Supreme Court; its justices, their decisions, and just what goes on behind closed chamber doors. From the appointment of judges to the process by which a case is put on the docket and finally reviewed, argued, and decided. It is an excellent overview of the Court, from its earliest days tucked away in the lower levels of the capitol building to its high-profile role in *Bush* v. *Gore*.

When I first began work at the court, I was nearly straight out of college, no student of law, and almost absolutely ignorant of the procedures, operations, and mechanisms of that august place. I wish I had had this book then to give me a better introduction to our noble judiciary and its influential role in our nation's history and our daily lives.

—Chris Chesak

Chris Chesak served in the Marshall's Office of the Supreme Court from 1993–1994 before embarking on a career in development for nonprofit conservation organizations. He is a graduate of Wesleyan University and now resides in Boise, Idaho.

Introduction

Most of us don't realize how much power nine unelected men and women wield in this country today. Just about every major decision that impacts our lives, our businesses, and our cities and towns has been decided through a series of court battles that end at the doorstep of the Supreme Court.

Congressional and state or local legislation can be overturned and government regulations can be stopped if someone successfully challenges them through the court system and finally makes it to the Supreme Court on appeal. Elections can even be decided behind closed doors at the Supreme Court, as we saw in 2000 when the Court decided to stop the counting of votes and award the election to President Bush against the decision of the Florida State Supreme Court.

Although many people think of the most controversial issues when the Supreme Court is mentioned, such as abortion, gay rights, or pornography, every year 100 cases are heard by the court that deal with these types of controversial issues as well as mundane ones, such as whether a case should be tried in the courts or arbitrated.

Building the Court, a Seven-Part Story

I'll take you through history to discover how this powerful institution was built and then peek behind its massive columns to explore how its decisions are made today.

Part 1 looks at **"Building the Court,"** which is an institution unique to the United States. While some countries are trying to imitate it today, our founding fathers developed this vision of one all-powerful court, which did not exist anywhere else in the world. Building that one-of-a-kind institution was not easy and has faced many challenges and changes over the years. Take a trip back in history to find out how this most powerful institution was built.

Most of the credit for **"Shaping the Court's Foundation"** can be given to the leaders of the Court that we'll meet in Part 2. You may think that legal scholars were responsible for its legacy, but actually the most successful shapers were known for the leadership skills. Meet the leaders and their contributions to today's Court legacy.

More than 7,000 cases knock on the doors of the Supreme Court each year. In Part 3, **"Peeking Behind the Columns,"** we'll go behind the scenes and see how all this work gets done. Starting with a peek behind the closed door of case conferences to see how cases are decided, we'll then move on to meet the key staff who help the justices get their work done each year.

Now that you know the basics of how the Court was built and how it does its work, we'll delve into the key decisions the Court made in recent years that impact our lives. Starting in Part 4 with **"Forming Government Rights,"** we'll see how the Federal government fights it out with states in an ongoing battle for control over issues such as electing our leaders, deciding on taxes, educating our kids, and determining our property rights.

Next we'll delve into the Court's role in **"Assembling a Social Structure"** in Part 5. Yes the Court does make decisions that control what we can do with our bodies, as well as who gets hired and who gets accepted at colleges. They also rule on our privacy rights and our freedoms.

Everyone wants to be tough when **"Dealing with Criminals"** and we'll review the rules for doing that in Part 6. We all get mad when a criminal goes free on a technicality. Learn what creates those situations and the recent Court rulings that impact evidence collection, arrests, and punishments.

Finally, we'll end our tour on the topic of **"Taking Care of Business"** in Part 7, which starts with looking at the rules that keep businesses moving and then moves on to the fine print of contract law and ends with rules that impact our work environment.

Helpers

I've designed a few aides to guide you more easily through this book:

Just the Facts

Facts and figures aren't everyone's favorite reading material. I've placed these helpers around the book for folks who like to read more about the details.

Court Connotations

Legalese can be hard to understand. I'll explain some of the more difficult terms.

Living Laws

I'll translate some of the key decisions in the laws we live by today.

Supreme Sayings

Quotes some of the people impacted by Court decisions, as well as some of the leading former and current justices.

Trademarks

All terms mentioned in this book that are known to be or are suspected of being trademarks or service marks have been appropriately capitalized. Alpha Books and Penguin Group (USA) Inc. cannot attest to the accuracy of this information. Use of a term in this book should not be regarded as affecting the validity of any trademark or service mark.

Part 1

Building the Court

The idea for one Supreme Court that would be the single, all-powerful court to which all appeals could be taken was unique to the new American colonies. Building that Court was a challenge that has gone through many changes. In this part, we'll look at how the court was designed, how you take a case to the highest court in the land, and how politics impact the makeup and decisions of that Court.

Chapter 1

Designing the Court

In This Chapter

- ◆ Magna Carta and the Constitution
- ◆ Court's jurisdiction
- ◆ Congress's role in court design
- ◆ Sizing it right
- ◆ Finding a home

Today the U.S. Supreme Court is the final word on whether an action taken by the Congress, the president or any one of the states is constitutional. The Court is a major force in the balance of power among our three branches of government—judicial (Supreme Court), legislative (Congress), and executive (president).

That was not always the case and its role was not clearly spelled out in the Constitution. In fact some of the framers of the Constitution even disagreed with moves to increase the power of the court, supporting instead states' rights.

In this chapter, we'll explore the formative years of the Supreme Court and how the initial architects of the Court built what is today a powerful court system.

Revisiting the Colonies

Before I get into the details about the formation of the Court, I need to set the stage for its design. The early settlers who came to the United States were from England—a country with no written constitution and a system of three separate courts:

- ◆ the King's Bench

- ◆ the Common Pleas court

- ◆ the Lord Chancery and the Chancery Court

In England at that time, civil matters were taken before the Court of Common Pleas and criminal matters were taken before the King's Bench. If someone wanted to appeal the civil findings in the Common Pleas court, a petition to the monarch could be made for special relief. These petitions were handled by the Lord Chancery and the Chancery Court.

Just the Facts _____

In England and Wales today the highest court official is the Lord Chancellor and Britain's highest court is under the control of the House of Lords. Prime Minister Tony Blair proposed in June 2003 that Britain separate the highest court from the political undercurrents of the House of Lords and create a Supreme Court. That proposal was still under consideration at the time this book was written.

The American settlers immediately determined that they wanted a written constitution, which was one of the key agreements in the Mayflower Compact. The first agreement put in writing in the new colonies was the 1639 Fundamental Orders of Connecticut that stated to "mayntayne the peace and union of such a people there should be an orderly and decent Government established according to God." The American Revolution was started with another key written document, the Declaration of Independence, which served as the precursor for the Constitution.

Supreme Sayings _____

"The concept of the Rule of Law—that laws should be enacted by democratically elected legislative bodies and enforced by independent judiciaries—is fundamental to a free society. The knowledge that there are certain basic rights of the individual that are enforceable even against the state has been the hallmark of our system of governance."
—Supreme Court Justice Sandra Day O'Connor in her book, _The Majesty of the Law_

The primary influence for that Constitution was the Magna Carta, which was signed by King John of England in 1215 to settle a power struggle with his warring barons. The Magna Carta limited the king's powers. It is this limit of powers that serves as a basis for the concept of our "Rule of Law" today. The colonists held steadfastly to what they believed the Magna Carta stood for—a government built around laws that protect the rights and liberties of its citizens.

Key principles found in the Constitution that stem from the Magna Carta include:

1. the establishment of an independent judiciary,

2. the requirement that people are tried quickly in criminal cases,

3. the requirement that people are given due process if charged with a crime,

4. guarantee of freedom of religion, and

5. the requirement that taxes are approved by a legislative body that is representative of the people.

In fact, the Magna Carta is still a major inspiration for Supreme Court rulings today. Supreme Court Justice Sandra Day O'Connor in her book, *The Majesty of the Law*, says the Supreme Court cited the Magna Carta in more than 50 written opinions in the last 40 years.

What's Set in Stone

Although the drafters of the Constitution had very specific designs for the legislative and executive branches, little was said about the structure of the judicial branch. The first section of Article III states, "The judicial power of the United States, shall be vested in one Supreme Court, and in such inferior courts as the Con-gress may from time to time ordain and establish. The judges, both of the supreme and inferior courts, shall hold their offices during *good behaviour*, and shall, at stated times, receive for their services, a compensation, which shall not be diminished during their continuance in office."

The second section of Article III gives an overview of judicial power that includes all cases:

◆ "in law and equity, arising under this Constitution, the laws of the United States, and treaties made, or which shall be made, under their authority;"

◆ "affecting ambassadors, other public ministers and consuls;" and

◆ "of admiralty and maritime jurisdiction."

Court Connotations _____

Essentially the idea of holding on to a judgeship during "**good behaviour**" grants a person the position for life. A judge can be impeached if he or she commits a crime or is found guilty of serious judicial misconduct, but only one judge in the history of the nation ever faced an impeachment trial—Samuel Chase. That was in 1805. The case was more a political battle between the two parties at the time, the Federalists and the Republicans, than a trial relating to a crime or charge of serious judicial misconduct. The impeachment attempt failed and no other federal judge in the history of the court has faced impeachment.

In Article III, the Supreme Court also was given a role in controversies:

- ◆ "to which the United States shall be a party;"

- ◆ "between two or more states;" and

- ◆ "between a state and citizens of another state; between citizens of different states; between citizens of the same state claiming lands under grants of different states, and between a state, or the citizens thereof, and foreign states, citizens or subjects."

The second section of Article III also spells out jurisdiction for various cases. Those "affecting ambassadors, other public ministers and consuls, and those in which a state shall be party, the Supreme Court shall have original jurisdiction. In all the other cases before mentioned, the Supreme Court shall have appellate jurisdiction, both as to law and fact, with such exceptions, and under such regulations as the Congress shall make."

Appellate jurisdiction limits the role of the Supreme Court to one of hearing appeals from lower courts. The Supreme Court cannot just pick out a controversial issue and make a decision. It must act on cases brought to the court based on actual disputes raised in actual court cases.

The Constitution also mandates that "trial of all crimes, except in cases of impeachment, shall be by jury; and such trial shall be held in the state where the said crimes shall have been committed; but when not committed within any state, the trial shall be at such place or places as the Congress may by law have directed."

There are no details of how the court system should be set up, how many courts there should be, or how many judges there should be. All these details were left to the first and future Congresses.

Legislating the Court System

Even though the politicians were cautious about how much power was to be given to the Supreme Court, they certainly wanted to quickly establish a court system. The first bill of the first Congress was the "Judiciary Act of 1789." The big debate then, as it still is today, was how much power should be given to the states and how much should be retained at the federal level.

Those advocating states' rights opposed giving the new federal courts too much power, while the proponents for a strong federal court system saw that as the only way to build a strong federal government. In order to bring together the union, a strong federal court system that had the power, if necessary, to overturn state court decisions was the only way to enforce uniformity of national standards. The alternative was 13 independent jurisdictions, which likely would have led to anarchy and a breakup of the union.

The 1789 Legislation: Justices, Districts, and Circuits

In the 1789 legislation, Congress mandated that the Supreme Court have a chief justice and five associate justices. Congress decided the Court would meet twice a year on the first Monday of February and the first Monday of August. The rest of the time the justices traveled around the country holding court. Congress thought it was important for justices to stay in touch with local laws and practices and not be set apart from the people by holding court only in the nation's capital.

The legislation divided the United States into 13 districts with a district court in each of these areas. Each of the 11 states had their own district court plus there was a district court for Kentucky and Maine, which at that time were part of other states. A district judge that lived in each of the districts was appointed.

A middle tier of the judiciary was also created called circuit courts, which would be the primary trial courts of the federal system. Each district was divided into three circuits, with the exception of Maine and Kentucky, which were not on the circuit. Two Supreme Court justices and the local district judge presided over these circuit courts. The Supreme Court justices practiced "circuit riding," which meant they had to travel the circuit they were assigned.

> **Just the Facts**
>
> Justices despised the travel entailed for "circuit riding." They had to travel thousands of miles bouncing in stagecoaches or on horseback to bring the federal judiciary to communities all over America. Just like a postman, they were expected to show up even in severe weather conditions including rain, snow, and sleet.

To alleviate fears that these new federal courts might threaten states's rights and restrict civil liberties, the Congress allowed for state courts to exercise concurrent jurisdiction over many federal questions. Federal courts were required to select juries based on the procedures used in the district's state courts and were required to guarantee citizens the right to face trial within the district where they lived.

The federal circuit courts also had jurisdiction over cases involving parties from two different states. The most controversial part of the legislation granted the federal courts the right to hear appeals from high courts of each state if a decision involved questions of the constitutionality of state or federal laws.

The Supreme Court at the time of the 1789 legislation considered very few cases and held little respect. Justices left the court after only a brief period of service. Several justices were politically active, making their decisions even more suspect. Thomas Jefferson and James Madison argued that the states, rather than the Court, should determine certain constitutionality issues.

The Judiciary Act of 1802 and the Appointment of John Marshall

In 1801, just before President-elect Thomas Jefferson took office, a move was made by President John Adams and his Federalist party to change the judiciary into one with expanded federal jurisdiction. When Jefferson took office, a time which also included a major power shift from Federalists to Republicans, the new Congress acted quickly to repeal the 1801 law and passed a new Judiciary Act of 1802, which nullified most of the 1801 act. The one change allowed to stand was a plan for six regional circuits and a reorganization that reduced the travel for Supreme Court justices.

Just the Facts

The president chooses all the justices, including the chief. The chief need not be a justice before being chosen chief.

President Adams was able to make a more permanent change in the standing of the court when he appointed Chief Justice John Marshall just before leaving office. This appointment is probably one of the most important in the history of the court. Marshall established the court's right to review the constitutionality of congressional legislation in a landmark case *Marbury* v. *Madison* (we'll delve more deeply into that case and Marshall's role on the court in Chapter 4). During Marshall's 34-year term he strengthened not only the judiciary branch, but the central government as well.

Supreme Sayings

"Two hundred years after his appointment as chief justice of the U.S. Supreme Court, John Marshall is one of the most universally admired men in American history. If George Washington was the leading figure at the time of Independence, and if Abraham Lincoln was the leader who saved the Union at its time of greatest peril, Marshall was the most important figure to hold it together during the difficult decades at the beginning of the 19th century."

—From the Washington Post review of the book, *John Marshall and the Heroic Age of the Supreme Court*

Six, Seven, Nine ... Do I Hear Ten?

Congress increased the size of the Supreme Court for the first time in 1807 when a seventh justice was added to help meet the needs of the growing country. A seventh regional circuit was also added with this legislation. Justices appointed after that date were also required to live in the circuit that they served.

As the country continued to build westward, there was more and more pressure to expand the federal court system. Although states west of the Appalachians had district courts, they were not part of the circuit court system. These states, which included Illinois, Indiana, Michigan, Ohio, Kentucky, Tennessee, Louisiana, and Mississippi, started to complain in the 1820s and 1830s that they wanted equal representation in the circuit court system. Finally in 1837, the eighth and ninth circuits were established and two justices were added to the Supreme Court for those circuits, increasing the number of justices to nine.

In 1863, the western states of California and Oregon finally got their circuit court when a tenth circuit was established with the intention of increasing the Supreme Court to 10 justices. The 10 justices only sat together on the court for one week in December 1863. After that, illnesses and vacancies kept the operating court size to nine justices or less.

After the Civil War, the Congress again passed a law in 1866 that reduced the number of Supreme Court justices to seven and the number of circuit courts to nine. The major political goal was to reapportion the circuits geographically to reduce the power of the southern states. Before the Civil War, five of the nine circuits consisted exclusively of slave states, which gave southern slaveholders the ability to dominate the Supreme Court. In 1866, the Congress' reorganization reduced the southern slave states hold on the court to only two circuits.

Finding the Right Size

In 1869, the Congress finally settled on the number of nine justices for the Supreme Court. It also decided to have separate judgeships for the U.S. Circuit Courts and reduced the requirement for "circuit riding" by Supreme Court justices.

After passage of this legislation, Supreme Court justices only needed to attend circuit court once every two years. This change was prompted by the growing backlog of cases. The *docket* for the Supreme Court was two to three years behind schedule. The district courts were also backlogged, which resulted in calls for more judicial districts. By adding this new level of circuit court justices, district judges could concentrate on their load and not have to worry about attending circuit. The same was true for Supreme Court justices.

The last major shift in the courts was the addition of the U.S. District Court of Appeals in 1891. This established an appeals level and for the first time gave the Supreme Court limited authority to decide which cases it would hear. Today that authority is much broader. We'll talk more about how a case gets to the Supreme Court in the next chapter.

Court Connotations

The Supreme Court's **docket** includes information about pending cases and those already decided. You can get information regarding the status of cases for the current term and the term immediately prior at www.supremecourtus.gov/docket/docket.html.

From 1790 until 2002, only 108 people have served as justices of the Supreme Court. On average, a new justice is appointed every 22 months, but the current Supreme Court has been stable since 1994, which is the longest period without a vacancy since 1837. At the end of each term there is always a retirement watch. Although many expected at least one justice to retire at the end of June 2003, none did.

Building a Home

The Supreme Court didn't have a permanent home until 1935, its 146th year of existence. Its first meeting place was the Merchants Exchange Building in New York City. When the national capital moved to Philadelphia, the court met first at the State House (Independence Hall) and later in the City Hall.

In 1800, the court moved to Washington, D.C., with the rest of the federal government. There it had six different meeting places in the Capitol Building and even met in a private residence during the War of 1812 when the British set fire to the Capitol.

In 1819 the court actually got its first formal chamber in the newly restored Capitol, which you can see today. It's called the "Old Supreme Court Chamber." Larger quarters were made available in the Capitol in 1860, which today is known as the "Old Senate Chamber." That was its home until 1935 when the Supreme Court Building was finally finished.

View of the "Old Supreme Court Chamber" 1810–1860, which can be seen today in the U.S. Capitol.

(Photograph by Franz Jantzen from the Collection of the Supreme Court of the United States)

Today's Court System

After 1989 there were more pieces of legislation tweaking our court system, but I won't bore you with all the details. Today the Supreme Court practices free reign on the cases it chooses to hear unless the case involves one of its two directly mandated Constitutional responsibilities—cases affecting ambassadors, other public ministers and consuls or cases in which a state is one of the parties (refer to the previous section in this chapter "What's Set in Stone").

There are 12 United States Circuit Courts of Appeal that hear appeals from the district courts. The 94 federal district courts serve as trial courts for criminal and civil cases that involve federal statutes, the U.S. Constitution or civil cases between citizens from different states involving claims of $75,000 or more.

In addition to these courts, there is a United States Court of Appeals for the federal circuit, which reviews civil cases dealing with minor claims against the U.S. government as well as appeals involving patent rights cases or international trade disputes.

Just the Facts

Only about 5 percent of cases tried in the United States are tried in federal courts. The rest are tried at the state level. Each state designs its own court system. A case that has been tried all the way up to the state's highest court (in most states it too is called the Supreme Court) can be appealed to the United States Circuit Court of Appeals if the issue of constitutionality is questioned.

Specialty federal courts also exist including the U.S. Bankruptcy Courts, U.S. Court of International Trade, and U.S. Court of Federal Claims, which handles federal cases involving claims over $10,000, conflicts from the Indian Claims Commission (adjudicates Indian claims against the United States) and government contractors. Other federal courts outside the judicial branch include the military courts, Court of Veterans Appeals, and U.S. Tax Courts.

The table that follows shows the breakdown of the courts.

United States Federal Courts

Supreme Court	United States Supreme Court
Appellate Courts	United States Courts of Appeals 12 Regional Circuit Courts of Appeals 1 U.S. Court of Appeals for the Federal Circuit
Trial Courts	U.S. District Courts 94 judicial districts U.S. Bankruptcy Courts U.S. Court of International Trade U.S. Court of Federal Claims
Federal Courts and Other Entities *Outside* the Judicial Branch	Military Courts (Trial and Appellate) Court of Veteran Appeals U.S. Tax Court Federal administrative agencies and boards

Now that we've set the stage for today's court, in the next chapter we'll explore the right of every citizen to "take a case all the way to the Supreme Court" and find out what happens when it gets there.

The Least You Need to Know

◆ In its early days, the Supreme Court did not hold a lot of respect nor did it wield a lot of power. Instead it was a pawn between two political parties—those who wanted a strong federal court system (Federalists) and those who wanted the court power to stay within the states (Republicans).

◆ Chief Justice John Marshall is credited as the key person who established not only the power of the Supreme Court, but also centralized the power in the federal government.

◆ The size of the court was not finally set at nine justices until 1869, and the court didn't have its final home in Washington, D.C., until 1935.

2

Taking a Case to Court

In This Chapter

- ◆ Chances of being heard
- ◆ Asking for a day in court
- ◆ Arguing your case
- ◆ Waiting for a verdict

You've probably heard at least one friend say in anger, "I'm going to file a suit and take it all the way to the Supreme Court." What are the chances of making good on that claim? The person making that boast actually has less than a one in 270,000 chance of doing what he or she promises.

More than 27 million cases are filed in U.S. federal and state courts around the country each year, and only 7,000 even get to the stage of petitioning for a Supreme Court hearing. Of those, less than 100 are actually accepted and heard by the court.

You can see the numbers are stacked against you being able to take a case to the Supreme Court, but it can happen if the issue is of enough significance and involves a critical constitutional question that merits consideration. Let's take a look at how cases actually make it to the doorstep of the Supreme Court and, once they are there, how they are argued before the Court.

Setting the Agenda

After seeing the odds, you're probably wondering if there is anything that can increase your chances of being heard by the highest court. Supreme Court Justice Sandra Day O'Connor answers that question in her book, *The Majesty of the Law,* by explaining the types of cases most likely to be heard.

One third of all cases are related to general federal law and business regulations. Cases that fill this part of the docket (case schedule) usually relate to new legislation. For example, cases dealing with issues surrounding Americans with disabilities, employee retirement income, age discrimination in the workplace, and occupational health and safety currently are the most prevalent topics in this area.

The next major portion of the docket is related to criminal procedure, which has held a steady count of about 25 cases each year since the 1960s. Another large segment of issues dominating the docket recently are cases relating to federalism, states' rights, and state or federal power. In recent years, these case types number between 20 and 25.

Supreme Sayings

"What accounts for this striking stability in the number of criminal cases on our docket? My guess is that criminal procedure is simply not perfectible. The Court must constantly reexamine the way in which law enforcement agencies, legislatures, and the court itself strike the right balance between the rights of defendants and the interests of society at large."

—Sandra Day O'Connor in her book, *The Majesty of the Law*

Cases less likely to make it to the Supreme Court in recent years are ones involving civil rights, which dominated the Court in the 1950s and 1960s when that issue was a political hot potato. O'Connor says there are basically three things likely to drive the court's docket:

1. Resolving conflicts between various federal circuit courts especially relating to antitrust laws, labor laws, and the Internal Revenue Service.

2. Change in the nation's agenda when the Congress or a state legislature passes new laws or the executive branch takes a bold new action.

3. Court lights a fire by starting a controversy. O'Connor gives the explosive decision of *Brown* v. *Board of Education,* which mandated the integration of schools, as a good example of a court-started blaze. I'll talk more about that case in Chapter 15.

Even if you think you have the perfect issue to bring to the Supreme Court, the largest barrier to actually making it there is the cost. Taking a case through the court system is expensive. Just to give you an idea of how expensive things can get, consider the court costs Microsoft was willing to pay in order to settle its case before reaching the Supreme Court. As part of the settlement it agreed to pay $25 million to help defray legal expenses for the states that accepted its settlement offer. I'll discuss the issues involved in this case in Chapter 23.

Although most cases are not as complex as the Microsoft case, even a relatively simple case involving just one question of constitutional law can cost hundreds of thousands of dollars to take it the way to the Supreme Court. Legal fees usually range from $300 to $500 an hour and can get even higher as you move through the *appeals process* in the higher courts. Then you must add to those fees court costs and other investigative and trial expenses.

Court Connotations

The **appeals process** involves filing briefs (written legal arguments) and then arguing these legal issues before judges after the initial trial in a courtroom. How many levels of appeals will depend upon where the case started. If a case started in a state court, then it must first be appealed in the state to the highest court there before being taken to the federal court level.

Petitioning the Court

After you've exhausted all the appeals levels and are finally ready to approach the Supreme Court, the most common way to do that is called a *writ of certiorari*, which is a legal document that discusses the reasons the case should be considered by the Supreme Court. The usual reasons for filing this writ include:

◆ A United States Court of Appeals decided a case in a way that conflicts with the decision of another United States Court of Appeals.

◆ A United States Court of Appeals decided a case in a way that conflicts with a state court of last resort (such as a state Supreme Court).

◆ A state court of last resort decided a case involving a federal question that conflicts with the decision on a similar question by a different state's court of last resort.

◆ A state court of last resort decided a case involving an important question of federal law that has not yet been heard at the Supreme Court level, but the Supreme Court Justices decide should be reviewed at that level.

You may be surprised to find out that the Supreme Court rarely considers a writ of certiorari that claims there was an error in the factual findings of a case or that the law was misapplied by a lower court judge. These types of questions are settled at the appeals court level.

Living Laws

Forty copies of a writ of certiorari must be filed with the court that includes a copy of the lower court opinion and statements discussing the legal question or questions to be reviewed and the reasons why the Supreme Court should hear the case. Format and content are clearly defined in the rules of the Supreme Court and rigidly enforced, even down to font, font size, and margins. If you'd like to review the rules, you can do that at the Supreme Court's website (www.supremecourtus.gov/ctrules/ctrules.html).

Another type of writ you'll occasionally hear about is the *writ of habeas corpus*, which asks the Supreme Court to step in without taking a case through the usual appeals court process. These types of writs are most commonly seen in relation to death penalty cases when a speedier ruling is needed. There are other types of writs that ask for a stay in a lower court opinion, which if successful means that the lower court ruling will not take effect until the case makes its way through the appeals process. The landmark case, *Gideon* v. *Wainwright*, discussed in Chapter 5 began using a writ of habeas corpus.

Court Connotations

A **stay** is court-ordered, short term delay in judicial proceedings. When issued by a Supreme Court justice, it delays a lower court ruling until the full Supreme Court is able to meet and discuss the issue in question. A stay of execution delays death penalty sentencing until the full Court meets.

If the Supreme Court issues a *stay*, it usually will also decide whether to take the case directly or let it be heard in the U.S. Court of Appeals first. One such recent case involved the 2000 presidential election when the Supreme Court stopped the vote count in Florida until it could decide the case. I'll discuss that case in greater detail in Chapter 12.

Picking Cases

Even if you've found a way to make the monetary commitment to take a case all the way to the Supreme Court and your case meets one of the criteria for filing a writ, you have no guarantee that the Supreme Court justices will agree to hear your case. As mentioned, more than 7,000 writs are filed throughout the year.

In order to review this overwhelming number of cases, the Supreme Court justices have pooled their *law clerks*. One of the responsibilities for these clerks is to write memos reviewing the writs.

Court Connotations

Each Supreme Court justice picks up to four **law clerks** each year to serve for one year and assist him or her with research. Law clerks who serve at the Supreme Court are the cream of the crop of recent law school graduates and usually have at least one year clerking for a lower court justice. In addition to top grades, recommendations from former professors and judges play an important part in the selection process.

These memos state whether there is a conflict among courts, weigh the importance of the questions to be determined, and cite related Supreme Court precedents related to the case. Chief Justice William Rehnquist says if he does think there is a valid reason to hear a case after reading the law clerk pool memo, he will then review the lower court opinion and possibly ask his law clerks to do further research. These writ memos are shared by all the justices except Justice John Paul Stevens, who prefers that his own clerks review each writ rather than accept the work of the pool.

Each week that the court is in session it decides in a weekly conference which cases it will hear. Conferences are attended by justices only. No court staff is allowed in the room. We'll take a closer look at what happens in these conferences in Chapter 8.

The court session runs from the first week of October until some time in late June or early July, depending upon when the court releases its final opinion for the session. The first conference held after the summer recess can go on for several days to review a long list of writs asking for court consideration. Although no decisions on writs are made during the summer, justices do review the case load that backs up during the summer break.

Chief Justice Rehnquist says in his book, *The Supreme Court*, that 2,000 writs can back up during the summer recess. Just before the first conference, Rehnquist makes up a list of cases that should be considered in the first conference after the summer, which is held the last week of September before the court goes back into session. Other justices can add to this list.

Supreme Sayings

"Whether or not to vote to grant certiorari strikes me as a rather subjective decision, made up in part of intuition and in part of legal judgment. One factor that plays a large part with every member of the Court is whether the case sought to be reviewed has been decided differently from a very similar case coming from another lower court: If it has, its chances for being reviewed are much greater than if it hasn't. Another important factor is the perception of one or more justices that the lower-court decision may well be either an incorrect application of Supreme Court precedent or of general importance beyond its effect on these particular litigants, or both."

—Chief Justice William Rehnquist in his book, *The Supreme Court*

In a normal week, a list of writs to be considered in a weekly conference usually totals 100 cases. Only 15 to 30 of these cases will actually be discussed and voted on. Others on the list that are not discussed will be denied without even a recorded vote, according to Rehnquist. A case must get the support of at least four justices to be placed on the docket of the Supreme Court.

View of the east wall, bench and frieze of the present Supreme Court Chambers.

(Photograph by Franz Jantzen from the Collection of the Supreme Court of the United States)

Getting Your Day in Court

If your case gets placed on the docket, the amount of time you'll have to wait to get your day in court will depend on the time of year the review is granted. For example a case granted review in September is usually heard in January or February. Cases granted review in June are usually heard in December. Sometimes cases will get a speedier hearing. For example, the justices decided in June 2003 to hear a case relating to a new campaign finance law in early September because its ruling could impact the November elections.

The Supreme Court hears up to four one-hour arguments a day, three days a week for two weeks. Then the justices work behind the scene for two weeks. This schedule is maintained for much of the court term.

Thirty minutes are granted to each side. The Chief Justice strictly enforces timing. Lawyers address the Court from a podium that has a white and red light. The white light goes on at 25 minutes to warn lawyers they only have five minutes left. When the red light goes on they are done. The Chief Justice will cut off the lawyer speaking in mid-sentence when the red light goes on.

In rare cases of significance a longer time can be set aside for oral arguments. One such case was the *United States* v. *Nixon* in 1974, when three hours were allocated for oral arguments. In that case President Richard Nixon argued unsuccessfully that he could withhold evidence needed for a criminal investigation citing *executive privilege*.

Court Connotations

Executive privilege is a right presidents claim to keep certain activity within the Executive branch secret.

At some times of the year there are longer breaks between hearing cases. Two cases are heard beginning at 10 A.M. and two cases are heard beginning at 1 P.M. on Mondays, Tuesdays, and Wednesdays. Cases are not heard on Thursdays and Fridays. Oral arguments are heard between October and late April; after that time the justices concentrate solely on preparing the written decisions not yet released.

In the week or weeks between arguments the justices meet in conference to discuss the cases heard, review future cases, or work on writing decisions assigned to them. Just as with discussions about writs, only the justices participate in the conferences. I'll delve more deeply into what happens in these conferences and the other responsibilities of justices in Chapter 8.

You Must Be Brief

Lawyers for cases chosen to be heard by the Supreme Court write a *brief* arguing their case, which cannot exceed 50 pages. The rules for these briefs are tightly controlled, and even the size of the pages and type of print is specified. The lawyer representing the person who petitioned the court submits his or her brief with a blue cover. The lawyer responding to the petition must submit his or her brief with a red color. In addition to the primary parties in the case (or cases—sometimes more than one case is combined if issues are similar), "friends of the Court" (*amici curiae*) can also file a brief of no more than 30 pages with a green cover. Any party having an interest in the case is allowed to file a "friend of the Court" brief. Friends of the court briefs are filed in a large number of cases that reach the Supreme Court. I'll be quoting from some of the more interesting ones when we talk about specific cases in the last four parts of the book.

Court Connotations

A **brief** is a written legal argument that summarizes the key arguments in the case. Briefs are used to counter the arguments of the opposing side and to provide the justices with reasons to rule in favor of the party for which the brief was written.

Each Supreme Court justice uses his staff to review briefs differently depending on working preferences. For example, Rehnquist explains that he lets his clerks split up the cases to be heard, then reads the opinion of the lower court and briefs submitted himself. After reading the submissions he meets with his law clerk assigned to the case to discuss its merits. Sometimes, if necessary, he will ask his clerk to do any additional research on the case if he thinks other legal issues are relevant or some issues not fully discussed.

Other justices ask their law clerks to do a "bench memo" summarizing the briefs and analyzing the key arguments with both pro and con discussions. Once the bench memo is complete the justice will then meet with the law clerk assigned to the case to discuss it further and decide if additional research is needed.

Before the case is ever heard orally, each justice prepares for oral arguments in the way he or she sees fit. Many lawyers believe the justices make up their mind before they even hear oral arguments, but Rehnquist says in his book he has changed his position after the oral arguments, but that usually happens only in cases involving areas of law in which he is least familiar.

Supreme Sayings

"I began to realize that some of my best insights came not during my enforced thinking periods in my chambers, but while I was shaving in the morning, driving to work, or just walking from one place to another. This phenomenon led me to revise my approach to preparation for argued cases by sharply cutting down my collateral reading in most of them, and simply allowing some time for a case to 'percolate' in my mind."

—Chief Justice William Rehnquist in his book, *The Supreme Court*

Choosing Your Advocate

Some people believe they should hire a lawyer specialized in arguing before the Sup-reme Court, but Rehnquist disagrees. Although experience is important, he believes that it is more important for the advocate to fully understand the case and its intricacies.

Just the Facts

Any lawyer can apply to practice before the Supreme Court if he or she has practiced before the highest court of a State, Commonwealth, Territory, or Possession, or the District of Columbia for at least three years. An application must include a certificate from a court official confirming the lawyer's background, a personal statement from the lawyer applying to the court, and two letters from judges or other qualified persons sponsoring the application. You can read about the application process at www.supremecourtus.gov/bar/baradmissions.html.

Rehnquist breaks down the types of advocates he has seen before the court during his 32 years on the bench into these four most common types:

1. **Lector**—These advocates represent their clients by merely reading the brief. They treat questions from the justices as interruptions to their speech.

2. **Debating Champion**—These advocates are so set on demonstrating their skills and knowledge of the subject that they don't listen carefully to questions. They prepare a series of stock answers and use one of them to reply to the question, but may not actually answer what the justice is asking.

3. **Casey Jones**—These advocates do know their subject, do listen and try to answer questions carefully, and do not read from a prepared text. The problem with this type is that in order to get all their points across, the Casey Jones types speak so quickly and make so many points they are "like an engineer on a non-stop train—he will not stop to pick up passengers along the way." Rehnquist says this type of advocate could make a much stronger presentation by slowing down, concentrating on fewer critical points, and allowing the brief to handle the rest. A lawyer who makes six points with three remembered by justices is in better shape than one who makes twelve points with only one remembered.

4. **Spellbinder**—These types of advocates are rare, Rehnquist says, but they are people who have learned "to talk with the Court rather than at the court."

Rehnquist also describes the perfect court advocate. I find it very interesting that Rehnquist decided to use "she" rather than "he":

"If the essential element of the case turns on how the statute is worded, she will pause and slowly read the crucial sentence or paragraph. She will realize that there is an element of drama in an oral argument, a drama in which for half an hour she is the protagonist. But she also realizes that her spoken lines must have substantive legal meaning and does not waste her relatively short time with observations that do not advance the interest of her client. She has a theme and a plan for her argument but is quite willing to pause and listen carefully to questions. The questions may reveal that the judge is ignorant, stupid or both, but even such questions should have the best possible answer. She avoids table-pounding and other hortatory mannerisms, but she realizes equally well that an oral argument on behalf of one's client requires controlled enthusiasm and not an impression of barely suppressed boredom."

Rehnquist says it is not necessary to hire a lawyer whose practice is solely before the Supreme Court. In fact, he says only justice department attorneys argue before the court more than once or twice a year. The key is to find an advocate who knows the cases and does the research to present the case well. Also, the advocate must remember that he or she is more interested in the case than any of the sitting justices.

Waiting for a Decision

After the case is heard, all that is left to do is sit and wait. There is no timetable for the amount of time one can expect between cases being heard by the court and the court releasing its decision.

The only requirement is that the court must release its written opinion by the end of the court term. If that deadline is not met, then the court would be required to rehear oral arguments during the next term before making its ruling, which does happen very infrequently if the justices can't agree on a decision and want to hear more. The landmark desegregation case, *Brown* v. *Board of Education* (discussed in Chapter 5), was first heard in the last year of Chief Justice Vinson's court, which couldn't make a decision, and then heard again in the first year of Chief Justice's Warren court.

Now that you know why it's so hard to get your case heard by the Supreme Court and how cases are chosen, in the next chapter, we'll look at the role politics play in not only choosing cases, but also choosing judges.

The Least You Need to Know

- More than 7,000 cases are considered for review by the Supreme Court, but only about 100 cases are accepted for review.

- Most cases accepted by the Supreme Court fall in one of these three categories—decisions that differ among lower courts, decisions that differ on federal law among various state high courts, and legal issues that have not yet been decided by the Supreme Court but should be.

- Choosing the right advocate to argue a case before the Supreme Court—one who knows how to properly present a case or has presented a case before—can make a significant difference in swaying justices' opinions.

Politics and the Court

In This Chapter

- ◆ Politics of judicial questions
- ◆ Infighting on the Court
- ◆ Role of external forces
- ◆ Senate confirmation battles

Although in a perfect world the Supreme Court is supposed to be deciding cases based on the constitutional issue without regard to politics, that ideal has never been attainable. Throughout U.S. history, politics have played a role in the court.

During some periods the justices actively opposed state and federal legislatures by regularly overturning laws passed if they disagreed with the politics of the legislation. In other periods, the court has practiced judicial restraint and permitted laws to stand provided there was no direct conflict with the Constitution.

We'll be exploring the politics of the court throughout this book. In the next section, we'll take a trip back in history, exploring how various justices shaped today's Supreme Court and the role politics played in shaping the Court. Then we'll go behind the scenes of today's Court. After that we'll review today's law in critical areas based on precedents set by the Supreme Court. Politics played a role in all cases, some more than others.

In this chapter, we'll concentrate primarily on the external politics that impact the Supreme Court.

It's All About Politics

As eighteenth century French historian Alexis de Tocqueville said, "scarcely any political question arises in the United States that is not resolved sooner or later into a judicial question." This observation is as true today as it was in the 1800s.

The Supreme Court cannot just jump into any political issue for which it would like to take a stand. Instead the Court must wait until the issue is brought to it on appeal from a lower court. By the time a case makes it to the Supreme Court, there are probably numerous cases working their way through various courts in several states. A major political issue rarely arrives at the court based on only one case. Usually the Supreme Court steps in when there is a conflict between court rulings from one or more state courts or one or more federal courts.

Just the Facts

During an event carried on C-Span in 2000 after the presidential election, a group of high school students from Maryland and Pennsylvania asked Justice Clarence Thomas how the political affiliations of both majorities in Congress and the president affect Supreme Court decisions. He answered, "That's a good question, the answer's none. They don't try to influence us, and they don't. We happen to be in the same city, [but] we may as well be on entirely different planets."

Sometimes a key political issue is sped through the lower courts to the Supreme Court because time is of the essence. A prime example of this was *Bush* v. *Gore* in 2000, when five justices of the Supreme Court decided the 2000 presidential election by stopping a recount of the vote in Florida.

The political tension in that case could easily be seen by reading the unsigned decision with one concurring opinion signed by Chief Justice William Rehnquist (joined by Antonin Scalia and Clarence Thomas) plus four dissenting opinions. The dissenting opinions were written by John Paul Stevens (joined by Ruth Bader Ginsburg and Stephen Breyer), David Souter (joined by Breyer and partially by Stevens and Ginsburg), Ruth Bader Ginsburg (joined by Souter and Breyer), and Stephen Breyer (joined partially by Stevens, Ginsburg and Souter). You can read the decisions online at http://caselaw.lp.findlaw.com/scripts/getcase.pl?court=US&vol=000&invol=00-949.

After sorting through these various opinions, the only thing the justices could agree on was that there were constitutional problems with the Florida election and the method being used to count the votes. The justices had difficulty specifying a proper remedy. I'll discuss the legal issues in greater detail in Chapter 12. Just to give you an idea of the political issues at stake and the potential impact on the Court, here is a quote from Breyer's dissent:

> "At the same time, as I have said, the Court is not acting to vindicate a fundamental constitutional principle, such as the need to protect a basic human liberty. No other strong reason to act is present. Congressional statutes tend to obviate the need. And, above all, in this highly politicized matter, the appearance of a split decision runs the risk of undermining the public's confidence in the Court itself. That confidence is a public treasure. It has been built slowly over many years, some of which were marked by a Civil War and the tragedy of segregation. It is a vitally necessary ingredient of any successful effort to protect basic liberty and, indeed, the rule of law itself. We run no risk of returning to the days when a President … might have said, "John Marshall has made his decision; now let him enforce it!" …. But we do risk a self-inflicted wound—a wound that may harm not just the Court, but the Nation."

There is no doubt the wounds from this decision are still open. When the country faces its next presidential election in 2004, this decision will certainly be a political undercurrent if not an outright rallying call for the opposing parties.

Internal Political Battles

No doubt the contentious split decision in the *Bush* v. *Gore* case brought into full view the division in the court. While the case conferences at which the justices present their views and vote are held in secret, their battles can clearly be seen when such vehement dissentions are issued in writing. Press reports immediately after the decision indicated that some justices were not even talking to each other.

The traditions of the Court have probably eased some of this tension, but decisions announced in June 2003 showed that the division in the Court is still very strong. Controversial decisions were decided by a five to four vote including one relating to affirmative action and a second to gay rights. I'll take a closer look at these cases in Chapter 18.

One daily tradition that helps to ease some of this tension is the practice of shaking each other's hands every day before the start of a session. This tradition was started during Chief Justice Melville Fuller's Court in the late 1800s. He believed this practice would ease tensions and it probably still does today.

> **Supreme Sayings** _____
>
> "There is one custom we have on the Court that was a pleasant surprise to me and that I treasure. Each day when there is an oral argument, just before we go out on the bench, and each day before we confer, every Justice shakes the hand of every other Justice. To an outsider, this may seem baroque and unnecessary, but you must realize we are a very small group. We see and interact with one another often and we all know we will continue to do so for the rest of our professional lives."
>
> —Sandra Day O'Connor in her book, *The Majesty of Law*

Another tradition is one that has been practiced by most chief justices when they lead the conferences. The chief justice speaks first and then the other justices speak based on their seniority. Some chief justices discouraged open discussion, while others encouraged it.

When a vote is finally taken, one justice in the majority will write the opinion. If the chief justice is in the majority, he selects the writer. If not, the writer is selected by the most senior justice. This is probably the most political decision made for each case. The justice who writes the decision has the greatest control over how the Supreme Court's position will be presented to the world. I'll be taking you behind the scenes of case decision-making in Chapter 9.

Friends of the Court

Outsiders who want to influence a court decision can only do so by filing what is called a "friend of the Court" brief. This type of brief can be filed by any individual who is interested in influencing the outcome of the case but is not an actual party to the suit. These briefs are called *"amicus curaie,"* which is the Latin term for friend of the court.

In a controversial case as many as 50 or more friend-of-the-court briefs can be filed. There are no limits to the number that can be filed as long as they are filed by the date set by the Court when the case is put on the docket. As we discussed in Chapter 2, these briefs must be filed with a green cover and can be no longer than 30 pages.

Politics of Appointments

The appointment of new justices to the Court is the time when the greatest degree of political influence can be imposed on the Court. While most presidents have tried to appoint justices who closely match their political views, frequently the justices do not

live up to expectations once they get on the
court. Historically, justices seem to gravitate to
the center of the Court after they have been
there for awhile. Some do hold to their strong
conservative or liberal views throughout their
Supreme Court service.

The president who appointed the most Supreme
Court justices is George Washington, who
appointed 10. Franklin Roosevelt is next in line
with nine appointments. Andrew Jackson and
William Taft both appointed six. Most times the
president will select a nominee from his own
party, but there have been 13 nominees who
were of a different party affiliation.

Just the Facts

Only four presidents have
not appointed a justice to
the Supreme Court—
William Harrison, Zachary
Taylor, Andrew Johnson,
and Jimmy Carter. Carter is the
only one who actually served a
four-year term. There were no
court retirements while he was in
office. Nixon appointed four justices and Ford appointed one.

Supreme Court researcher Henry Abraham found that in the history of the Court
there have been 144 nominees and 30 of them never made it to the Court. Eleven
were not even acted upon, which means only 19 were actually rejected.

The reasons for rejection vary. In some cases, the nominee was not considered qualified. While there are no legal or constitutional requirements for an appointment to a
federal judgeship, there is an unwritten expectation that the appointee will have a law
degree. It is not mandatory to have practiced law or be a member of the bar.

Some rejections are not even based on the nominee, but instead relate to opposition
to the nominating president. Frequently, contentious political issues are what stop a
nomination. Special interest groups who oppose a nomination can also play a major
role during the appointment process.

Henry Abraham, in his book *Justices, Presidents and Senators*, names three primary
forces that influence the judicial selection process:

1. Influence of public and private leaders.

2. American Bar Association's Standing Committee on Federal Judiciary (first established in 1945-1946. More about this committee to come.)

3. Advice from current and former Supreme Court justices.

The first factor is the one most visible to the public. If a president does not nominate
someone who can make it through the Senate confirmation process, that person will
never sit on the Court. Although we haven't witnessed a Supreme Court nomination
process since 1991, we've certainly seen how the Senate handles political appointments

for the lower federal courts. Many of President Clinton's appointees were held up at the committee level and never made it to the floor of the Senate.

Supreme Sayings

"The Senate should not be faulted for carefully scrutinizing those nominated. We are not a rubber stamp. The constitution requires the Senate to advise and consent to the President's nominees. The Senate thus has an obligation to take its role seriously, and the Judiciary Committee has a mandate to review each and every nominee."
—Senator Orrin Hatch (R-Utah) in *The New York Times* on January 11, 1998

While more than 100 Bush appointees have been confirmed by the Senate since he took office in 2001, the Democrats in the Senate are holding up four of the most conservative nominees using a procedure called *filibuster*.

Court Connotations

Filibuster is a tactic that can be used by Senators to extend debate on an issue indefinitely and prevent a vote. There is no Senate rule that can force a vote. Debate must first be cut off and that requires a 60 vote majority. When the Senate is closely divided, it can be very difficult to get those 60 votes. The practice dates back to the 1800s. The term comes from "filibusteros" used by early nineteenth century Spanish pirates who held ships hostage for ransom.

Most expect a similar tactic will be used if President Bush tries to nominate a staunch conservative when a seat on the Supreme Court becomes available. Many expected William Rehnquist or Sandra Day O'Connor to retire when the court finished its 2003 session at the end of June. Others thought both might retire. Both conservative and liberal political activists ramped up for the possible Supreme Court nomination fight, which never happened. No one announced retirement and it is unlikely someone will in 2004, a presidential election year.

President Bush set the stage for the current battle when he announced he would no longer seek advice from the American Bar Association's (ABA) Standing Committee on Federal Judiciary, which other presidents have used to varying degrees since 1945. The committee is a 15-member group with representatives from each of the 11 judicial districts plus one from the federal circuit, one from the District of Columbia Circuit, one extra appointee for the Ninth Circuit and a chairperson. Some have criticized the power this committee has had in the past because the ABA represents less than half of the nation's lawyers.

After the committee receives a nomination for screening, it asks the nominee to respond to a detailed questionnaire followed by a lengthy interview. Then the committee conducts extensive interviews with judges, law school deans, practicing attorneys and some nonlawyers. Finally the committee reviews the nominee's previous rulings (if currently a sitting judge) and other legal writings. The committee then issues a recommendation of "well qualified," "not opposed," "not qualified."

Rejecting Bork

The most recent rejection of a Supreme Court nomination was President Ronald Reagan's nomination of Robert Bork in 1987 to replace Justice Lewis Powell, Jr., who, as a moderate, was considered a swing voter on the Court.

Reagan tried to sell Bork as a moderate, but lost that opportunity when Senator Edward Kennedy openly opposed the nomination by declaring (from the book *Battle for Justice: How the Bork Nomination Shook America*):

> "Robert Bork's America is a land in which women would be forced into back alley abortions, blacks would sit at segregated lunch counters, rogue policemen could break down citizen's doors in midnight raids, school children could not be taught about evolution, writers and artists could be censured at the whim of government."

Bork was a well-respected and qualified judge who sat on the U.S Court of Appeals after being unanimously confirmed by the Senate in 1982. His prior claim to fame occurred during the Nixon administration when he served as solicitor general and became acting attorney general during the "Saturday Night Massacre."

Just the Facts

The "Saturday Night Massacre" occurred near the end of the Watergate investigation. Nixon feared Special Prosecutor Archibald Cox was close to finding out the truth about his involvement in the break-in into the Democratic headquarters at the Watergate. Cox had just requested the secret tapes of Oval office conversations, which ultimately proved Nixon's culpability. Nixon ordered then Attorney General Elliot Richardson to fire Cox. Richardson said no and resigned. The Deputy Attorney General William Ruckelshaus also refused and resigned. Bork carried out Nixon's wishes.

Politically, his appointment to the Supreme Court proved impossible. While he was well qualified, the timing was bad. Reagan was near the end of his term and embroiled in another scandal called the Iran-Contra Affair. During Reagan's term, the United States provided financial support for military activities of the Nicaraguan contra rebels between the period of October 1984 to October 1986, when there was a pro-hibition on such aid. The money came from selling arms to Iran, which was against the stated U.S. policy. This scandal weakened Reagan's administration and helped to doom the Bork nomination.

Democrats had just taken over the Senate after the 1986 elections. Senate Democrats did not like Bork's conservative philosophy, especially his positions on abortion, affir-mative action, and First Amendment rights, so they rejected the nomination. Bork now serves as a senior fellow of the American Enterprise Institute for Public Policy Research, which is a conservative Washington, D.C., think-tank.

Many consider this rejection the start of the war for control of judicial nominations. Republicans regained control of the Senate in 1994 and blocked many of Clinton's nominations for federal judgeships in retaliation for the Bork rejection. This set up a tit-for-tat game that still drives the politics of federal judicial appointments today.

Now that you have a better understanding of the influence of politics on the court, let's step back in history and explore the early days of the Supreme Court.

The Least You Need to Know

- ◆ Most controversial political questions ultimately are decided by the courts as cases make their way through the U.S. judicial system.

- ◆ Since Supreme Court justices serve for life, there are times of internal strife, but it's rarely seen by the public. The case of *Bush* v. *Gore* (regarding the 2000 presidential election) brought those struggles into the limelight.

- ◆ External groups that want to influence court decisions can do so by filing a friend-of-the-court brief.

- ◆ Appointments to the Supreme Court and other federal judgeships often face a battleground in the U.S. Senate, especially if the appointee is seen as too liberal or too conservative.

Part 2

Shaping the Court's Foundation

Molding the Court was left to the great leaders of the Court. Some were legal scholars, but many of the key shapers of the Court were known for their leadership qualities and not their legal scholarship. In this part, we'll discover who helped to shape the Court and the role each of the Chief Justices and other great minds played in building the Court.

Chapter 4

Marshall Court

In This Chapter

- ◆ Molding the Court
- ◆ Dividing the power
- ◆ Establishing the right of judicial review
- ◆ Building a strong federal government

The Supreme Court honors historical lawgivers in its main chamber. Biblical figures include Moses and Solomon. Other country's lawgivers are represented by their political leaders or monarchs such as Confucius, King John, Napoleon, and Charlemagne. Only the United States is represented by a lawgiver that was a judge—Chief Justice John Marshall.

That shows how much power and respect we give to the Supreme Court of the land. This wasn't always so. Marshall is credited through his early leadership with developing our unique court structure—where the Supreme Court can overturn the legislature and has the final word on the constitutionality of a law.

We'll step back in time and visit the early days of the Supreme Court, review John Marshall's contributions and discuss the key cases that gave the court its power and the United States its foundation.

Setting the Stage

Let's start by looking at the stature of the court before Marshall took over as chief justice. Remember we mentioned in Chapter 1 that the court met only twice a year, in February and August. When it met for the first time on February 2, 1790, there were no cases to be decided. The same was true for the next two sessions. Instead the Supreme Court justices did most of their work on the road "riding the circuit," as we discussed.

While the justices delivered their first opinions in August 1792 in a case titled *Georgia* v. *Bradford*, it was not until February 1793 that the justices actually decided their first important case. The Bradford case was a request from the state of Georgia for an *injunction* to stop the recovery of money by a British subject, whose estate had been confiscated. Georgia was given the temporary injunction by the Supreme Court in that first case.

> **Court Connotations**
>
> An **injunction** is an order issued by a court that orders someone to do something or prohibits someone from doing something. For example an injunction may be ordered to prevent the cutting down of trees, prevent the polluting of a stream or stop a group from picketing if their plans go beyond the bounds of free speech and assembly.

Opinions in the early days of the court were not delivered formally in writing, as they are today. Instead during the first 10 years of the Court each justice gave his opinion orally at a session of the Court. During the first 10 years of the Court it heard only about 100 cases. As we've already discussed, today's Court hears that many in one year. At that time the Court heard all cases brought before it. Today the Court has much more discretionary power over which cases it will hear and picks only about 100 out of 7,000.

The first actual ruling on a case came in February 1793 in *Chisholm* v. *Georgia*. This case established the right for citizens of one state to sue another state. Chisholm, a resident of South Carolina, sued Georgia because he had delivered goods to Georgia but Georgia didn't pay for the goods. Georgia claimed immunity from begin sued. The Supreme Court ruled that Georgia was subject to suit.

The right to sue states didn't last long though. This ruling led to such an uproar by the states that the Congress passed the *Eleventh Amendment* to the Constitution on March 4, 1794. This amendment bans suits from being filed by individuals of another state or of a foreign country against a state. Just 339 days later on February 7, 1795, the amendment was ratified and took effect January 1798.

The Supreme Court first ruled on the right to overturn a state legislature in 1796 in the case *Ware* v. *Hylton*. In this case a citizen of Virginia owed money to a British subject. Virginia had enacted a law that confiscated British property, including any debts owed by its citizens to British subjects. The British subject filed suit to collect his money.

> **Court Connotations** _____
>
> **Constitutional amendments** alter the language of the original draft of the U.S. Constitution. The Constitution can be changed either through an amendment proposed by two-thirds of both houses of Congress or by a call for a constitutional convention by two-thirds of the state legislatures. The legislatures don't have the right to draft the new amendment, but they can ask the Congress to convene a special amendment proposal convention. So far every amendment to the constitution has been made by Congress. No one even knows what the logistics would be if a call were made for a constitutional convention.

The Supreme Court overturned the state law because the Treaty of Paris, which established peace after the Revolutionary War, protected such debts. Justice Samuel Chase in his opinion said, "A treaty cannot be the supreme law of the land if any act of a state Legislature can stand in its way." Just think what the United States would be like today if each state could decide whether or not it wanted to abide by a treaty signed by the federal government.

Interestingly, John Marshall, who at that time was a practicing attorney in Virginia, argued against overturning the state law by questioning the right of the judiciary to invalidate a state law because that right has not been given to it by the Constitution. As we'll discuss below, John Marshall is most famous for the court ruling that established the Supreme Court's right to overturn a law passed by Congress. He also ruled the right to overturn a state legislature in a second famous case we'll discuss later.

A Supreme Lack of Priority

Justices did not keep their position on the court very long. Many left because they complained about the travel. The first chief justice, John Jay, resigned to become governor of New York. Can you imagine a Supreme Court justice giving up his or her seat to run for political office today?

In addition to having very few cases that needed to be decided, many of the justices who served on the Supreme Court in the first 10 years did not make the Court their first priority. Chief Justice John Jay served from 1789 to 1795 before leaving court to be governor of New York. While on the court, he also served as Special Ambassador to England in 1794.

Chief Justice Oliver Ellsworth, who served from 1796 to 1800, also served as a special U.S. envoy in France for the last year of his term. In that year Justice William Cushing, who served on the court from 1789 to 1810, was too sick to attend the August term. In addition, Justice Samuel Chase was too busy working on President John Adams' reelection to be at the August session. Since there were only six justices, the Supreme Court could barely function during the year before John Marshall was appointed to the court.

This lack of priority for a court appointment led Alexander Hamilton to write in *The Federalist*, "The judiciary is beyond comparison the weakest of the three departments of power." Without a strong leader, the Supreme Court was destined to fail.

Marshall Steps In

When John Adams appointed John Marshall chief justice in 1801 (just before he left the presidency), Marshall took over a weakened court that was so low on the priority list Congress did not even see the need to provide it with a place to meet. No building was planned for it when the Congress appropriated money to build the federal buildings in its new capital, Washington, D.C., in 1800. Instead its chambers were relegated to a committee room beneath the House Chamber.

One of Marshall's first acts to take control of the situation was to change the way the Court dished out its opinions. Rather than have each justice read his own opinion, Marshall got the justices to agree the court should have one opinion delivered orally. During his tenure, Marshall delivered the opinions on all the critical cases. A judge did have the right to read a dissenting opinion.

Low esteem for the Supreme Court was not its only problem. The Court also played the role of political football between the Federalists and the Republicans. In 1800 the Federalists lost the battle and were getting ready to give up control of both the executive and legislative branches.

Official portrait of Chief Justice John Marshall painted by Rembrant Peale.

(Photograph by Vic Boswell from the Collection of the Supreme Court of the United States)

Just the Facts

Marshall studied law for only about a month at the College of William and Mary in Virginia before being admitted to the bar in 1780. He then practiced law for 20 years in Virginia, representing land owners. He was the oldest of 15 children from one of the leading families of Fauquier County, Virginia. His love of the country and support for a strong federal government came primarily from his boyhood friendship with George Washington, who he served under as a captain at Valley Forge.

One of the Federalists' last acts before losing control was to pass the Judiciary Act of 1801 on February 13, 1801, which made major changes in the makeup of the judiciary. While the act did include the desired reform that relieved Supreme Court justices of their dreaded circuit court duties, it also created a new layer of judges at the district and circuit court levels that could quickly be appointed by outgoing Federalist President John Adams. This would give the Federalists at least some control of the judiciary branch after they left office.

Within two weeks, John Adams nominated and the Congress confirmed the appointments of these new judges. The task had to be done so quickly that the commissions for many of these new judges were completed on John Adams' last day in office by, guess who, Secretary of State John Marshall. He had been appointed as Secretary of State in 1800 and continued to serve in that post even after being appointed chief justice.

Court Connotations

A lame-duck Congress is a Congress that meets after the election in November and before the new Congress takes over.

These last minute appointees were dubbed the "midnight judges" by the Republicans because the *lame-duck Congress* worked late into the night to confirm all the judges just before a March 3 midnight deadline when the newly elected President Thomas Jefferson would take office. One story about the incident even says that John Marshall was asked to leave his office at midnight by Levi Lincoln, Jefferson's incoming Attorney General, but this is probably a tale told by some Republicans to make the changeover more dramatic.

This last-minute flurry of activity did leave a mess for both sides to clean up and set the stage for a landmark decision of the Supreme Court, *Marbury* v. *Madison*, which we'll discuss later. The Republicans repealed the Judiciary Act of 1801 on March 8, 1802, abolished the new courts and made no provision for the newly appointed judges. Instead Congress passed the Judiciary Act of 1802, moving the Court's next term, which had been scheduled to begin June 1802, to February 1803. The Republicans did not want the Supreme Court to rule immediately on the constitutionality of the 1802 law because they also had plans to impeach some federal judges and possibly even Supreme Court justices, which they hoped to do before the Supreme Court could meet to make a ruling on the Judiciary Act.

Republicans hoped that by impeaching some justices they could have more support for their position on the Court. The Marshall Court did uphold the constitutionality of the Judiciary Act of 1802 in a March 1803 decision, *Stuart* v. *Laird*.

Only one federal judge was actually impeached because of gross misconduct. There was an attempt to impeach the most political Supreme Court justice at the time, Samuel Chase, who worked to reelect John Adams. Bernard Schwartz writes in his book, *A History of the Supreme Court*, that Senator William Branch Giles, Jefferson's leader in the Senate, told John Quincy Adams that the Chase impeachment was part of a greater plan to replace judges with ones more to the liking of the Republicans. He quotes a letter from John Quincy Adams to his father, "The assault upon Judge Chase was unquestionably intended to pave the way for another prosecution, which would have swept the Supreme Judicial Branch clean at a stroke."

Luckily for the nation, there were enough defectors from Jefferson's own party to defeat the conviction of Chase. The Senate had 25 Republicans and nine Federalists. The Constitution requires a two-thirds majority for impeachment, so 23 votes were needed for success. Republicans could only find 19 votes in favor of impeachment because 6 decided to vote against impeaching Chase, so the impeachment move was defeated.

Supreme Sayings

"Why the six Republicans broke party ranks and voted not guilty on all counts is not completely clear. Most believe that a good part of their reluctance to convict was a recognition that a healthy nation required a truly independent judiciary—a judiciary whose members could make decisions, sometimes even politicized decisions that could later be assailed as legally erroneous, without fear of reprisal."

—Sandra Day O'Connor in her book, *The Majesty of the Law*

As we discussed in Chapter 3, the most political time for the Court is when a new justice is being confirmed by the Senate. Imagine what the Supreme Court would be like if impeachments were more common each time the control of Congress changed parties. The legislative branch would have much greater power over the politics of the Court if a judge who displeased the current Congress politically could be impeached for his or her politics. Although this might please you if you disagree with the politics of some of today's justices, the balance of power would then be out of whack and the legislative branch could wield much more power over the judicial branch.

Taking Control

While Supreme Court action was delayed by Republicans when they stopped the court from meeting in the summer of 1802 after repealing the 1801 law, a case was filed by one of the judges who did not get his commission. John Marshall left 42 commissions on his desk when he left the office as Secretary of State. He didn't have enough time to deliver them. Jefferson told his new Secretary of State, James Madison, to deliver only 25 of the commissions left by Marshall. Four of the 17 judges who did not get their commissions filed suit in the Supreme Court asking for a *writ of mandamus*.

Court Connotations

A **writ of mandamus** is a common law practice that dates back to English law. A judge can force an official to carry out his or her official duties if the writ is granted.

The case in which the Supreme Court ruled on this issue was titled *Marbury* v. *Madison*. William Marbury was one of the slighted justices. James Madison was named as Jefferson's Secretary of State because he had the duty to deliver the commissions. Since Madison refused to deliver them, Marbury asked for a writ to force Madison to deliver the commissions. The case sat in the Supreme Court clerk's office for two years before it was argued. The Court was not even allowed to conduct business for the more than a year because the Congress had moved its summer 1802 session to February 1803.

There were three key questions to be decided by the court:

1. Was Marbury entitled to his commission? The answer to this was an easy yes. The first Article of the Constitution empowers Congress to create federal offices. Marbury was appointed and confirmed by the Senate and his commission was signed by the Secretary of State.

2. Was there a legal remedy for Marbury to remedy Madison's refusal to deliver the commission? This too was an easy yes, since the key purpose of a court is to provide a remedy if someone is wronged.

3. Was the writ of mandamus the right remedy? Marshall surprised everyone by answering no to this question primarily because he said Marbury filed his action in the wrong court. The Supreme Court only had appellate jurisdiction based on the Constitution, so it could not rule directly on this writ. Marbury did have the right after this ruling to file the case in a lower court.

By concluding the court did not have jurisdiction, Marshall declared Section 13 of the Judiciary Act unconstitutional. The section gave the Supreme Court the right "to issue writs of mandamus, in cases warranted by the principles and usages of law, to any courts appointed, or persons holding office, under the authority of the United States." Marshall said in his opinion that this section was unconstitutional because the Constitution specifically only gives the Supreme Court appellate jurisdiction is this type of case. "It is emphatically the province and duty of the judicial department to say what the law is …. The constitution is superior to any ordinary act of the legislature."

This ruling was the first glimpse into the brilliance of Marshall that would become a hallmark of his court. Everyone expected him to rule in favor of Marbury because he was an appointee of John Adams and a Federalist. By giving the Republicans a victory, he actually won a more important victory for the future of the Supreme Court—the right to overturn federal legislation. While the precedent to review state legislation had been established by earlier court rulings, this was the first time the Court took a firm stance on its right to overturn federal law.

The Republicans were so glad to win their case little notice was made of the more critical ruling. No one seriously challenged the right of the Supreme Court to declare an act of Congress unconstitutional.

William Marbury never did get his commission and is not well known except for this landmark case. James Madison, as you probably know, served as Secretary of State under Thomas Jefferson for eight years before being elected president.

Marshall went on to firmly establish the right of the Supreme Court to rule state legislation unconstitutional in *Fletcher* v. *Peck*. In this case, the Georgia legislature granted four land companies territory that included most of present day Alabama and Mississippi. The land deal was tied to corruption in the state and a newly elected legislature in 1796 rescinded the agreement. The companies fought to regain their rights to the land, which was ceded to the United States in 1802 for $1,250,000. As part of this cession agreement, the companies were to receive 5 million acres, but they were not happy with the settlement, so they rejected it and filed a suit.

> **Supreme Sayings**
>
> "What transformed *Marbury* from a simple 'jurisdiction' case, sending the plaintiff back to a lower court, into a constitutional landmark was John Marshall's determination to force a showdown with Thomas Jefferson—his political foe and personal enemy—over the most basic question in politics: Who rules?"
> —Peter Irons in his book, *The People's History of the Supreme Court*

In 1810, the Supreme Court ruled that even though the land deal was conceived in fraud, the companies' claims to the land were valid because Georgia's grant of the land was a binding contract. The Marshall Court overturned the 1796 state legislation that rescinded the companies' rights to the land. Congress eventually settled with the companies by paying them more than $4 million for their claim.

Empowering the National Government

Now that Marshall had clearly established the Court's power to rule on the constitutionality of the law, his next major battle was to ensure the federal government had the power it needed over state governments to build a strong national government. The first case that landed on the doorstep of the Supreme Court that allowed him to rule on this critical principle was *McCulloch* v. *Maryland*.

The controversy in this case involved the right of the United States to set up a central bank. In 1791 Secretary of the Treasury Alexander Hamilton proposed the first charter Bank of the United States. Jefferson opposed the idea, saying the Constitution did not give Congress the power to charter such a bank. Hamilton argued that Congress did have that power under the Necessary and Proper clause of the Constitution, which allows Congress to make "all laws which shall be deemed necessary and proper for carrying into execution the foregoing powers, and all other powers vested by this Constitution in the government of the United States."

President Washington backed Hamilton and the bank was given a 20-year charter, which expired in 1811 and was not renewed by Jefferson. In 1816, President Madison realized that the federal government did need a central bank and recommended that Congress charter a second Bank of the United States, which established branches throughout the country. This bank served as a depository for federal funds and had the right to print bank notes.

State-chartered banks opposed the move and asked their legislatures to restrict the federal bank's operations. Maryland did just that by imposing a tax on bank operations. James McCulloch, who was the cashier at the Baltimore branch of the Bank of the United States, refused to pay the tax, which eventually landed the entire issue in the lap of the Supreme Court.

Just the Facts

State-chartered banks did end up winning 20 years later when it came time for Congress to revisit the central bank's charter in 1832. Andrew Jackson thought the central bank had too much economic power and campaigned against it. State bankers were happy to support his campaign, as were westerners and farmers who also were opposed to the federal bank's control. Jackson won election campaigning on this issue against the pro-bank candidate Henry Clay. Congress did recharter the bank in 1832, but Jackson vetoed the bill. The second central bank closed its doors in 1836.

Marshall's court ruled that not only did the federal government have a right to establish a central bank, but that this bank could not be subjected to state taxation. He clearly established the right of federal supremacy by ruling that "states have no power, by taxation or otherwise, to retard, impede, burden, or in any manner control, the operations of the federal government, or its agencies, and instrumentalities."

Of course there were many more critical rulings throughout Marshall's 34 years on the court, but we don't have room to review each of the Marshall Court cases here. Instead, we'll be taking a closer look at how case law established during the Marshall court, as well as other Supreme Courts over the years, has shaped the body of laws that serve as a foundation for our government today. Each of the last four sections of the book focuses on a different theme—government rights, social issue, criminal cases, and business issues.

In the next chapter, we'll look at the court of another giant in the shaping of the Supreme Court and today's laws—Chief Justice Earl Warren, who served from 1953 to 1969.

The Least You Need to Know

◆ The first 10 years of the Supreme Court were not auspicious, and even the men selected to serve on the court did not value the appointment.

◆ John Marshall was a visionary and the first to see the true potential of the Supreme Court. The rulings of his court not only established the Court's power, but also the federal government's power.

◆ The first major case for John Marshall's court was *Marbury* v. *Madison*, which established the right of the Supreme Court to overturn Congressional legislation.

◆ Federal powers were given a strong boost with the Marshall Court's ruling in *McCulloch* v. *Maryland*.

Chapter 5

Warren Court

In This Chapter

- ◆ Judicial restraint versus activists
- ◆ Separate educational facilities are inherently unequal
- ◆ Establishing state appointed council
- ◆ Requiring Miranda warnings
- ◆ Proving malice in libel cases involving public officials

The Supreme Court shifted away from its focus on property rights to personal rights when Chief Justice Earl Warren took over the court in 1953. Prior to the Warren Court a majority of the cases centered around building a foundation for property law.

That all changed with the Warren court's first landmark case—*Brown* v. *Board of Education* in 1954, which opened the battle for school desegregation. After working hard to get a unanimous ruling in that case, Warren continued to work his magic to lead the court in a series of cases that guaranteed numerous personal rights, which primarily focused on the Bill of Rights.

After introducing you to Earl Warren and the politics of the Warren Court, I'll take a brief look at the critical cases that helped make this court the second most extraordinary court in U.S. history—second only to the Marshall Court.

From Politician to Chief Justice

Earl Warren was not known for legal scholarship, but instead for his ability to manage the court and sway other justices to his way of thinking. His appointment to the court came as a payback for helping President Dwight D. Eisenhower secure the nomination of the Republican Party by throwing the California delegation's votes to Eisenhower at a critical time during the Republican convention. At the time, Warren was governor of California.

Chief Justice Earl Warren's official portrait painted by C. J. Fox.

(Photograph by Vic Boswell from the Collection of the Supreme Court of the United States)

Before becoming governor, Warren served as California's attorney general. He advocated, along with many other California politicians, the forced evacuation of people of Japanese decent into *internment camps* just after the Japanese attacked Pearl Harbor, which drew the United States into World War II. While chief justice he led the battle for personal rights, which makes this earlier support seem contradictory to his reputation as a vanguard in safeguarding the Bill of Rights and our personal freedoms.

Court Connotations

Internment camps were set up by President Franklin D. Roosevelt in 1942 when he signed an executive order to establish the War Relocation Authority, which had the responsibility to remove Japanese Americans from their homes and place them in camps. These camps housed more than 110,000 Japanese Americans who lived along the Pacific Coast. Some of these Japanese Americans had lived in the country since the early 1900s and some were second-generation Japanese born in America.

Warren held two law degrees from the University of California at Berkeley and briefly practiced law before joining the Army to serve in World War I. After the war he spent 20 years in government service starting as a deputy district attorney and moving up to the lead position of attorney general in 1939. Warren was first elected California governor in 1943 on the Republican ticket and was reelected two more times on both the Republican and Democratic tickets. Safe to say he was a very popular California politician.

Eisenhower appointed Warren to the Supreme Court on September 30, 1953, which was just five days before the Court's term began. He replaced Chief Justice Frederick Vinson, who died on September 8, 1953. I'll talk more about Vinson in Chapter 7. Warren didn't have formal confirmation hearings at that time because the Senate was in recess. His formal confirmation wasn't until March 1954.

A Court Divided

Not unlike today's Supreme Court, which is almost evenly split between liberals and conservatives with many controversial Supreme Court rulings decided on a five to four vote, the Court Warren first took over was also divided in half with two strong factions. Luckily when the final number of Supreme Court justices was decided by Congress in the 1800s the decision favored an odd number of justices, which means one side of any issue can put together a majority decision.

Today's well-known fence sitter is Justice Sandra Day O'Connor, who straddles the fence on many issues and whose support is frequently needed to get a majority vote on a ruling. This can be a powerful role on a divided court because the fence sitter can demand certain changes in order to moderate the winning position.

In Warren's day the two factions split on the issue of judicial restraint versus the activist approach. The judicial restraint wing, who believed the law must be stable, was resistant to changing past precedents. The activists, who believed the law cannot stand still, supported changes in precedent as society changed.

Supreme Sayings

"I think he came to realize very early, certainly long before I came here [1958], that this group of nine rather prima donnaish people could not be led, could not be told, in the way the Governor of California can tell a subordinate, do this or do that."
—Justice Potter Stewart from *A History of the Supreme Court*

Before Earl Warren got to the court, Justice Felix Frankfurter was firmly in charge of the justices who believed in judicial restraint and Justices Hugo Black and William Douglas led the activist wing. Earl Warren quickly chose sides and joined the activists.

The key swing vote for Warren during the first half of his term was Justice Tom Clark, who was appointed by Truman in 1949. Clark was Truman's Attorney General before being nominated for the Court. Warren could count on him for many of the cases related to personal rights, but occasionally, Clark would take the role of sole dissenter when Warren did not successfully convince him to join the activist view.

The court stayed evenly divided until 1962 when Frankfurter retired from the court at the age of 79 and one other justice from his faction also retired. As replacements, President John Kennedy appointed one justice who joined the judicial restraint group, Justice Byron White, and one who joined the activist group, Justice Arthur Goldberg. This helped to solidify Warren's activist wing and gave him the power base he needed at the Court.

Just the Facts

Byron White sat on the fence for much of his time on the court from 1962 to 1993. He opposed many of the Warren Court decisions relating to criminal procedure and was in the majority of 807 five to four decisions during his 31 years on the Court. White, even though he was a Democratic appointee who was expected to join the liberal side of the Court, became a solid force for judicial restraint during the Warren Court and worked to overturn many of the decisions of that Court after Warren left.

Warren essentially led two courts—one evenly divided for about the first half of his term and one strongly activist for the second half. While the landmark desegregation case was decided early in his term on the court, most of the critical personal rights cases were decided after enough activists had joined the court in 1962.

Desegregating Schools

Let's take a close look at Warren's first landmark case, *Brown* v. *Board of Education*. This case was heard for the first time during the last year of Vinson's term, but the justices could not come to a decision and put the case back on the docket to be re-argued the next year. Before the next court session started, Vinson died and Warren was appointed to take his place.

In the early 1950s racial segregation in public schools was the norm across the United States. Even though all schools in a district were supposed to be equal, generally black schools were far inferior to white schools.

The case was brought in Topeka, Kansas, on behalf of a black third-grader named Linda Brown, who had to walk a mile to her black elementary school even though a white elementary school was only seven blocks from her house. Her father, Oliver Brown, tried to enroll her at the white school, but the principal refused to take her.

Oliver Brown's next stop was the National Association for the Advancement of Colored People (NAACP), who helped the Browns challenge the decision in court. Other parents in Topeka joined Brown and the NAACP requested an injunction to stop the segregation of Topeka's public schools. The U.S. District Court heard the case in June 1951. The NAACP argued that segregated schools sent the wrong message to black children—that they were inferior to whites.

Supreme Sayings

"… if the colored children are denied the experience in school of associating with white children, who represent 90 percent of our national society in which these colored children must live, then the colored child's curriculum is being greatly curtailed. The Topeka curriculum or any school curriculum cannot be equal under segregation."

—Dr. Hugh W. Speer, an expert witness for the NAACP during the trial

The Board of Education's response was that segregation in Topeka's schools and elsewhere prepared black children for the segregation they would face during adulthood. They also said that black Americans such as Frederick Douglass, Booker T. Washington, and George Washington Carver were still able to achieve their greatness even though they were products of segregated schools.

The district court ruled that while they agreed that segregation had a detrimental effect upon colored children by giving them a sense of inferiority, they must rule in favor of the Board of Education because of a long standing precedent *Plessy* v. *Ferguson*, which allowed separate but equal school systems for blacks and whites. The Supreme Court had not yet reversed that position.

Just the Facts

Plessy v. *Ferguson*, decided by the court in 1896, allowed an entire system of segregation of public facilities including schools, libraries, bus stations, and bathrooms. The lone dissenter on this case was Justice John Harlan (who served on the court from 1877 to 1912) who wrote, "Our Constitution is color-blind, and neither knows nor tolerates classes among citizens. In respect of civil rights, all citizens are equal before the law …. The present decision … will not only stimulate aggressions, more or less brutal and irritating, upon the admitted rights of colored citizens, but will encourage the belief that it is possible, by means of state enactments, to defeat the beneficent purposes which the people of the United States had in view when they adopted the recent amendments of the Constitution."

This was the controversy that faced Warren during his first year on the court. After the case was heard in December 1953, Warren lead his first conference to discuss the case. At the start of the conference Warren told the justices that he just wanted to discuss the case informally, but did not plan to take a vote. By the end of the conference Warren counted five or maybe six of the nine votes in favor of desegregation. He knew if the Supreme Court was going to rule in favor of desegregation he wanted it to be a unanimous ruling.

After the first conference he worked behind the scenes for about a month to garner support for the unanimous decision. Warren structured the second conference to concentrate on remedy rather than the more contentious question of overturning *Plessy*. The greatest concern of those in the judicial restraint camp was the possibility of devastating social upheaval if the court forced desegregation. To get around that concern and secure unanimity, the conclusion at that second conference was the court would support desegregation but ask for reargument about how to desegregate. This would give time for the country to adjust to the idea of desegregation and give flexibility about how it could be obtained.

Warren took the assignment to write the decision and continued to work behind closed doors with the other justices to draft an opinion that all would sign. He wanted to avoid any chance of dissenting opinions. Finally on May 17, 1954, Warren read the decision, which concluded:

> "We come then to the question presented: Does segregation of children in public schools solely on the basis of race, even though the physical facilities and other

'tangible' factors may be equal, deprive the children of the minority group of equal educational opportunities? We believe that it does …. We conclude that in the field of public education the doctrine of 'separate but equal' has no place. Separate educational facilities are inherently unequal."

The Supreme Court did not fully overturn *Plessy*, but only struck down the "separate but equal" doctrine for public education. The Court did not specify a time frame for deseg-regation, but did declare segregation, which was allowed or mandatory in 21 states, unconstitu-tional. By not stating a time frame for desegre-gation the Court found middle ground giving time for the public and the states to adjust to the change and figure out the best way to do it.

Supreme Sayings

Senator Harry Byrd of Virginia declared the *Brown* decision "the most serious blow that has yet been struck against the rights of the states in a matter vitally affecting their authority and welfare."

The firestorm of words started quickly. Southern senators and governors quickly pounced on the decision. Most said they would never agree to desegregation and some even thought a second civil war was possible. The next year the Supreme Court published its second ruling related to how desegregation should be implemented and left it to the district courts to manage the process. The two decisions opened the flood gates and the country faced years of battles, both in the courts and on the streets, before true desegregation existed in the school system. By the 1960s the Warren Court declared all types of segregation in public facilities unconstitutional. We'll talk more about this issue in Chapter 18.

Mandating Criminal Rights

The next major focus for the Warren Court was criminal justice and the rights of people accused or convicted of a crime. The first landmark case in this area was *Griffin* v. *Illinois*. Griffin was convicted of a bank robbery by an Illinois state court. He wanted to appeal the decision, but could not afford to pay for a court transcript. He asked for a free transcript and his request was denied by the state court, so he appealed the decision to the Supreme Court.

Warren believed that a defendant who could afford to pay for a transcript had an advantage of one who could not. The Supreme Court ruled in 1956 that it violates the Constitution for a state to refuse a transcript to a defendant who cannot afford to pay for it. The transcript is needed to adequately prepare an appeal.

This gave precedent for the decision in the next major case on the issue, *Gideon* v. *Wainwright*. In this case Clarence Gideon was charged in a Florida state court because he was accused of breaking into a poolroom with the intent to commit a *misdemeanor*, which was a *felony* under Florida law. Gideon could not afford to hire an attorney and asked for one appointed by the court. The state court refused saying that Florida law only allowed council appointed by the court when charged with a *capital offense*. Gideon challenged this ruling to the Supreme Court.

Court Connotations

Misdemeanors are minor crimes with the least severe level of penalty, usually small fines and sometimes a short jail sentence. **Felonies** are more serious crimes with stronger penalties, larger fines and longer jail terms. **Capital offenses** are the most serious crimes, usually related to murder or other crimes in which the death penalty could be imposed. Whether a crime is a misdemeanor, felony, or capital offense is determined by each state. Federal law also has similar designations for crimes against the government.

Gideon was forced to defend himself at trial. He was declared guilty and sentenced to five years in state prison. After the trial he petitioned the Florida Supreme Court for a writ of habeas corpus saying that the state's refusal to appoint counsel denied him rights "guaranteed by the Constitution and the Bill of Rights by the United States Government." The Florida State Supreme Court denied him relief. He then took his case to the United States Supreme Court.

Supreme Sayings

"The right of one charged with crime to counsel may not be deemed fundamental and essential to fair trials in some countries, but it is in ours. From the very beginning, our state and national constitutions and laws have laid great emphasis on procedural and substantive safeguards designed to assure fair trials before impartial tribunals in which every defendant stands equal before the law. This noble ideal cannot be realized if the poor man charged with crime has to face his accusers without a lawyer to assist him."
—Supreme Court in its opinion on *Gideon* v. *Wainwright*

The Warren Court ruled in 1963 that not only was Gideon entitled to legal representation, but that because his request for court-appointed representation was denied by the state court, his conviction was overturned. This ruling overturned a 1942 case *Betts* v. *Brady* in which the Supreme Court ruled that a defendant was not entitled to state-appointed council. The two cases were similar. Betts was charged with a felony in Maryland state court and denied state-appointed counsel even though he could not afford counsel.

The landmark criminal rights case you're probably most familiar with is *Miranda* v. *Arizona*. This is the case that established the requirement for reading a person his or her *Miranda* warnings when taken into custody.

Ernesto Miranda was convicted on charges of kidnapping and rape. He had been arrested and interrogated for two hours without being advised that he had the right to have an attorney present. After two hours he confessed and that confession was used to convict him. The Supreme Court overturned his conviction because it found that the prosecution could not use statements made by a person in police custody unless certain minimum procedural safeguards were in place.

Living Laws

Today the safeguards that make up the Mirada warnings are:

◆ the right to remain silent;

◆ the fact that anything you say may be used in evidence against you;

◆ the right to request the presence of an attorney, either retained by yourself or appointed by the court;

◆ the right, even after beginning to answer questions, to stop answering questions or request an attorney.

This was definitely one of the most controversial decisions of the Warren Court. His successors, Chief Justices Warren Burger and William Rehnquist, have called for it to be overturned. We'll talk more about their attempts to overturn this ruling in the next chapter. In section six, we'll be discussing cases involving criminal proceedings.

Focusing on Personal Rights

I've given you an overview of some of the key cases decided during the Warren Court. His court reviewed many more cases guaranteeing individual rights. These included freedom of press, speech, and religion in addition to the rulings on desegregation and criminal proceedings.

One landmark ruling involving freedom of the press during the Warren Court was *New York Times Co.* v. *Sullivan* in 1964. The Court ruled that under the First and Fourteenth Amendments, a state court cannot award damages to a public official for defamatory falsehoods relating to his or her official conduct unless the official can prove *actual malice*.

Court Connotations

Actual malice is a statement that was made with the knowledge that it was false or with reckless disregard to whether or not it was true or false.

L.B. Sullivan was one of three people elected commissioner of the City of Montgomery, Alabama. His responsibilities included supervision of the police department. On March 29, 1960 *The New York Times* printed a full-page advertisement entitled, "Heed the Rising Voices," about the civil rights movement in Alabama. Sullivan sued four Alabama clergymen and the *Times* for damages alleging that he had been libeled by statements in the advertisement.

Sullivan claimed that two of the ten paragraphs in the ad libeled him. The first paragraph in question was:

> "In Montgomery, Alabama, after students sang 'My Country, 'Tis of Thee' on the State Capitol steps, their leaders were expelled from school, and truckloads of police armed with shotguns and tear gas ringed the Alabama State College Campus. When the entire student body protested to state authorities by refusing to reregister, their dining hall was padlocked in an attempt to starve them into submission."

And the second paragraph was:

> "Again and again, the Southern violators have answered Dr. King's peaceful protests with intimidation and violence. They have bombed his home, almost killing his wife and child. They have assaulted his person. They have arrested him seven times—for "speeding," "loitering" and similar "offenses." And now they have charged him with "perjury"—a felony under which they could imprison him for ten years. ..."

As you can see, Sullivan's name was not mentioned, but he alleged that since he was the commissioner in charge of police he was libeled. Some of the statements in the ad were proved to be falsehoods, including:

♦ Students sang the National Anthem and not "My Country 'Tis of Thee."

♦ Nine students were expelled for demanding service at a lunch counter in the Montgomery County Courthouse not for the demonstration at the Capitol.

♦ Most of the student body protested, not the entire student body, by boycotting classes on a single day, not by refusing to reregister for classes.

♦ The campus dining hall was never padlocked.

♦ Police were deployed near the campus in large numbers on three occasions, but never "ringed" the campus.

- ◆ Dr. Martin Luther King Jr. was arrested only four times, not seven times.

- ◆ Dr. Martin Luther King Jr. claimed he was assaulted for loitering outside a courtroom, but one of the officers that made the arrest denied there was such an assault.

- ◆ While Dr. King's home had been bombed twice when his wife and children were there, these bombings happened before Sullivan was commissioner.

The advertisement was placed by a New York advertising agency and cost $4,800. The agency submitted the advertisement with a letter from A. Philip Randolph as chairman of the Committee to Defend Dr. Martin Luther King Jr. and the Struggle for Freedom in the South, which signed the ad along with 64 named persons. Randolph said these people had given permission for the use of their names, but each testified that they had never granted permission and did not know about the ad until they were asked to retract their statements. Neither the *Times* nor the advertising agency confirmed the accuracy of the ad.

The case first was heard before the Circuit Court of Montgomery County, which awarded Sullivan damages of $500,000. This ruling was affirmed by the Supreme Court of Alabama. The *Times* appealed to the United States Supreme Court.

The Supreme Court unanimously overturned the lower court ruling. In writing the opinion for the Court, Justice Brennan said:

> "… we consider this case against the background of a profound national commitment to the principle that debate on public issues should be uninhibited, robust, and wide open, and that it may well include vehement, caustic, and sometimes unpleasantly sharp attacks on government and public officials …. The present advertisement, as an expression of grievance and protest on one of the major public issues of our time, would seem clearly to qualify for the constitutional protection. The question is whether it forfeits that protection by the falsity of some of its factual statements and by its alleged defamation of respondent.

> "Authoritative interpretations of the First Amendment guarantees have consistently refused to recognize an exception for any test of truth—whether administered by judges, juries, or administrative officials—and especially one that puts the burden of proving truth on the speaker."

This case reaffirmed the Court's strong support for Freedom of Speech when key public issues are being debated even if some falsehoods work their way into the public debate. Public officials today cannot sue for libel unless they can prove malice.

Sometimes the issue of whether or not someone is a public official will be challenged in the courts today.

Leaving the Court

Warren definitely liked to control the situation. He even thought he could be involved in the decision of who would replace him. He sent a letter of resignation in June 1968 hoping to give President Lyndon B. Johnson the opportunity to appoint his successor rather than the next president.

His decision backfired. Johnson nominated Abe Fortas (already an Associate Justice), but he was never confirmed. Opposition to his nomination was primarily from southern Democrats and conservative Republicans, who stalled a vote in committee, which is still a common practice today when the Senate is considering judicial appointments (filibustering).

The Senate Judiciary Committee vote was stalled by opponents of Fortas until after the summer break. By the time the committee took up the nomination in September, information was uncovered that Fortas was paid to teach a seminar at American University with funds partially contributed by clients of Fortas' former law practice. Opposition mounted to his nomination and the Senate was unable to cut off debate because several Senators decided to filibuster the nomination. Fortas asked Johnson to withdraw his name.

Warren served one more year on the court and President Richard Nixon appointed his successor—Warren Burger. Next we'll look at how Burger changed the tone of the court and worked to reverse much of what Earl Warren accomplished.

The Least You Need to Know

- ◆ Earl Warren, whose background was in politics rather than the judiciary, was known for his political management skills and his willingness to change court precedent even if at times it resulted in major social and political upheaval.

- ◆ The Warren court is best known for reversing years of school segregation with the landmark *Brown* v. *Board of Education* decision.

- ◆ The Warren Court also decided many key cases related to criminal proceedings that are still a major part of U.S. criminal law today, including the Miranda warnings.

- ◆ Public officials cannot sue for libel unless they can prove malice.

Chapter 6

Burger Court

In This Chapter

♦ Shaking up the Court

♦ Middle-of-the-road takes control

♦ Court decision leads to presidential resignation

♦ Legalizing abortion

After successfully stopping the nomination of Abe Fortas as Chief Justice, the Republicans won overwhelmingly in the next election and President Richard Nixon got to appoint Chief Justice Earl Warren's successor. He wanted to find someone who would reshape the court in his image and he chose Warren Burger.

Burger was not a forceful leader and was never able to overturn any of the Warren Court's rulings. Instead his court was led by the moderate justices who tried to find middle ground. While it might not have been his intention when he took over the court, his court's ruling on abortion set off a social struggle that continues to split the nation today.

By the end of the Burger court the idea of judicial restraint died and the appointment of activist justices seemed to be the norm for the foreseeable future. This battle between conservative versus liberal activism still divides the court, and the country, today.

Let's take a look at how all this got started and how the Burger Court was steered by the middle, and then I'll review a couple of landmark cases, including one that led to the first resignation of a U.S. president.

Chief Justice Warren E Burger's official portrait by photographer Robert Oaks.

(From the Collection of the Supreme Court of the United States)

Political Firestorm That Fizzled

Richard Nixon knew that he needed to replace at least two justices in order to stop the liberalism of the Warren Court. While Warren's resignation sat on his desk when he arrived at the White House, one definite appointment wasn't enough for him, so he started a campaign to get rid of the other liberal judges.

Bob Woodward writes in his book, *The Brethren*, that Nixon's Attorney General John Mitchell assisted *Life Magazine* with a story that exposed an annual payment of $20,000 to Abe Fortas from a foundation funded by millionaire Louis Wolfson, who was then under investigation by the Securities and Exchange Commission (SEC). Wolfson told friends that Fortas would help him. After the *Life Magazine* story, "Fortas of the Supreme Court: A Question of Ethics," Fortas was quietly pressured to resign from the court.

Nixon chose Harry Blackmun to replace Fortas, but he turned out to be a disappointment. Rather than join the conservative activist wing, he instead sided with the justices looking to find middle ground and was reluctant to reverse court precedent.

Once Nixon had his two appointments in place, he didn't want to stop there, according to Woodward. If he could force two other liberal justices off the court, he'd really be able to make a long-term impact on the judicial branch. William Douglas, who had served on the court for 30 years, was criticized for his $12,000 per year directorship on the board of the Albert Parvin Foundation. Douglas resigned from the foundation to avoid any question of ethics and stayed on the Court.

Next on the attack agenda was William Brennan because of a real estate investment he held with Fortas and some other lower justices. To avoid any question of ethics, Woodward writes in *The Brethren*, Brennan not only divested the real estate investment, he also sold all his stocks, resigned from the board of Harvard University, and quit a part-time summer teaching post at New York University.

Court Connotations

Brethren, or brother, is a term used by the justices, who were an exclusively male club until 1981 when the first female justice, Sandra Day O'Connor, was appointed during Burger's term. Some wondered if her appointment would end the tradition. Today even with two women on the court the tradition holds.

Nixon's desire to quickly reconstitute the makeup of the court failed. He did finally get to appoint two more justices in 1971, Lewis Powell and William Rehnquist, who replaced one Roosevelt liberal, Hugo Black, and one Eisenhower conservative, John Harlan. Powell, too, turned out to be disappointment because he joined the justices in the middle rather than the Burger activist conservative wing.

Controlling at the Center

As we've discussed in Chapter 3, the politics inside the court are primarily driven by who gets to pick the person who will write the court's decision. If the chief justice is not in the majority, he loses his control of that decision. Instead it falls to the most senior associate justice. This tradition gave those justices sitting in the middle the greatest role in shaping the Burger court. In many instances Burger actually ended up voting with the middle to gain control of decision-writing. As we'll discuss, he joined the landmark *Roe* v. *Wade* decision legalizing abortion so he could pick Harry Blackmun to write the decision.

The senior justice for the middle-of-the-road group was Eisenhower appointee Associate Justice Potter Stewart. He was joined by Kennedy appointee Byron White. By 1975, when President Gerald Ford appointed John P. Stevens, this middle group had a block of five votes. In addition to Stewart, White, and Stevens were two other Nixon appointees: Blackmun and Lewis Powell.

Even though Nixon appointed four justices, only two joined the conservative activist wing. Rehnquist voted solidly as conservative activist. Burger played politics and frequently joined the center court justices so he could control the final decision-writing. President Lyndon Johnson's appointee Thurgood Marshall and President Eisenhower's appointee William Brennan both kept true to the liberalism of the Warren Court. Stevens and Rehnquist are still on the court today.

While Rehnquist as chief justice still leads firmly from the conservative side, Stevens has moved steadily to the left. Today he is found far more often voting with the liberal block. Some actually see Stevens as a loner. He holds the record for writing more lone opinions, either dissenting (opposing the decision) or concurring (agreeing with the decision, but adding some unique twist).

Supreme Sayings

"Widely considered a 'sure swing vote' in the Court's center, Stevens fairly rapidly proved to be found far more frequently with the 'liberal bloc,' increasingly so with the passing of time .... A 'gadfly to the brethren,' a personal loner, a legal maverick, he forever challenges his colleagues .... He has written more dissenting and concurring opinions than any of his colleagues. To dissent, of course, is one thing; but to engage in the veritable flood of concurring opinions that have emanated from Stevens's pen is quite another—for they all too often muddy the constitutional law waters and lay themselves open to the charge that they are ego trips."

—Henry J. Abraham, author of *Justices, Presidents, and Senators: A History of the U.S. Supreme Court Appointments from Washington to Clinton*

Dethroning a President

Ironically President Nixon, who so much wanted to remake the Court in his own image, was forced to resign because of a landmark decision of the Supreme Court. Even Chief Justice Burger ended up siding against him in the unanimous decision of the *United States* v. *Nixon* in 1974. Rehnquist did not participate in that decision (he recused himself).

You probably remember that Nixon was reelected to office in 1972 after a landslide defeat of Democrat George McGovern. Dirty tricks played by Nixon's reelection committee ultimately destroyed his presidency. On June 17, 1972 burglars broke into the Democratic Party campaign headquarters at the Watergate complex in Washington,

D.C. The actual break-in was given little notice by the press until *The Washington Post* investigative team led by Bob Woodward and Carl Bernstein found links to top government officials.

The Nixon administration repeatedly denied any connection to the burglary, but information connecting the administration started to dribble out. Woodward and Bernstein found a secret informant they called "Deep Throat" to help expose the Nixon administration. To this day no one knows who Deep Throat was, even though there has been lots of speculation.

The Congress and the public pressured Nixon to appoint a special prosecutor. During the special prosecutor's investigation, it was learned that Nixon secretly taped conversations in the Oval Office. On March 1974, a federal grand jury indicted seven Nixon associates for conspiracy and named President Nixon an unindicted co-conspirator. At the same hearing the prosecutor asked for a subpoena so he could hear those tapes because he believed they were relevant to the criminal investigation. Nixon turned over edited transcripts of some of tapes, but refused to turn over the tapes asserting the right of *executive privilege*.

Court Connotations

Executive privilege is claim not mentioned in the Constitution, but one that presidents invoke on the constitutional principle of separation of powers. Presidents believe that this privilege permits them to resist requests for information by the Congressional and judicial branches.

The district court denied the claim for executive privilege and the case was taken to the Supreme Court. The court needed to decide two critical issues:

- ♦ Was the judiciary the ultimate arbiter of the Constitution? This was easy to reaffirm using the Marshall Court's ruling in *Marbury* v. *Madison*.

- ♦ Could the president withhold materials germane to a criminal investigation using the claim of executive privilege? The court ruled that no person, not even the president, was above the law.

Some thought Nixon would not comply, but within eight hours of the Supreme Court ruling on July 24, 1974, Nixon said he would turn over the tapes. Transcripts of 64 tape recordings were released on August 5 and damaging information was found on the tapes that linked the White House to the Watergate cover-up and the fact that Nixon was involved in that cover-up as early as June 23, 1972. Three days later, after it was clear he had lost all Congressional support, Nixon announced his resignation before he could be impeached.

In deciding the case, the Supreme Court did state that the president has limited executive privilege in areas of military or diplomatic affairs, but found that due process in criminal law took precedence over that privilege. Here's a brief quote from that decision read by Chief Justice Burger:

> "In this case we must weigh the importance of the general privilege of confidentiality of Presidential communications in performance of the President's responsibilities against the inroads of such a privilege on the fair administration of criminal justice. The interest in preserving confidentiality is weighty indeed and entitled to great respect. However, we cannot conclude that advisers will be moved to temper the candor of their remarks by the infrequent occasions of disclosure because of the possibility that such conversations will be called for in the context of a criminal prosecution.

> "On the other hand, the allowance of the privilege to withhold evidence that is demonstrably relevant in a criminal trial would cut deeply into the guarantee of due process of law and gravely impair the basic function of the courts. A President's acknowledged need for confidentiality in the communications of his office is general in nature, whereas the constitutional need for production of relevant evidence in a criminal proceeding is specific and central to the fair adjudication of a particular criminal case in the administration of justice. Without access to specific facts a criminal prosecution may be totally frustrated. The President's broad interest in confidentiality of communications will not be vitiated by disclosure of a limited number of conversations preliminarily shown to have some bearing on the pending criminal cases."

The Court's decision and the nation's first presidential resignation certainly sent shockwaves through the country. There is no question its impact is still felt to some extent politically today, but another controversial case from the Burger Court has created even more political divisions that continue to divide the country today—*Roe* v. *Wade*.

Starting the Abortion Debate

Long before *Roe* v. *Wade* made it to the doorstep of the Supreme Court, the issue was creating controversy throughout the United States. Women who could afford it found a way to get an abortion in states where it was legal or secretly in private doctors' offices. Poor women who could not afford to travel, but chose to have an abortion, did so at illegal make-shift clinics that frequently did not meet even the minimum standards of cleanliness. Many women were hospitalized or died after these illegal abortions. In fact, statistics in 1965 showed that 17 percent of deaths related to pregnancy and childbirth could be tied to abortion. The laws that made it a criminal offense for a doctor to perform an abortion were 100 years old or more in most states.

Just the Facts

By the late 1960s, efforts were being made in almost every state to decriminalize abortion. Supporters from health care providers, women's rights advocates, clergy members, and the legal community lobbied state legislatures to overturn laws that were in place before 1900. Most of these laws dated back to the mid-1800s. Prior to that time, abortion was allowed in this country before "quickening" or first fetal movements. Between 1967 and 1973, four states appealed their abortion laws—Alaska, Hawaii, New York, and Washington. Lawsuits challenging the remaining laws were working their way through about a dozen states.

Jane Roe, who is now identified as Norma McCorvey (she went public in 1984), was a single woman from Texas who found out she was pregnant for the third time. Her mother had custody of her first daughter and the father of her second daughter took custody of that child. McCorvey was a high school dropout from a broken home and spent a good part of her childhood in reform schools.

When she went to her doctor and said she didn't want the third child, he said he wouldn't help her. She approached a second doctor who sent her to an attorney with the expectation that he would help her find someone to adopt the baby, but she did tell the attorney she wished abortions were legal in Texas. He put her in touch with the two attorneys who ended up arguing the case all the way to the Supreme Court—Linda Coffee and Sarah Weddington. These attorneys were working with the First Unitarian Church, which was planning to challenge the Texas law with a public campaign. Coffee and Weddington thought a court case would give them needed publicity for the campaign.

After McCorvey, Weddington and Coffee met, they decided to file suit against the Dallas County district attorney Henry Wade, seeking an injunction to bar him from enforcing the Texas statute. The statute making abortion a criminal act dated back to 1854 and carried a penalty of two to five years in jail. In the complaint filed on March 3, 1970 in federal court, Roe alleged that the law denied her "right to safe and adequate medical advice pertaining to the decision of whether to carry a given pregnancy to term" and asked the court to declare it unconstitutional citing rights related to the First, Fourth, Fifth, Eighth, Ninth and Fourteenth Amendments. They certainly wanted to be sure something stuck.

The federal court ruled in Roe's favor based on the *Ninth Amendment* and the state of Texas appealed the case to the United States Supreme Court. In their unanimous decision on June 17, 1970, the United States Appeals Court panel of judges ruled that Texas abortion laws "must be declared unconstitutional because they deprive single women and married couples of their right, secured by the Ninth Amendment, to choose whether to have children."

The primary case used as precedent for this decision was *Griswold* v. *Connecticut (1965)*, which involved the appeal of the criminal conviction of the executive director of the Planned Parenthood League of Connecticut for providing contraceptives to married couples. In that case the Supreme Court ruled that a state statute making it a crime to use birth control violated a couple's right to privacy, using the Ninth Amendment as the basis for that ruling.

Court Connotations

The **Ninth Amendment** to the Constitution states, "The enumeration in the Constitution, of certain rights, shall not be construed to deny or disparage others retained by the people." This amendment was used in previous cases to grant individuals fundamental rights to be protected from governmental infringement.

Roe v. *Wade* made it to the doorstep of the Supreme Court in October 1970, but it wasn't until May 21, 1971 that the court announced it would review the case. It also decided to review a Georgia case, *Doe* v. *Bolton*. Georgia's law had been modernized and allowed abortions to protect a woman's health or in the case of rape, but required there be a three-doctor panel to determine if abortion would be allowed. It also imposed restrictions on abortion procedures. Arguments were set for December 13, 1971. At that point the court had only seven justices. Hugo Black and John Harlan had resigned within six days of each other in September 1971 because of cancer and both died before the end of 1971.

Just like the previously controversial desegregation case, the justices could not come to a decision and decided to rehear the case in the next session. By the time the case was heard for the second time, Rehnquist and Powell were on the bench.

Blackmun, who had been assigned to write the decision by Burger after the first conference, continued to research the issue through the summer. In the conference after hearing the case for the second time, Blackmun urged his brethren to strike down the abortion laws. He got five justices to go along with him and then Burger joined the majority so he could have influence over the writing of the opinion.

The key controversy was the question of "viability." The court had to determine at what point a fetus is viable, which is when the court would permit restrictions on abortion. In writing the decision, Blackmun developed the idea of breaking up pregnancy into three trimesters. During the first trimester (first three months), Blackmun placed no restrictions on abortion, leaving decisions entirely up to a woman and her doctor. During the second trimester (middle three months), Blackmun said states could regulate abortion to protect a women's health. Blackmun only allowed states to prohibit abortions in the third trimester—unless childbirth endangered a woman's health.

Living Laws

Roe legalized abortion nationwide. At the time the decision was handed down, most states outlawed abortion except to save a woman's life or for limited reasons such as preserving the woman's health, instances of rape, incest, or fetal anomaly. *Roe* declared these laws unconstitutional, making abortion services safer and more accessible to women throughout the country. The legal precedent set by this case affected more than 20 subsequent Supreme Court cases involving restrictions on access to abortion.

Rather than use the Ninth Amendment as a basis for ruling the Texas law unconstitutional, Blackmun instead based his decision on the Fourteenth Amendment's due process clause, which guarantees the right to the concept of personal liberty. Seven of the nine justices signed onto Blackmun's decision, including Burger. Rehnquist and White dissented. Blackmun wrote in his decision:

> "This right of privacy, whether it be founded in the Fourteenth Amendment's concept of personal liberty and restrictions upon state action, as we feel it is, or, as the District Court determined, in the Ninth Amendment's reservation of rights to the people, is broad enough to encompass a woman's decision whether or not to terminate her pregnancy. The detriment that the State would impose upon the pregnant woman by denying this choice altogether is apparent. Specific and direct harm medically diagnosable even in early pregnancy may be involved. Maternity, or additional offspring, may force upon the woman a distressful life and future. Psychological harm may be imminent. Mental and physical health may be taxed by child care. There is also the distress, for all concerned, associated with the unwanted child, and there is the problem of bringing a child into a family already unable, psychologically and otherwise, to care for it. In other cases, as in this one, the additional difficulties and continuing stigma of unwed motherhood may be involved. All these are factors the woman and her responsible physician necessarily will consider in consultation."

The firestorm of political debate started by this decision still festers in the United States today. When the decision came down, the country was evenly divided. In the first Gallup Poll after the decision, 46 percent of the respondents supported the right of a woman and her doctor to choose to have an abortion in the first trimester, while 45 percent opposed. A Gallup Poll released in May 2003 found that 80 percent of the population thinks that abortion should be legal under any (23 percent) circumstances or certain (57 percent) circumstances. Only 19 percent say that abortion should be illegal under all circumstances.

> **Just the Facts**
>
> Norma McCorvey joined the anti-abortion movement in the mid-1980s. She filed a suit in 2003 trying to overturn *Roe* v. *Wade*. In her motion to a Dallas federal court, she claimed changes in the law and advances in medicine made the original decision unjust. She said in a rally to support her suit, "I'm so sorry that I filed that affidavit. I long for the day that justice will be done and the burden from these deaths will be removed from my shoulders." McCorvey's recent motion was quickly denied. Most saw it as a publicity stunt and not a serious court case.

Serious attempts to overturn *Roe* v. *Wade* so far have failed, even though a number of cases have made it to the Supreme Court. Restrictions have been placed on women's rights in these later cases, such as the need for young women to get parental consent to have an abortion. Many believe one more conservative justice will be enough to overturn *Roe* v. *Wade*, but that will depend upon which justice is being replaced.

Activism Takes Over the Court

The Warren Court threw down the gauntlet in moving the court in a liberal direction. The Burger Court tried unsuccessfully to take up the challenge and reverse the Warren's Court successes, especially in the area of criminal rights. Burger's lack of strong leadership left a fractured court that was not able to live up to the dreams of Nixon's conservative constituency.

Reagan rekindled those efforts when he elevated Rehnquist to the position of Chief Justice and appointed conservatives Sandra Day O'Connor and Antonin Scalia. Rehnquist's court still does not have the votes to overturn *Roe* v. *Wade* and most of the Warren Court decisions, but that could change if the Bush Administration is able to shift the balance toward the conservative wing with any appointments he gets to make to the court. If Rehnquist leaves the court, as is expected by many, appointing a conservative would not shift the balance, but if one of the moderate or liberal justices leaves, the Court's balance could be changed for years to come.

Either way, the age of judicial activism, whether liberal or conservative, is firmly in place and likely will dominate judicial appointments for a long time, if not forever. The judiciary has certainly become much more political since the social revolution started by the Warren Court. In the next chapter, we'll briefly discuss other chief justices who influenced the building of the court.

The Least You Need to Know

- ◆ Earl Warren was replaced by Chief Justice Warren Burger, who sought to overturn many of the Warren Court's decisions. He was never successful because his Court instead was led by the moderate justices.

- ◆ The Burger court rocked the country when it ruled that Nixon must release his taped conversations relating to Watergate, which ultimately led to Nixon's resignation.

- ◆ The legalization of abortion was another landmark decision of the Burger Court—a decision that still divides the country today.

Chapter 7

Ebbs and Flows of Court Leadership

In This Chapter

- ◆ Chief justice dozen
- ◆ Dreading Dred Scott
- ◆ Understanding laissez faire
- ◆ Stopping worker protections

A dozen chief justices served between John Marshall and Earl Warren. All had some impact on the building of our judicial system, some more than others, but none as great as those two giants of the court.

The activist times starting with the Warren Court and continuing today are not the first time there have been activist periods on the Court. The Court has ebbed and flowed between periods of judicial restraint and judicial activism throughout its history. The activist periods occurred primarily when the country faced economic, political, or social crisis, such as the buildup to the Civil War, the aftermath of two World Wars, and the Great Depression.

I'll take you on a quick trip back in history to briefly discuss the other courts led by the other chief justices and review key decisions of these courts.

Taney Court, 1837 to 1864

Chief Justice Roger Taney had the difficult position of following the true star of the Court. Not an easy act to follow. Many feared he would try to overturn much of Marshall's work building the stature of the court, especially because of this sentence he wrote about the Supreme Court during a controversy involving the Bank of America, "the opinion of the judges has no more authority over Congress than the opinion of Congress has over the judges, and on that point the President is independent of both. The authority of the Supreme Court must not, therefore, be permitted to control the Congress or the Executive." If he followed through on this belief, he would overturn the Marshall decisions that strengthened the Court.

Official portrait of Chief Justice Roger Taney painted by George P. A. Healy.

(Photography by Vic Boswell from the Collection of the Supreme Court of the United States)

Supporters of what Marshall accomplished feared the court was doomed, but these fears proved unwarranted because judicial restraint ruled the day and the Taney Court was reluctant to overturn precedents set by the Marshall Court. The primary contribution of the Taney Court to the foundation of U.S. law was the belief that property should not be secondary to the needs of man.

Charles River Bridge v. Warren Bridge

One landmark case that reinforced that belief was *Charles River Bridge* v. *Warren Bridge*. The Charles River Bridge was run by a corporation held by Harvard College and some of Boston's leading citizens. The corporation ran a toll bridge over the Charles River in Boston based on a charter granted in 1785. The bridge owners made huge profits and the stock in the corporation rose tenfold.

The public was outraged by the monopoly granted this small group of people and in 1828 the Massachusetts legislature granted a charter for a second bridge over the Charles River to the Warren Bridge Company. The second charter mandated that the new bridge would become a free bridge shortly after construction. A free bridge, of course, hurt the business of the Charles River Bridge Corporation, so they filed suit claiming that the legislature had broken its contract, which the corporation believed had prohibited the construction of another bridge. The case made it to the Supreme Court for oral arguments on January 24, 1837.

Living Laws

In *Charles River Bridge v. Warren Bridge* the Taney Court established a key principal that drives property decisions today: Property rights must, when necessary, be secondary to the needs of the community. Today this decision placing community needs over personal property rights still stands as a key precedent in cases involving personal property versus local needs. We most often see this precedent come to life when people must sell their property to a government entity, frequently at reduced market value, to make way for road construction, water projects, and other needs of the community.

In its decision handed down on February 12, 1837, the Taney Court held that property rights must, when necessary, be secondary to the needs of the community. The Court decided that the legislature did not give exclusive control over the waters of the river nor did it invade corporate rights by interfering with the company's ability to make a profit. The Taney Court's decision was critical to the country's need for encouraging economic development. In this case the new bridge met the community's need for finding new channels for travel and trade.

This case was just one of many decided during the years of the Taney Court that established the rights of corporations, as well as the limits that could be put on those rights. His court was the first to rule that corporations could operate outside the state in which they were chartered. It also set the groundwork for the legal theory that a corporation is on the same footing as a person when taken to court. We'll talk more about business cases and corporate law in Chapters 24 to 26.

Dred Scott v. Sandford

The first 20 years of the Taney Court showed to all its critics that they were wrong to think Taney would work to diminish the stature of the Court. Then a case that will live in infamy did diminish the Court when it made it to the Supreme Court's doorstep in 1857—*Dred Scott* v. *Sandford*, a case that ultimately hastened the start of the Civil War.

The case started in 1846, when a 50-year-old slave named Dred Scott filed suit for his freedom and the freedom of his wife. At that time, some areas of the country permitted slavery, while others prohibited it. Scott was purchased from a family named the Blows when they were living in St. Louis by Dr. John Emerson, who was a military surgeon.

While Emerson owned him, Scott moved with his new owner to posts in the free territories where slavery was prohibited. While in the free territories, Dred Scott married Harriet Robinson, who was also a slave and had two children, Eliza and Lizzie. He never challenged his status as a slave while living in those territories. In 1842, the Scotts returned to St. Louis with Dr. Emerson and his new wife Irene. Dr. Emerson died in 1843 and Irene started hiring out Dred Scott, his wife and their children.

By that time the Scotts had lived in the free territories for a total of nine years. Scott could not read and had no money, but was helped by his minister, John Anderson. His original owners, the Blows, were among the friends who helped the Scotts through the 11 years of legal battles. Scott lost in St. Louis court the first time the trial was heard in 1847, but that ruling was overturned because hearsay evidence was presented. The Scotts won their freedom in a second trial. Mrs. Emerson appealed the case to the Missouri State Supreme Court, which reversed the ruling and returned the Scotts to slavery. The court ruled that Missouri law allowed slavery and it would uphold the rights of slave owners.

Just the Facts

No one is certain what drove the Scotts to finally file suit for their freedom, but on April 6, 1846, Dred Scott and his wife Harriet filed suit against Irene Emerson. Three reasons have been given as possibilities—that they didn't like being hired out, that Mrs. Emerson was planning to sell them, or that he offered to buy out his family's freedom and was refused. Many believe that friends in St. Louis who opposed slavery encouraged Scott to sue for his freedom. Missouri courts had ruled in the past in favor of the doctrine "once free, always free." Because Scott had lived in the free territories, he counted on those past rulings when he filed.

Dred Scott wasn't giving up on freedom for himself or his family. He found a new team of lawyers who hated slavery. The new legal team filed suit in St. Louis Federal Court in 1854. Mrs. Emerson's brother, John F.A. Sanford, who was executor of the Emerson estate, lived in New York, which gave them the option of filing in Federal Court because he lived in another state. The Federal Court ruled in favor of the Sandfords and Dred Scott appealed it to the United States Supreme Court.

Taney's Court was filled with a majority of justices from south of the Mason-Dixon Line. Taney was born in Maryland, where his family owned a tobacco farm and were slave owners. The Supreme Court in a 7 to 2 decision ruled against freeing Dred Scott from slavery for three reasons:

1. Blacks, regardless of whether they are free or slaves, are not and could not be citizens.

2. Temporary residence of a slave in the free territories did not bestow freedom.

3. Congress, under the Fifth Amendment, did not have the authority to deprive citizens of their property. This ruling wiped out the slavery provisions of the *Missouri Compromise*.

Court Connotations

The **Missouri Compromise** was the brainchild of Henry Clay. Missouri was admitted as a slave state, while at the same time Maine was admitted as a free state. This kept the balance of 12 free states and 12 slaves states. As future states were added over the next 30 years, the balance had to be kept with one free state and one slave state admitted at the same time. States north of the 36 degrees 30 minutes north latitude, which was the southern boundary of Missouri, were free states. States south of that line could decide for themselves.

Taney read the court's ruling, which included this finding:

"[Negros] had for more than a century before been regarded as beings of an inferior order; and altogether unfit to associate with the white race, either in social or political relations; and so far inferior that they had no rights which the white man was bound to respect; and that the Negro might justly and lawfully be reduced to slavery for his benefit. He was bought and sold, and treated as an ordinary article of merchandise and traffic."

The case split the Democratic Party, which was in power at the time. The northern faction opposed slavery, while the southern faction supported it. A new faction of the

Republication Party had been founded in 1854 to lead the fight to prohibit the spread of slavery. The rift in the Democratic Party caused by this decision helped to fuel the election of Abraham Lincoln, who ran on the Republican ticket. After this election, South Carolina was the first to secede from the Union, followed by the other Southern States, which led to the Civil War.

Just the Facts

In 1850, Irene Emerson married a northern Congressman, Calvin Chaffee, who opposed slavery. After winning the case in the Supreme Court, the new Mrs. Chaffee turned the Scotts over to the Blows, who gave the Scotts their freedom in May 1857. Dred Scott died of tuberculosis in 1858 and never lived to see the Civil War that was fought after this decision.

Chase Court, 1864 to 1873

Taney's successor, Samuel Chase, was one of the least distinguished chief justices. His legal experiences were considered by many to be that of a glorified collection agent. Most of his career was spent on building his political base. He was a former Secretary of the Treasury and the head of the new Republican Party that helped get Lincoln elected.

Chase clearly sent signals that he wanted to be president of the United States and many thought his decisions were more based on what he thought would be politically expedient rather than on legal precedent. He lost respect for himself and the role of the chief justice of the Supreme Court. Chase died while still on the court.

Waite Court, 1874 to 1888

Ulysses Grant again wanted to use the appointment of chief justice for repaying political favors, just as Lincoln had done. Luckily for the court he failed to get his appointments confirmed and instead named Morrison Waite. Waite was considered competent legally, but was not a strong leader. The Court's rulings during his tenure primarily were seen as tools to heal the rifts of the Civil War and the Reconstruction period that followed. He did help to restore some of the damage done to the image of the court by the Dred Scott ruling and the political maneuverings of Chase.

Fuller Court, 1888 to 1910

Melville Fuller was the first chief justice appointed who had never held a federal office before being appointed, yet many believe he was one of the most effective chief justices to serve on the court. Fuller studied at Harvard Law School and had a prominent legal practice in Chicago before being appointed by President Grover Cleveland.

Photograph of Chief Justice Melville Fuller by Harris and Ewing.

(From the Collection of the Supreme Court of the United States)

He was known as a great mediator and led the case discussions in conferences to find a route to compromise. Fuller started the tradition that each justice greet and shake hands with every other justice each morning. This tradition is still followed today and helps to strengthen the idea of brethren.

The Fuller Court started a new phase of judicial activism with its strong support for the principle of *laissez faire*, which opposes any form of government interference in the economy. This basis of capitalism believes it is dangerous to subject any aspect of corporate power to public control. It also opposes any restriction upon the rights of private property. Justices regularly overturned any legislation that might try to limit corporate or private property rights.

Court Connotations

Laissez faire is an economic principle on which capitalism is based. It opposes governmental regulation of or interference in commerce unless necessary to enable the operation of a free enterprise system based solely on its own economic laws.

Pollock v. Farmer's Loan & Trust Co.

One landmark case for the Fuller Court was *Pollock* v. *Farmer's Loan & Trust Co.*, which was used to declare the Income Tax Act of 1894 unconstitutional. I'll bet anyone who would like to get rid of the income tax today wishes this case was still the precedent.

The Constitution gives states the power to impose direct taxation, but limits the federal government's right to impose direct taxes unless they are apportioned among the states based on their representation in Congress. Congress passed the Income Tax Act of 1894 to tax people with incomes over $4,000 with no provision for apportionment. The Fuller Court ruled the Income Tax Act unconstitutional. This ruling stood until 1913 when the *Sixteenth Amendment* to the Constitution was adopted.

Court Connotations

The **Sixteenth Amendment** to the Constitution states, "The Congress shall have power to lay and collect taxes on incomes, from whatever source derived, without apportionment among the several states, and without regard to any census or enumeration." The amendment was in direct response to the 1895 case *Pollock* v. *Farmer's Loan and Trust Co.*, and established that the federal government could tax without having to apportion the tax among the states.

Before even the Sixteenth Amendment was adopted, the Court realized it had put the country close to the possible danger of bankruptcy. To alleviate that threat, the Court became creative with how it defined "direct tax" and ended up allowing certain types of taxes on private property, called "excise taxes," which the court determined were based on the "incident of ownership." Types of taxes the court allowed included revenue stamps on the sales of merchandise (sales taxes) and inheritance taxes.

Lochner v. New York

The most discredited case of the Fuller Court was *Lochner* v. *New York* in 1905. Many think the only Supreme Court case more discredited than this one is the *Dred Scott* case. Before I get into the facts of the case, I need to set the stage. In the early 1900s it was not unusual for bakers to work over 100 hour per week in bakeries that were often located in the basements of tenement houses.

New York passed a law in 1895 to try to protect workers and reform what it saw as unhealthy and unfair working conditions. This law limited the number of hours a baker could work to ten per day or 60 per week. Opponents of this law said this was unwarranted government interference in the free market.

Lochner filed suit against the state of New York on the basis that the law was unconstitutional because it violated his "liberty to contract" between his business and his employees. He cited the due process clause of the Fourteenth Amendment, which guarantees the right to property. He said this guarantee protects the individual's right to buy and sell their labor (or property) freely.

The Supreme Court ruled in favor of Lochner in a split 5 to 4 decision and ruled the New York law unconstitutional. Justice Rufus Peckham wrote the Court's opinion and said:

> "The general right to make a contract in relation to his business is part of the liberty protected by the Fourteenth Amendment, and this includes the right to purchase and sell labor, except as controlled by the State in the legitimate exercise of its police power …. There is no reasonable ground, on the score of health, for interfering with the liberty of the person or the right of free contract, by determining the hours of labor, in the occupation of a baker. Nor can a law limiting such hours be justified as a health law to safeguard the public health, or the health of the individuals following that occupation."

The *Lochner* decision was fully repudiated by the Supreme Court by the mid 1950s, but even the Fuller Court started chipping away at it in 1908 in the case *Muller* v. *State of Oregon*.

Muller v. State of Oregon

In this case, Oregon passed a law that limited the number of hours women could work in certain commercial businesses. Curt Muller, who owned a laundry in Portland, Oregon, refused to obey the limitations of the law and sued. This law was one of many that had been passed around the country to protect children, women, and people working in hazardous occupations such as mining. *Muller* v. *State of Oregon* was chosen by the Supreme Court to test the constitutionality of this legislation. The court ruled the Oregon law constitutional and said:

> "As healthy mothers are essential to vigorous offspring, the physical well-being of women is an object of public interest. The regulation of her hours of labor falls within the police power of the State, and a statute directed exclusively to such regulation does not conflict with the due process or equal protection clauses of the Fourteenth Amendment."

This partially reversed the earlier finding in *Lochner* granting states the right to limit certain labor contracts for certain "social" purposes. Apparently the Court believed women and babies had more social significance than male bakers.

White Court, 1910 to 1921

After President William Taft won the presidential election in 1908, he decided he wanted to fix the problems at the Supreme Court. His biographer, Henry Pringle, noted in his book, *The Life and Times of William Howard Taft*, that Taft wrote this about the court: "The condition of the Supreme Court is pitiable and yet those old fools hold on with a tenacity that is most discouraging." Taft was a respected jurist, who served as a circuit judge and understood the importance of judicial appointments. Teddy Roosevelt hand-picked Taft, who was Secretary of War, as his successor.

Taft decided to promote Edward White, who served as an associate justice since 1894, to the position of chief justice. White served on the southern side during the Civil War and was seen as an ex-confederate. White brought civility back to the court and worked to build consensus when case discussions were held in conference. His court was run sharply different than the Fuller Court, whose activism frequently resulted in closely divided decisions like the *Lochner* decision just discussed.

Standard Oil v. U.S.

The *Standard Oil* v. *U.S.* case is the most famous of the cases decided by the White Court. By the time this case made it to the Court, Standard Oil controlled over 90 percent of the oil market and related businesses. The case was brought by Teddy Roosevelt's Justice Department in 1906, but it wasn't until 1909 that a Missouri court ruled in favor of the United States and ordered the breakup of Standard Oil. The case didn't make it to the Supreme Court until 1910 and was decided on May 15, 1911.

> **Just the Facts**
>
> John D. Rockefeller's oil monopoly was exposed by investigative journalist Ida Tarbell, whose work is considered one of the best pieces of investigative journalism ever seen in this country. She wrote a series of stories in *McClure's* magazine that were later published in a book, *The History of Standard Oil*, which is no longer in print, but you can read parts of it at www.history.rochester.edu/fuels/tarbell/MAIN.HTM.

The case was brought against the Standard Oil Company of New Jersey and 33 other corporations, John D. Rockefeller, William Rockefeller, Henry Flagler, and four other defendants, who were in charge of the company. The Supreme Court had more than 12,000 pages of testimony to review regarding business transactions over a 40-year period.

The Supreme Court's final 8 to 1 decision ordered the breakup of Standard Oil Company of New Jersey and its related 36 domestic companies and one foreign company within six months. The court found that Standard's misdeeds included the following:

- Rebates, preferences, and other discriminatory practices that favored certain railroad companies;

- Restraint and monopolization by control of pipe lines, and unfair practices against competing pipe lines;

- Contracts with competitors in restraint of trade;

- Unfair methods of competition, such as local price cutting at the points where necessary to suppress competition;

- Espionage of the business of competitors, the operation of bogus independent companies, and payment of rebates on oil;

- The division of the United States into districts, and limiting the operations of the various subsidiary corporations to such districts limiting price competition; and

- Enormous and unreasonable profits earned by the Standard Oil Trust and the Standard Oil Company as a result of the alleged monopoly.

The case was one of many that was brought to the courts after the passage of the Sherman Anti-Trust Act of 1890. This act made restraint of trade illegal and monopolizing trade a felony.

> **Just the Facts**
>
> Standard Oil is the only major corporation that was broken up based on a Supreme Court ruling. Monopoly issues that including rulings on boxing, aluminum, and many other businesses have made it to the court over the years. If you are interested in researching other monopoly and anti-trust cases, here is a good place to start: www.ripon.edu/faculty/bowenj/antitrust/caselist.htm.

Taft Court, 1921 to 1930

Taft is not remembered as a great president, but he never really wanted to be there. His first love was the Supreme Court and he finally made it there in 1921 when he was appointed as chief justice by President Warren G. Harding. Taft was a strong leader at the court and many said he was the strongest leader since Taney.

Taft's court led an attack on regulatory legislation. His court invalidated minimum-wage laws for women in industry, overturned consumer laws, ruled unconstitutional laws protecting the unemployed from being exploited by employment agencies, and even overturned tax laws.

Adkins v. *Children's Hospital*

The most extreme example of the Taft Court's regulatory attack was *Adkins* v. *Children's Hospital* in 1923. In 1918, Congress passed a law that guaranteed a minimum wage to women and children employed in the District of Columbia. When making its ruling, the Court found this law infringed on the constitutional right of liberty of contract by requiring employers of adult women to satisfy the minimum wage standards, which the Court ruled a "price-fixing law."

Chief Justice Taft, Oliver Wendell Holmes, and Edward Sanford dissented from this decision, saying that Congress did have the policing power to correct recognizable evils. The case held as precedent until 1937 and prevented social legislation from being introduced in legislatures around the country.

Taft's major legacy to the court was its future building. Using his political skills he worked with the head of the Senate Judiciary Committee to get appropriations for the Supreme Court building. He never lived to inaugurate the new building though. That honor went to his successor in 1935. Taft was forced to resign from the Court in February 1930 for health reasons and died a month later.

Hughes Court, 1930 to 1941

President Herbert Hoover selected Charles Even Hughes as the next chief justice. He had a reputation for running the court in a military-like matter. He led the case-decision conferences by spelling out what he considered to be the key issues of the case and did not allow discussion to deviate from those points.

Hughes took over the court when the country was in a state of economic crisis following the stock market crash of 1929. The conservative activists on the Court had just prevailed with *Adkins* and were ready to take on any laws they found offensive. The court ruled unconstitutional all of Franklin Roosevelt's *New Deal* legislation up to 1937.

Roosevelt then went on the offensive and tried to pack the Court by proposing legislation on February 5, 1937 that would allow him to appoint a justice for every justice over 70 who did not retire. If this had passed Roosevelt would have been able to appoint six new Supreme Court justices. The president lost the battle, but his warning to the Court changed the Court's attitude. Before the Court-packing plan was considered in Congress, the Hughes Court ruled in 12 separate cases overturning every piece of New Deal legislation. By the time the fight was over in Congress, even though Roosevelt did not get his bill, the Hughes Court upheld every piece of New Deal legislation.

Prior to the successful enactment of New Deal legislation, the government's primary role was national defense. The government also supported the status quo including some limitations to be sure there was some semblance of fair play. Essentially the principle of laissez faire prevailed. That principle did not stand the test of time to solve the pressing economic problems and bring the country out of the Great Depression.

Court Connotations

The **New Deal** was a series of legislative initiatives proposed by Roosevelt to get people back to work by establishing various federal work projects. Roosevelt also formed the Federal Emergency Relief Administration to provide federal monetary assistance to the most desperate people. Social Security also became law during this period of time.

Stone Court, 1941 to 1946

President Franklin Roosevelt promoted Harlan Stone to the seat of chief justice in 1941 because he was a leader in the fight against the principle of laissez faire as the basis for the constitution. Stone was first appointed to the Court as an associate justice in 1925 by President Calvin Coolidge.

Although Stone was widely recognized as the intellectual leader of the Court, he did not prove to be an effective chief justice. The Court was strongly divided throughout his tenure. World War II also stymied any major decisions by the Court because it did not want to appear to question the government in the time of war.

One major case during this time was *Korematsu* v. *United States (1944),* in which the Court ruled that the government had the right to intern citizens of Japanese ancestry in Relocation Centers.

Vinson Court, 1946 to 1953

When Stone died suddenly in 1946, Fred Vinson was appointed by Roosevelt. He was quickly looked down upon by the other justices because they did not respect his legal abilities. Vinson had been a Congressman and a circuit court judge and was Secretary of the Treasury just before his appointment.

The Vinson Court set the record for the highest number of split decisions to that time in the history of the Court. Only 19 percent of the decisions of his court were unanimous.

In this chapter, I briefly introduced you the chief justices who served between Marshall and Warren. Next we'll explore some of the great minds of the court who served as associate justices.

The Least You Need to Know

- There were a dozen chief justices who served on the Supreme Court between the time of the two greats—John Marshall and Earl Warren.

- The Court rules that slavery was legal and that Negroes could not be considered citizens in its infamous *Dred Scott* decision.

- The Fuller Court led the Supreme Court's strong support for the principle of laissez faire.

- The Court upheld the principle of *laissez faire* up until a battle with Franklin Roosevelt, who wanted to pack the Court to force the justices to support his New Deal plan. The principle of *laissez faire* was used to overturn many laws protecting the rights of workers.

Chapter 8

Great Minds of the Court

In This Chapter

- ◆ Hugo Black
- ◆ Louis Brandeis
- ◆ Benjamin Cardozo
- ◆ Oliver Wendell Holmes
- ◆ Joseph Story

Only 108 justices have served on the Supreme Court over its 224-year history. I've already introduced you to the chief justices. In this chapter, I'm going to introduce you to the five top minds of the court. My choices are based on an article from the *American Bar Association Journal*, "The All-Time, All-Star, All-Era Supreme Court."

This list named nine justices, including four chief justices—Marshall, Taney, Hughes, and Warren. Since you've already met those four, I'll be concentrating on Hugo Black, Louis Brandeis, Benjamin Cardozo, Oliver Wendell Holmes, and Joseph Story. I've named them in alphabetical order, but I'll be reviewing their careers and key decisions in chronological order.

Joseph Story (1811-1845)

As we discussed in Chapter 4, Marshall had minimal legal training and was not known for his legal research abilities. That hole was filled for Marshall by Joseph Story, who was widely regarded for his legal scholarship.

Before being appointed to the Supreme Court, Story served as a Congressman, as Speaker of the Massachusetts House, and as a leader of the bar. We discussed the rivalry between the Federalists and Republicans regarding states in Chapter 4. Republican President James Madison appointed Story, thinking he would be a champion of the state's rights side, but he instead became a close ally to John Marshall and helped to lead the charge for a strong federal government.

> **Supreme Sayings** _____
>
> "Mr. Jefferson stands at the head of the enemies of the Judiciary, and I doubt not will leave behind him a numerous progeny bred in the same school. The truth is and cannot be disguised, even from vulgar observation, that the Judiciary in our country is essentially feeble, and must always be open to attack from all quarters .... Its only support is the wise and the good and the elevated in society; and these, we all know, must ever remain in a discouraging minority in all Governments."
>
> —From a letter written by Joseph Story that was reprinted in the 1845 book, *Life and Letters of Joseph Story*

Martin v. Hunter's Lessee

Story didn't take long to let his views on state's rights be known. One of his most famous decisions was *Martin* v. *Hunter's Lessee* in 1816. Virginia confiscated all lands owned by foreigners after passing a series of laws making it illegal for land to be held by foreigners. David Hunter benefited by that decision when he was granted 800 acres that the state had confiscated from Denny Martin Fairfax, a British subject.

Fairfax sued Hunter for the return of the land. When Fairfax died, his heir, Philip Martin, continued the fight. Martin argued that Fairfax's ownership was protected by treaties signed between the United States and Great Britain, which guaranteed British subjects the right to hold land in America. The Virginia Court of Appeals upheld the state's land grant to Hunter, but was overturned by the United States Supreme Court in 1813.

The Virginia Court refused to obey the United States Supreme Court ruling, saying the United States Supreme Court had no right to review the decisions of state courts under the United States Constitution. Virginia lost on that argument when Story ruled that section 25 of the Judiciary Act of 1789, which gave the United States Supreme Court appellate jurisdiction over state courts, was valid when a state court denied the validity of a federal statute. This ruling firmly established the appellate jurisdiction of the United States Supreme Court. Justice Story said in his opinion for the court:

> "The questions involved in this judgment are of great importance and delicacy. Perhaps it is not too much to affirm that, upon their right decision rest some of the most solid principles which have hitherto been supposed to sustain and protect the Constitution itself. ... The Constitution of the United States was ordained and established not by the States in their sovereign capacities, but emphatically, as the preamble of the Constitution declares, by 'the people of the United States.' ... The Constitution was not, therefore, necessarily carved out of existing State sovereignties, nor a surrender of powers already existing in State institutions, for the powers of the States depend upon their own Constitutions, and the people of every State had the right to modify and restrain them according to their own views of the policy or principle. On the other hand, it is perfectly clear that the sovereign powers vested in the State governments by their respective Constitutions remained unaltered and unimpaired except so far as they were granted to the Government of the United States. ... These deductions do not rest upon general reasoning, plain and obvious as they seem to be. They have been positively recognized by one of the articles in amendment of the Constitution, which declares that: 'The powers not delegated to the United States by the Constitution, nor prohibited by it to the States, are reserved to the States respectively, or to the people.'"

Justice Story also in this decision talks about the fact that the Constitution was deliberately written in general language so that it could stand the test of time and serve many generations:

> "The Constitution unavoidably deals in general language. It did not suit the purposes of the people, in framing this great charter of our liberties, to provide for minute specifications of its powers or to declare the means by which those powers should be carried into execution. It was foreseen that this would be a perilous and difficult, if not an impracticable, task. The instrument was not intended to provide merely for the exigencies of a few years, but was to endure through a long lapse of ages, the events of which were locked up in the inscrutable purposes of Providence. It could not be foreseen what new changes and modifications of power might be indispensable to effectuate the general objects of the charter, and restrictions and specifications which at the present might seem salutary might in the end prove the overthrow of the system itself. Hence its powers are expressed in general terms, leaving to the legislature from time to time to adopt its own means to effectuate legitimate objects and to mould and model the exercise of its powers as its own wisdom and the public interests, should require."

In addition to his support for a strong national government, Justice Story's other key contribution for the developing nation was his expertise in commercial law. His early rulings helped to shape today's corporate laws. He was the first to establish that a corporation could operate freely as individuals across state boundaries. His view of corporate America helped the country expand and build a strong economy. I won't delve deeply into corporate law here, but instead will discuss key cases in Part 7, "Taking Care of Business."

Justice Story's legal contributions did not stop at the Supreme Court. In 1829 he became the first *Dane Professor of Law* at Harvard College. He continued to serve on the court and teach at Harvard. He also wrote a series of legal texts, many of which were used as textbooks in U.S. colleges until 1905 when the texts became outdated because of changes to the Constitution and related constitutional law.

Story served on the Court for 33 years. He died in September 1945 while he was still serving on the Court.

Court Connotations

The position of **Dane Professor of Law** was established at Harvard College in 1829 with a donation from Nathan Dane, who gave a total of $15,000 over his lifetime to Harvard Law School. These donations paid for the Dane professorship and the founding of Dane Hall. Nathan Dane served in positions for both the Massachusetts and U.S. government. His service included being a delegate from Massachusetts for the Continental Congress from 1785 to 1787.

Oliver Wendell Holmes (1902-1932)

President Theodore Roosevelt appointed Oliver Wendell Holmes to the United States Supreme Court in 1902. Prior to that time, Holmes served as a Massachusetts Supreme Court judge and taught at Harvard College. Holmes also served on the Twentieth Massa-chusetts Regiment during the Civil War and was wounded three times.

He received his degree from Harvard Law School in 1867, but his law practice was never very successful. He gained his fame when he was invited to give a series of lectures at the Lowell Institute, which were published in a book called *The Common Law* in 1881. The Lowell Institute was established in Boston in 1836 to bring distinguished lecturers to the city.

Photograph of Associate Justice Oliver Wendell Holmes by Harris and Ewing.

(From the Collection of the Supreme Court of the United States)

Supreme Sayings

"The life of the law has not been logic; it has been experience. The felt necessities of the time, the prevalent moral and political theories, institutions of public policy, avowed or unconscious, even the prejudices which judges share with their fellow men, have had a good deal more to do than the syllogism in determining the rules by which men should be governed. The law embodies the story of a nation's development through many centuries, and it cannot be dealt with as if it contained only the axioms and corollaries of a book of mathematics."

—From the first of 12 Lowell Lectures delivered by Oliver Wendell Holmes on November 23, 1880

Holmes was known for both his intellect and humor. He strongly believed in the principle that law was built on experiences and not logic. He believed it was important to look at the facts of a changing society rather than to cling to old slogans and formulas. Holmes worked to convince people that the law should develop along with the society it serves. He also championed the idea of "judicial restraint" because he believed judges should avoid letting their personal opinions impact their decisions.

Lochner v. New York

Some of Holmes' most famous writings as a Supreme Court Justice are pulled from his dissents on landmark cases. Two of those we discussed in the preceding chapter.

The first is *Lochner* v. *New York*. In that case the Supreme Court overturned a New York law that mandated maximum work hours for bakers. Holmes dissented on that decision and said:

> "This case is decided upon an economic theory which a large part of the country does not entertain. If it were a question whether I agreed with that theory, I should desire to study it further and long before making up my mind. But I do not conceive that to be my duty, because I strongly believe that my agreement or disagreement has nothing to do with the right of a majority to embody their opinions in law. ... But a constitution is not intended to embody a particular economic theory, whether of paternalism and the organic relation of the citizen to the State or of laissez faire. It is made for people of fundamentally differing views, and the accident of our finding certain opinions natural and familiar or novel and even shocking ought not to conclude our judgment upon the question whether statutes embodying them conflict with the Constitution of the United States."

Adkins v. Children's Hospital

The second case (discussed in the previous chapter) also involved legislation that tried to mandate working conditions, *Adkins* v. *Children's Hospital*. In this case, the Supreme Court ruled that Congress could not establish minimum wage rates. Holmes disagreed and wrote this in his dissent:

> "The question in this case is the broad one, whether Congress can establish minimum rates of wages for women in the District of Columbia with due provision for special circumstances, or whether we must say that Congress has no power to meddle with the matter at all. To me, notwithstanding the deference due to the prevailing judgment of the Court, the power of Congress seems absolutely free from doubt. The end, to remove conditions leading to ill health, immorality and the deterioration of the race, no one would deny to be within the scope of constitutional legislation. The means are means that have the approval of Congress, of many States, and of those governments from which we have learned our greatest lessons. When so many intelligent persons, who have studied the matter more than any of us can, have thought that the means are effective and are worth the price, it seems to me impossible to deny that the belief reasonably may be held by reasonable men. If the law encountered no other objection than that the means bore no relation to the end or that they cost too much, I do not suppose that anyone would venture to say that it was bad. I agree, of course, that a law answering the foregoing requirements might be invalidated by specific provisions of the Constitution. For instance, it might take private property without just compensation. But in the present instance, the only objection that can be urged is found

within the vague contours of the Fifth Amendment, prohibiting the depriving any person of liberty or property without due process of law."

Abrams v. United States

Another famous Holmes dissent was in the case of *Abrams* v. *United States* in 1923. This case involved the publishing of two political publications during World War I that supported the Germans.

Just the Facts _____

All five of the defendants in *Abrams* v. *United States* were born in Russia. They lived in the United States for 5 to 10 years, but none had applied for citizenship. Four of the defendants admitted they were rebels, revolutionists, and anarchists who did not believe in government in any form. One did testify that he believed in a socialist government, but not a capitalist government like that of the United States.

The Supreme Court held that these publications were unlawful on the basis that the information was:

- "disloyal, scurrilous and abusive language about the form of Government of the United States,"

- "intended to bring the form of Government of the United States into contempt, scorn, contumely and disrepute;"

- "intended to incite, provoke and encourage resistance to the United States in said war."

This time his dissent was signed by Supreme Court Justice Louis Brandeis, who we'll discuss next. They often dissented jointly while on the court together. Holmes said:

"But, as against dangers peculiar to war, as against others, the principle of the right to free speech is always the same. It is only the present danger of immediate evil or an intent to bring it about that warrants Congress in setting a limit to the expression of opinion where private rights are not concerned. Congress certainly cannot forbid all effort to change the mind of the country. Now nobody can suppose that the surreptitious publishing of a silly leaflet by an unknown man, without more, would present any immediate danger that its opinions would hinder the success of the government arms or have any appreciable tendency to do so. Publishing those opinions for the very purpose of obstructing, however, might indicate a greater danger, and, at any rate, would have the quality of an attempt. …

"In this case, sentences of twenty years' imprisonment have been imposed for the publishing of two leaflets that I believe the defendants had as much right to publish as the Government has to publish the Constitution of the United States now vainly invoked by them. … It is an experiment, as all life is an experiment. Every year, if not every day, we have to wager our salvation upon some prophecy based upon imperfect knowledge. While that experiment is part of our system, I think that we should be eternally vigilant against attempts to check the expression of opinions that we loathe and believe to be fraught with death, unless they so imminently threaten immediate interference with the lawful and pressing purposes of the law that an immediate check is required to save the country."

Buck v. Bell

Holmes was also known for facing some darker moments. One of his worst decisions was *Buck* v. *Bell* in 1927. This case involved the right of the state of Virginia to sterilize a "feeble-minded white woman" against her will. The Supreme Court ruled in favor of allowing the sterilization. Holmes wrote the Court's opinion and said:

"We have seen more than once that the public welfare may call upon the best citizens for their lives. It would be strange if it could not call upon those who already sap the strength of the State for these lesser sacrifices, often not felt to be such by those concerned, in order to prevent our being swamped by incompetence. It is better for all the world, if instead of waiting to execute degenerate offspring for a crime, or to let them starve for their imbecility, society can prevent those who are manifestly unfit from continuing their kind. The principle that sustains compulsory vaccination is broad enough to cover cutting the Fallopian tubes. Three generations of imbeciles are enough."

This ruling did not sit long on the books. The first move to overturn was in 1942 in the case *Skinner* v. *Oklahoma*, which involved an Oklahoma law that allowed forced sterilization of habitual criminals. Skinner was an armed robber and chicken thief. The Supreme Court decided in favor of Skinner, ruling that procreation was a "fundamental right of man" and that forcible sterilization violated Skinner's Fourteenth Amendment rights.

Holmes resigned from the court in January 1932 after serving for 29 years. He left the court at the age of 90 and died three years later in March 1935 just four days before his 94th birthday.

Louis Brandeis (1916-1939)

Louis Brandeis entered Harvard Law School at the age of 19 and graduated at the top of his class. He built a hugely successful law practice and was a successful investor as well, amassing a $3 million fortune in the early 1900s. This allowed him to pursue causes that he believed in. He strongly sympathized with the trade union movement, supported women's rights, fought for minimum wage laws and championed the cause for anti-trust legislation. When he fought for these causes, he rarely charged legal fees to his clients. He believed in using the law to protect the powerless from the powerful.

Supreme Sayings

Louis Brandeis argued in his 1914 books, *Other People's Money* and *Business: A Profession* that a retailer should be certain "the goods which he sold were manufactured under conditions which were fair to the workers—fair as to wages, hours of work, and sanitary conditions."

Associate Justice Louis Brandeis's official portrait painted by Eben Cumins.

(Photograph by Vic Boswell from the Collection of the Supreme Court of the United States)

Muller v. Oregon

One famous case that he argued before being appointed to the Supreme Court was *Muller* v. *Oregon*, which we discussed in the preceding chapter. For this case he introduced the "Brandeis Brief," which included just two pages arguing the constitutional issues and 100 pages arguing the facts of the case. Today the Brandeis Brief style is still considered a model for constitutional cases. Prior to that time, legal briefs concentrated on constitutional arguments and did not focus on the facts of the case.

His tactic worked. Using the facts, Brandeis argued the "reasonableness" of legislative action on this issue.

The Supreme Court ruled unanimously in favor of his clients and upheld Oregon's law, which regulated hours and working conditions for women. Prior to *Muller* v. *Oregon*, the Court had ruled against worker protection laws because they were considered a violation of due process.

When President Woodrow Wilson appointed Louis D. Brandeis to the court in 1916, he set off one of the most contentious battles for a Supreme Court nomination. Not only were business leaders out to stop the nomination, but, as the first Jew appointed to the court, there was a major anti-Semitic undercurrent to much of the opposition.

Even though he had graduated at the top of his class from Harvard Law School, the President of Harvard circulated a petition among leading Bostonians opposing the nomination. The four-month confirmation battle was one of the ugliest in history. Leading newspapers including *The Wall Street Journal* and *The New York Times* helped to lead the fight against Brandeis.

At that time the Supreme Court nominee did not testify before Congress, as is true today. Instead others testified on his behalf. Brandeis stayed quiet during the four months of verbal assaults and finally did get Congressional approval in a near party line vote of 47 to 22, with only one Democrat opposing Brandeis.

Just the Facts

Henry Abraham writes in his book, *Justices, Presidents, and Senators*, that Brandeis' daughter Susan was at a meeting in New York City when she heard about his confirmation. A woman seated next to her commented when she heard the news, "I hear they confirmed that Jew Brandeis to the Supreme Court." Susan said in response, "You are speaking to the right person. Mr. Brandeis happens to be my father."

Olmstead v. United States

Once on the Court, Brandeis quickly aligned with Holmes and they became the famous dissenting duo. They frequently joined each other in written dissents. One of Brandeis' more famous dissents was in the case *Olmstead* v. *United States* in 1928, which was the first wiretapping case in the Supreme Court.

This case took place during the time of Prohibition when the sale, distribution, and consumption of alcoholic beverages was banned by law. Olmstead was a bootlegger (one who made and sold alcohol illegally) who was convicted based on evidence gathered by the FBI using a wiretap on his telephone.

His lawyer argued that wiretapping amounted to illegal search and violated his rights under the *Fourth Amendment*. The Court ruled that electronic eavesdropping did not violate protections against illegal search because it did not involve physical entry. The Court held that by speaking on the phone, Olmstead had broadcast his conversations to the general public. Chief Justice Taft wrote in the majority opinion, "The language of the amendment cannot be extended and expanded to include telephone wires, reaching to the whole world from the defendant's house or office. The intervening wires are not part of his house or office, any more than are the highways along which they are stretched."

Court Connotations

The **Fourth Amendment** to the constitution states, "The right of the people to be secure in their persons, houses, papers, and effects, against unreasonable searches and seizures, shall not be violated, and no warrants shall issue, but upon probable cause, supported by oath or affirmation, and particularly describing the place to be searched, and the persons or things to be seized." This is the amendment that is used to protect you against illegal search and seizure in your own home.

In his dissent, Brandeis argued:

> "The evil incident to invasion of the privacy of the telephone is far greater than that involved in tampering with the mails. Whenever a telephone line is tapped, the privacy of the persons at both ends of the line is invaded and all conversations between them upon any subject, and, although proper, confidential and privileged, may be overheard. Moreover, the tapping of one man's telephone line involves the tapping of the telephone of every other person whom he may call or who may call him …. The makers of our Constitution undertook to secure conditions favorable to the pursuit of happiness. They recognized the significance of man's spiritual nature, of his feelings, and of his intellect. They knew that only a part of the pain, pleasure and satisfactions of life are to be found in material things. They sought to protect Americans in their beliefs, their thoughts, their emotions and their sensations. They conferred, as against the Government, the right to be let alone—the most comprehensive of rights, and the right most valued by civilized men. To protect that right, every unjustifiable intrusion by the Government upon the privacy of the individual, whatever the means employed,

must be deemed a violation of the Fourth Amendment. And the use, as evidence in a criminal proceeding, of facts ascertained by such intrusion must be deemed a violation of the Fifth."

Even though Brandeis' dissent was not the opinion of the court, it is one of the most frequently cited opinions in Supreme Court rulings, including landmark cases such as *Griswold* v. *Connecticut, Miranda* v. *Arizona, and Roe* v. *Wade.* We'll explore the impact of his dissent in greater depth in Chapter 21.

Brandeis served on the court for nearly 23 years before retiring in 1939 at the age of 82. He died two years later in 1941.

Benjamin Cardozo (1932-1938)

Benjamin Cardozo's family history dates back to the Revolutionary War in which his ancestors fought against the British. His father was a New York Supreme Court justice but was forced to resign in 1872 under threat of impeachment.

Benjamin Cardozo received his law degree from Columbia Law School and was admitted to the bar in 1891. After proving his success as a courtroom lawyer, Cardozo was elected to the New York Supreme Court in 1913. He served as associate judge and chief judge on the New York Court of Appeals for 18 years, writing over 500 opinions for the court.

Just the Facts

William Borah, who at the time was one of the most powerful Senate Committee chairmen, strongly supported Cardozo's nomination. He helped to convince President Hoover to make the nomination, according to Henry Abraham in his book, *Justices, Presidents, and Senators.* Abraham says when Hoover showed Borah the list of possible candidates to replace Oliver Wendell Holmes, Cardozo was on the bottom of the list with the notation "Jew, Democrat, New York." Borah told him he was handed the list upside down and convinced Hoover to appoint Cardozo, according to Abraham.

His reputation grew nationwide and there was widespread support for this nomination to the Supreme Court. Support for his nomination came from all sides: labor, business, liberals, and conservatives. Taft refused to nominate Cardozo while he was president in the 1920s because he viewed him as too liberal. Herbert Hoover reluctantly nominated him in 1932 because by that time the groundswell of support was too large to fight off.

Even though he was Jewish, he met with none of the anti-Semitism that Brandeis experienced. His nomination sailed through the Senate unanimously without debate ten seconds after it was taken up on the floor of the Senate. Once on the court, Cardozo aligned with Brandeis and another leading liberal, Harlan Stone.

Palko v. Connecticut

One of the key cases for which Cardozo wrote the Court's opinion was *Palko* v. *Connecticut* in 1937. Frank Palko faced a charge of first-degree murder, but was convicted instead of second-degree murder and sentenced to life imprisonment. The state of Connected appealed the decision because of errors made at trial and won a new trial for Palko. The appeal was passed on errors by the trial judge because he excluded the defendant's confession, excluded certain testimony that would have impeached the defendant's credibility, and instructed the jury incorrectly regarding the difference between first and second degree murder.

Palko was convicted of first-degree murder and sentenced to death after the second trial. Palko's attorneys appealed the second trial to the Supreme Court on the belief that the second conviction violated the protection against double jeopardy guaranteed by the Fifth Amendment to the constitution. They believed this protection applied to state cases because of the Fourteenth Amendment's due process clause.

The Supreme Court upheld Palko's second conviction and the majority opinion was written by Cardozo. In his opinion, Cardozo wrote:

> "The state is not attempting to wear the accused out by a multitude of cases with accumulated trials. It asks no more than this, that the case against him shall go on until there shall be a trial free from the corrosion of substantial legal error. … This is not cruelty at all, nor even vexation in any immoderate degree. If the trial had been infected with error adverse to the accused, there might have been review at his instance, and as often as necessary to purge the vicious taint. A reciprocal privilege, subject at all times to the discretion of the presiding judge … has now been granted to the state."

Before he died in 1938, Cardozo wrote over 100 opinions during his short six-year period on the Court.

Hugo Black (1937–1971)

Hugo Black earned his law degree from the University of Alabama and then became one of Birmingham's leading trial lawyers. He set a goal of being elected senator by the age of 40. In the South, that meant he had to join the Democratic Party. He also believed that to be electable, he had to join the Ku Klux Klan (KKK), which he thought was necessary to further his political career.

While Black was serving in his second Senate term, Franklin Roosevelt was elected president. Black became an ardent supporter of Roosevelt's New Deal programs and led the fight to help Roosevelt pack the court and change its opposition to New Deal legislation. Even though he lost the fight, when it came time for Roosevelt to nominate his first justice to the Supreme Court, he picked Hugo Black, knowing he would support him on the Court. During his four terms, Roosevelt appointed nine justices.

Black's appointment was opposed by Negro physicians of the National Medical Association because of his KKK connection, and a small group of blacks protested his appointment on the day of the Senate debate. The KKK connection had not come up during judiciary committee deliberations and, at that time, there was no proof of his membership.

Just the Facts

Black's involvement in the KKK was very limited. He joined the KKK on September 13, 1923, marched in a few parades and spoke at meetings. His speeches were on liberty and encouraged the KKK to be a law-abiding organization. He opposed whipping and other violent activities of the KKK.

Opposition to his appointment was also raised because he served on the Senate at the time a change was made in the Supreme Court retirement provisions. Since he could benefit from the change, some questions were raised about blocking his appointment. The Constitution forbids a Congressman from being appointed to a U.S. office for which benefits were increased by that same Congress. After intense debate, Black was confirmed by a vote of 63 to 16.

After Black took the Supreme Court oath, the newspaper *Pittsburgh Post-Gazette* exposed Black's KKK membership. There were major protests, but the issue was pushed to the side as war fears before World War II began to build in the country.

Chambers v. Florida

Black's service on the Court proved that he was not a bigot. He opposed racial segregation and championed minority rights. One case that helped prove his position was *Chambers* v. *Florida* in 1940. Chambers was one of about 30 to 40 blacks arrested after an elderly white man was robbed and murdered in Pompano, Florida.

Some of the blacks were held in the Dade County jail and questioned for more than a week, sometimes throughout the night, until confessions were secured. The prisoners were not allowed to confer with an attorney or to speak with friends or relatives.

They were questioned one at a time, surrounded by 10 men. They were continually threatened and physically mistreated. After about a week of this type of treatment, four of them finally confessed in desperation and for fear of their lives.

Formal charges had not been brought before the confessions. Two days after the confessions, the four men were indicted and arraigned. Two pleaded guilty and two pleaded not guilty. One of the ones that pleaded not guilty changed his plea to guilty, leaving Chambers as the sole one to be tried. He was convicted of murder based on his confession and the testimony of the three other confessors.

The Florida State Supreme Court overturned the first conviction when it learned that the confessions were not voluntary and had been obtained by coercion and duress. After some court maneuvering, the case was moved to a different count and tried. Even with the change of venue the four men were convicted, so the Supreme Court of Florida upheld the conviction. The case was then appealed to the United States Supreme Court.

The Supreme Court overturned the conviction of all four black men. In writing his opinion for the court, Black said:

> "The determination to preserve an accused's right to procedural due process sprang in large part from knowledge of the historical truth that the rights and liberties of people accused of crime could not be safely entrusted to secret inquisitorial processes. The testimony of centuries, in governments of varying kinds over populations of different races and beliefs, stood as proof that physical and mental torture and coercion had brought about the tragically unjust sacrifices of some who were the noblest and most useful of their generations. The rack, the thumbscrew, the wheel, solitary confinement, protracted questioning and cross questioning, and other ingenious forms of entrapment of the helpless or unpopular had left their wake of mutilated bodies and shattered minds along the way to the cross, the guillotine, the stake and the hangman's noose. And they who have suffered most from secret and dictatorial proceedings have almost always been the poor, the ignorant, the numerically weak, the friendless, and the powerless."

Hugo Black staunchly defended the First Amendment right to free speech during the *McCarthy Era*. His support was so strong that some say he and his fellow justice William Douglas were under FBI surveillance during the 1953 Rosenberg case. The Rosenbergs were convicted as spies and electrocuted in 1953. The Supreme Court never heard the case. As we've discussed, four justices must vote in favor of hearing a case before being put on the docket. Hugo Black became sick before the conference was held to discuss the case and was not available to vote. Without his vote, there weren't enough votes in favor of taking the case.

Court Connotations

The **McCarthy Era** got its name from Senator Joseph McCarthy, who led a witch-hunt to expose people with communist views after World War II. Many who were proved to be members of the Communist Party lost their jobs. Anyone called before McCarthy's committee in the House of Representatives had to prove their loyalty to the country by naming other members of the communist party in order to keep their jobs. He accused Harry Truman of being soft on communism and portrayed him as a dangerous liberal, which helped to elect Republican Dwight Eisenhower as president.

Black became seriously ill and retired from the Supreme Court in 1971 after serving 34 years. He died eight days after retiring.

Now that you've met the shapers of the court, let's go behind the scenes and explore how the present-day court operates. We'll start with how cases are decided.

The Least You Need to Know

♦ Justice Joseph Story was a close confidant of John Marshall. His legal scholarship bolstered Marshall's efforts to build a strong federal government.

♦ Justice Oliver Wendell Holmes believed in the principle that law was built on experiences and not logic. He thought it important to consider societal changes and not cling to old beliefs.

♦ Justice Louis Brandeis faced stiff opposition to his nomination because he was perceived as anti-business. He also faced anti-Semitism as the first Jew appointed to the Court. He believed in using the law to protect the powerless from the powerful.

♦ Justice Benjamin Cardozo was widely respected for his work as associate judge and chief judge of the New York Court of Appeals. Even though he only served for six years, he wrote about 100 decisions for the Supreme Court.

♦ Justice Hugo Black, who was a member of the KKK while in Alabama, proved to be a champion of minority rights while on the Court.

Part 3

Peeking Behind the Columns

The majority of the Court's work is done privately, behind closed doors. Case decisions are made even outside the earshot of Court staff. In this part, we'll take a tour behind the grand columns of the court and see how cases are decided, who staffs the court, and who helps the justices research cases and write their opinions.

Deciding Cases

In This Chapter

- ◆ How decisions are made
- ◆ Case conference styles
- ◆ Putting it in writing
- ◆ Bird's-eye view of today's Court

You may think that after oral arguments are heard, the Supreme Court justices go behind closed doors and argue vehemently about their positions on the issues in the case conferences. Actually, that is rarely the case. Most justices arrive at conferences already having made their decision on how they will vote and rarely change their mind.

The case conference is the place where the justices let their decision be known and find out how the other justices plan to vote. The majority is set by these votes and the justice chosen to write the Court's opinion is selected by the chief justice, if he is in the majority, or the most senior justice in the majority.

Let's take a closer look at how all this works.

Understanding the Process

First, let's review the actual steps taken by the Supreme Court to make a decision. We've already talked about taking a case to court in Chapter 2 and how the justices pick a case to be heard. Also, we talked about the oral argument step in the process.

After oral arguments are completed, there are five additional steps in Supreme Court decision-making. The steps are:

1. **Case conference**—These are held twice a week when the justices are hearing oral arguments: Wednesday afternoons for cases heard on Monday, and Friday afternoons for cases heard on Tuesday and Wednesday. Tradition mandates even where each justice sits depending on seniority, as well as when each justice gets to speak. The chief justice speaks first, followed by each justice depending on seniority. Only the justices themselves attend these conferences. No staff people are allowed, so each justice must be fully prepared before the conference to discuss each case.

2. **Writing the opinion**—After each justice has stated his or her views on the case, the vote is clear. If the justices are unanimous in their decision, the chief justice will assign the justice to write the Court's opinion. If the vote is divided, the senior justice in the majority decides who will write the opinion. Since this is the way the public will learn how the Court voted, the written opinion can have great influence on how the Court's decision will impact future related cases by the precedents set in the written opinion. The selection of the writer is usually the most important part of the decision-making process.

Court Connotations

A **concurring opinion** is an opinion that agrees with the position of the Court but varies on the legal reasons for deciding that way. A **dissenting opinion** is an opinion that disagrees with the opinion of the Court.

3. **Circulating opinion(s)**—Although there is one person assigned to write the Court's opinion, there may be several writing *concurring* or *dissenting opinions*. Concurrences and dissents are not required. Justices only write one if they believe they have a key legal point to make that is not in the Court's opinion. When justices complete their writing, whether a concurring or dissenting opinion, the drafts are circulated to the other justices.

4. **Joining opinions**—If a justice agrees with the written opinion, he or she will send a memo agreeing to join the opinion. If a justice agrees but wants changes in how the decision is written, a memo is sent stating what changes would be needed in order for the justice to join. How successful a justice will be in getting

a change depends on how close the vote was in the case conference. If the decision was closely divided, such as a 5 to 4 vote, then the justice writing the majority opinion will be more accommodating in making changes to keep the majority status of the opinion intact. In some cases this process is one of mediation to get as many justices to join a decision as possible. During this process a dissenting opinion can become the majority opinion if the dissenter is more successful in getting justices to join.

5. **Announcing the opinion**—After all opinions are complete, the justice who writes the Court's opinion will read it in an open Court session followed by any concurring or dissenting opinions read by their authors.

This process has been the tradition of the court since the time of Chief Justice Taney, but its formations began even during Chief Justice Marshall's reign.

> **Just the Facts** _____
>
> If you've watched the court, you've probably noticed that the most controversial cases are decided in the final days of a court session, usually in the month of June. The reason this happens is due to the delays usually caused during the writing process to get as many justices as possible to sign an opinion. Each time changes are made to the initial draft to satisfy comments of one justice, the draft must be circulated again. One justice who joined the initial draft could then pull out and refuse to join the new draft with the changes, so it can take awhile to find a compromise acceptable to the most justices. More on this in the later section "Writing the Opinions."

Differing Conference Styles

While the seniority-first structure of the case conference stayed the same throughout the history of the Court, the control of this process changed depending upon who was chief justice. In some Courts, no one was allowed to speak until all justices stated their initial opinions. In other Courts, justices were questioned on points made during their presentation.

Some chief justices led conferences more like law school professors, encouraging arguments on key legal issues that could go on for hours. Other chief justices were known for driving the conference with an iron fist by stating what they thought were the key legal issues up front and not allowing anyone to deviate from those issues.

While there isn't much detail about the case conferences during the times of Chief Justices Marshall and Taney, it is widely acknowledged they were strong leaders of the Court. Marshall was known for his ability to mediate a unanimous decision. Taney was known as a strong leader who led a more divided Court. These two great leaders were followed by two very weak ones, Chief Justices Chase and Waite. In fact, Associate Justice Miller is quoted in the book, *History of the Supreme Court of the United States: Reconstruction and Reunion*, as saying about Chase, "He liked to have his own way, but when he came upon the bench it was admirable to see how quietly and courteously the Court resisted his imperious will." Miller goes on to say that Chase was "not possessed of any more authority than the rest of the court chose to give him."

Chief Justice Fuller brought back respect to the position of chief justice when he started on the court in 1888 and is known as one of the most effective chief justices, who used wit and charm to run the conferences. Fuller biographer, Willard Leroy King quotes Justice Holmes on Fuller, "there was never a better presiding officer, or rather, and more important in some ways, a better moderator inside the conference chamber, than this quiet gentleman from Illinois."

Supreme Sayings

Oliver Wendell Holmes said about Chief Justice Fuller, "He had the business of the Court at his fingers' ends; he was perfectly courageous, prompt, decided. He turned off the matters that daily called for action easily, swiftly with least possible friction, with imperturbable good humor, and with a humor that relieved any tension with a laugh." —From the book *The Justices of the United States Supreme Court 1789-1969: Their Lives and Major Opinions* by Leon Friedman and Fred Israel

Fuller started the practice of shaking hands each morning, which helped to ease the tensions on the court. He ran conferences with an iron fist and cut off debate when he thought the issues seemed to be clearly spelled out.

Following Fuller was Chief Justice Edward White, who was known to run a less rigid conference. White had been a Senator and used his political skills to promote agreement on cases. He allowed freer discussion in conferences and didn't cut off debate. This allowed for a more relaxed court.

The strongest chief justice after Taney was William Howard Taft. Holmes wrote that the case conferences were more pleasant under Taft than any other chief justice. Supreme Court historian Alpheus Mason, who wrote the book, *William Howard Taft: Chief Justice*, said Taft strictly controlled case conferences, never hesitating to cut off discussion when the issues were clear, according to Holmes. Mason quotes in a letter

from Holmes, "never before ... have we gotten along with so little jangling and dis-
sension." Taft's success was helped by the fact that most of the justices shared his
conservative views.

Taft's successor, Chief Justice Hughes, also
was known for running very tight conferences. Justice Brandeis said Hughes did most
of the talking. He rarely allowed discussion to
stray from the points he made at the beginning
of the case discussion.

The military-style rule of Hughes was followed
by a very loosely led conference by Chief
Justice Stone. He was a law professor who
treated the conference like a law school seminar. Stone was known to debate at length any
justice who disagreed with him.

Supreme Sayings

Conferences led by Hughes
were "not a debating society. To
see [Hughes] preside was like
witnessing Toscanini lead an
orchestra."

—From an interview with Associate Justice Felix Frankfurter
conducted by Alpheus Mason

Stone's successor Chief Justice Vinson was considered to be even worse at leading
conferences because he presented cases in a shallow way. Bernard Schwartz writes in
A History of the Supreme Court that Vinson's Court was the most fragmented in the
Court's history. Only 19 percent of the cases in his Court were decided unanimously.

When Chief Justice Warren took over, things changed dramatically. His skilled leadership showed clearly in how he led court conferences. The other justices respected
his leadership because he led efficiently with a clear knowledge of the issues presented
in the cases at conference. The *Washington Post* wrote that, "Warren helped steer cases
from the moment they were first discussed simply by the way he framed the issues."

Just the Facts

Chief Justice Burger introduced the Xerox machine to the Court in 1969. Supreme
Court historian Bernard Schwartz believes that addition "had a baneful, though
unintended, effect upon the operation of the Burger Court. One privy to the working of the Warren Court quickly notes the crucial importance of personal exchanges among the Justices—both in conference discussion and, even more so, in
the postargument decision process. Such exchanges became less significant in the Burger
Court." This continues today in the Rehnquist Court, where memos flow more readily than
personal exchanges among the justices—according to many court observers.

Warren's skilled leadership was followed by Chief Justice Burger, who became known
for holding conferences with very little exchange of opinion. Justice Scalia was quoted
in *The New York Times* on February 2, 1988, about Burger's conferences, "In fact,

to call our discussion of a case a conference is really something of a misnomer, it's much more a statement of the views of each of the nine justices, after which the totals are added and the case is assigned."

The effectiveness of a chief justice can clearly be seen in the way he runs the case conferences. Leadership and the ability to mediate case decisions is one overriding factor that makes for a great chief justice. All the top shapers of the Court were known for their ability to effectively lead case conferences.

Writing the Opinions

After the case conference, the assignments to write the opinions are handed out within a week of the conference. As noted previously, if the chief justice is in the majority, he makes the assignment; otherwise the assignment is made by the senior justice in the majority.

When the writing is assigned to a justice, he or she then assigns the work of writing the initial draft to one of his or her clerks. The justice discusses the opinions voiced during the case conference and gives the clerk directions for researching and writing the draft opinion. After the justice edits the initial draft, it is sent out to the other justices for comments.

Those who agree will send a memo asking to join the opinion. Those who agree but want changes will note the difficulties they have with the argument. Those who disagree will send a memo indicating they will not join the decision.

After getting all the comments, the justice in charge of writing the opinion can choose to make changes to satisfy some comments and try to increase the number of justices who will join the opinion, or the justice can decide to ignore the comments and accept the fact that a justice will not join the opinion.

While most of the exchanges are done with memos in today's Court, justices do occasionally meet in smaller groups to work out compromises and opinion language. These meetings were known to be more common and effective in the days of the Warren Court, as well as during the times of other Courts throughout the history of the Supreme Court.

Deciding Cases in Rehnquist's Court

I've left the discussion of the workings of the Rehnquist Court for last. Rehnquist gave us an incredible view behind the scenes in his book, *The Supreme Court*.

I'll summarize his description, which gives us a rare look at how today's Court operates. Rehnquist also served as an associate justice on the Warren and Burger Courts.

The justices meet in a conference room next to the chamber of the chief justice. After shaking each others hands, they sit at a long, rectangular conference table. Chief Justice Rehnquist sits at one end and the Senior Associate Justice John Paul Stevens sits at the other end. If Stevens is not in attendance, next in line is Sandra Day O'Connor. The rest sit in order of their seniority with the three most senior on one side and the others opposite them.

Photograph of the current Supreme Court justices. Back row from left: Ruth Bader Ginsburg, David Souter, Clarence Thomas and Stephen Breyer. Front row from left: Antonin Scalia, John Paul Stevens, William Rehnquist, Sandra Day O'Connor, Anthony Kennedy.

(Photograph by Richard Strauss of the Smithsonian Institution from the Collection of the Supreme Court Historical Society)

There are no clerks, secretaries, or staff of any kind in the room during a conference. The most junior associate justice is designated to open the door if a staff person knocks to get their attention. The junior justice also must dictate to staff any orders decided when the conference is over, such as which cases will be put on the docket.

Rehnquist, as chief justice, starts off the discussion of a case in which oral arguments have been completed. He reviews the facts and decisions of the lower courts, outlines his understanding of case law and indicates whether he will vote to affirm the decision of the lower court or reverse it. Once he is finished, the next most senior associate justice in the room gives his summary and vote, followed by all other associate justices in order of seniority.

Supreme Sayings

"When I first went on the Court I was both surprised and disappointed at how little interplay there was between the various justices during the process of conferring on a case. Each would state his views, and a junior justice could express agreement or disagreement with views expressed by a justice senior to him earlier in the discussion, but the converse did not apply; a junior justice's views were seldom commented upon, because votes had been already cast up the line. Probably most junior justices before me must have felt as I did, that they had some very significant contributions to make, and were disappointed that they hardly ever seemed to influence anyone."

—Chief Justice William Rehnquist in his book, *The Supreme Court*

During Rehnquist's conferences, it is a general rule that all justices are given a chance to speak before there is any cross-questioning or interpretation. However, Rehnquist can't enforce that rule as chief justice and occasionally a justice will question another justice during his initial remarks.

Rehnquist does not believe the case conference changes many votes, but occasionally a justice will shift his vote after hearing another justice's argument. Occasionally justices will change views to be part of the majority, but Rehnquist says there is not institutional pressure to do that.

Once all justices have had a chance to speak, Rehnquist will announce the vote as he has heard it. In a simple case, the vote can be a calculation of yeses and noes, but Rehnquist points out that few cases are that simple. Most involve a number of issues, and the most frequently heard quote is "some things will have to be worked out in the writing." This reaffirms what I said earlier that the justice assigned to write the case is a pivotal player in how the decision will be presented to the public.

As chief justice, Rehnquist assigns the writing assignments for most of the cases. Only cases in which he is not in the majority are assigned by others. He says that the Court is unanimous in a good number of cases and he is in the majority of many more. If there are three or four dissents on a case, it is less likely that he will be in the majority and more likely one of the senior justices in the moderate ranks will assign the case.

For controversial cases, Rehnquist votes fairly consistently with other conservatives on his court—Antonin Scalia and Clarence Thomas. Sandra Day O'Connor, who started on the Court voting more regularly with the conservative wing, has voted more often with the moderates on controversial cases in recent years.

Supreme Sayings

"… my years on the Court have convinced me that the true purpose of the conference discussion of argued cases is not to persuade one's colleagues through impassioned advocacy to alter their views, but instead, by hearing each justice express his own views, to determine there from the view of the majority of the Court. This is not to say that minds are never changed in conference; they certainly are. But it is very much the exception and not the rule …."

—Chief Justice Rehnquist in his book, *The Supreme Court*

Ruth Bader Ginsburg and Stephen Breyer lead the charge for the liberal viewpoint on Rehnquist's court. In addition to O'Connor, the key swing voters are John Paul Stevens, Anthony Kennedy, and David Souter. While the Rehnquist Court has chipped away at some of the more controversial decisions of the Warren Court, it has not succeeded in overturning any of them.

Now that you know how the basic case decisions are made, we'll use the next chapter to explore how the justices are staffed.

The Least You Need to Know

- After oral arguments are heard, there are five steps in the process of decision-making at the Supreme Court: case conference, writing assignments, opinion circulation, joining opinions, and announcing opinions.

- Each chief justice has his own style for leading a case conference, but in all courts seniority and tradition rule the order of discussion.

- Assigning case writing is a pivotal decision made by the chief justice or the senior associate justice in the majority.

- Writing of the Court's opinion in the most controversial cases can take a long time and several drafts before the final version is set.

- Rehnquist states that few minds are changed during the case conferences. He says the conference's primary purpose is for the justices to state their opinions and vote on the Court's decision.

Chapter 10

Staffing the Court

In This Chapter

- ◆ Top spot—administrative assistant
- ◆ Filings—clerk of the Court
- ◆ Opinions—reporter of decisions
- ◆ Building manager—marshal
- ◆ Other key staff of the Court

Considering that the Supreme Court is one of three of the branches of government, you may be surprised to find out that its staff totals only about 400 people and about half of those people report to the marshal. Staff reporting directly to the Supreme Court justices numbers relatively few.

In this chapter, we'll explore how the Court is staffed and the work done by that staff. All of the key staff officers at the Court are officially appointed by the Chief Justice.

Starting at the Top

The highest ranking staff person at the Court is the administrative assistant to the chief justice. Since August 14, 2000, that person has been Sally M.

Rider, who was appointed by Chief Justice Rehnquist. Prior to taking that position, Rider was the Assistant United States Attorney and Deputy Chief of the Civil Division, Office of the United States Attorney for the District of Columbia. Rider is the first woman to hold the position of Administrative Assistant to the Chief Justice.

The administrative assistant aids the chief justice with the overall management of the court, provides research to support any public addresses or statements the chief justice makes, and monitors any developments in the field of judicial administration and reform. She also assists the chief justice in fulfilling his other statutory responsibilities, which include chairman of the *Judicial Conference of the United States*, chairman of the board of the *Federal Judicial Center*, and chancellor of the *Smithsonian Institution*.

Court Connotations

Judicial Conference of the United States makes policy with regard to the administration of the United States courts and supervises the director of the Administrative Office of the United States Courts.

Federal Judicial Center is the research and education agency for the federal judicial system. It conducts and promotes education and training for judges and court employees, develops recommendations about court operations, and conducts or promotes research on federal judicial procedures, court operations and history.

Smithsonian Institution is best known for its museums in Washington, D.C., and New York. In addition to running its 16 museums and the National Zoo, the institution does extensive behind-the-scenes research through its institutes.

Rider began her legal career as a staff counsel for the United States House of Representatives' Committee on Interior and Insular Affairs in 1986. From there she moved to the Torts Branch of the Civil Division of the Department of Justice in 1987. She served as an Assistant United States Attorney in the Office of the United States Attorney for the District of Columbia during two different periods, from 1990 to 1995 and 1998 to 2000. In between those periods she was on the legal staff of the Office of the Legal Advisor for the Secretary of State. Rider received her law degree from the University of Arizona College of Law.

Clerk to the Court

Next in line in the court pecking order is the clerk to the Court. The clerk is responsible for managing the receipt and dispersal of the over 7,000 filings the court receives each year. About two-thirds of these filings come from people who cannot afford to pay the fees, of which a third are prison inmates. The clerk's staff separates the paid from the unpaid filings before passing them on to the justices' staffs. If a case is selected by the justices to be heard, the clerk puts the case on the docket and manages the inflow of briefs related to that case. If an attorney wants an extension to a deadline set by the Court, the clerk is the person who must be contacted.

In addition to sorting out and managing the filings, the clerk is also responsible for applications from attorneys who want to be admitted to the Supreme Court bar so they can practice before the Court. The clerk's office gets about 5,000 bar applications per year. Once the application is accepted, the attorneys can be sworn in by the clerk near their home when he travels outside of Washington, D.C., or they can travel to capital to be sworn in at the Supreme Court Building. About 1,300 choose to travel to Washington, D.C., each year, where they are greeted by the Chief Justice before the Clerk swears them in to the bar. Approximately 225,000 attorneys have been admitted to the Supreme Court bar since 1925, although few ever appear before the Court to argue a case.

William K. Suter was appointed Court Clerk in 1991 after retiring as a major general from the U.S. Army. Suter was the assistant judge advocate general of the Army from 1985 to 1990, and prior to that he was chief judge of the U.S. Army court of Military Review and commander of the U.S. Army Legal Services Agency. He earned his law degree from Tulane University and completed his graduate law program at the Judge Advocate General's School at the University of Virginia in Charlottesville, Virginia. Suter speaks frequently at law schools, bar associations, business organizations, as well as professional, international, and student groups.

Reporting Court Decisions

The reporter of decisions is the next most critical person to the case operations of the Court. He is responsible for the task of being sure Court opinions are released without typographical or grammatical errors and also that the opinions conform to the Court's stylistic rules. In addition to form and appearance, the reporter's office also ensures the accuracy of quotations and citations used in the opinions.

In addition, the reporter prepares the "syllabus," which is a brief synopsis of the key points of law at the top of each ruling that precedes the text of each opinion. The reporter of decisions is not the same as stenographic reporters who record and transcribe actual court proceedings.

The Congress officially authorized the post of reporter in 1817. Prior to that time the Court's decisions were published privately and sold by independent reports. When the position was first established, the reporter had six months to print and publish decisions of the Court and was required to make 80 copies available to the Secretary of State for distribution to the Library of Congress and other government officials. Today, when a decision is released, it's published on the Court's website for all to see within hours of its release. You can find those opinions at www.supremecourtus.gov/opinions/opinions.html.

> **Just the Facts**
>
> The first official reporter for the Court was Henry Wheaton. He had the exclusive right to print and sell his work during his 10 years of service. In *Wheaton* v. *Peters* (1834), Richard Peters challenged Wheaton's exclusive rights to publish and won. The Court ruled in 1834 that no one possessed a copyright to the work of the Court. Richard Peters served as reporter from 1828 to 1843 and published his volumes of Court decisions dating back to the 1790s.

In 1834, the Court issued an order requiring justices to file their opinions in writing. Prior to this time all opinions were given orally. The only written copies of Supreme Court decisions before that order were transcribed by reporters.

After the Civil War, Congress agreed to pay the reporter $2,500 per year and gave him eight months to publish opinions. The Congress also increased the number of copies to be printed to 300. All printing and publishing costs were the responsibility of the reporter. Finally in 1874, Congress appropriated funds for the publication costs and began the printing of the official court publication, "United States Reports." Today you can download this publication at www.supremecourtus.gov/opinions/boundvolumes.html.

In 1948, Congress gave up its control of the reporter and authorized the Court to fix his salary, as well as granting the right for the reporter to hire assistants. The job title changed to "Reporter of Decisions" in 1953 to differentiate the work from that of stenographers.

Today the Reporter of Decisions is Frank D. Wagner.

Keeping Things Working

The marshal of the Court is responsible for the operations of the Supreme Court Building. The marshal's office, which supervises about half of the Court's staff, is responsible for space management, maintenance and cleaning, renovation, property and supplies, procurement and contracting, telecommunications, parking, managing the motor pool, and coordinating Court events. The marshal also directs the

Supreme Court Police, which has about 100 officers that provide security for the Supreme Court employees, as well as the buildings and grounds. This office also manages the finances of the Court, disburses the payroll, and pays the bills.

You will see the marshal at all court sessions. She is responsible for gaveling the Court to order and announcing its presence with the same "cry" today as in the early days of the Court:

> "*Oyez*, Oyez, oyez. The Honorable, the Chief Justice and the Associate Justices of the Supreme Court of the United States. All persons having business before this honorable Court are admonished to draw nigh and give their attention, for the Court is now sitting. God save the United States and this honorable Court."

Court Connotations

Oyez is actually an Anglo-Norman word derived from "oyer" or "to hear." It literally means "hear ye" and was used during the Middle English period beginning about 1425.

Pamela Talkin serves as marshal for the Court and has held the position since 2001. She is the first woman to serve in that position. Talkin was Associate Justice Clarence Thomas' chief of staff when he chaired the Equal Employment Opportunity Commission (EEOC). She was also a member of the Federal Labor Relations Authority and a president of the Association of Labor Relations Agencies.

Keeping the Books

Every legal entity needs books and the library of the Court holds an extensive collection with over 500,000 volumes. The Court's librarian, Judith Gaskell, was appointed by the Chief Justice in 2003 and has a staff of 25.

The library is available not only to the justices, but can also be used by their law clerks, members of the bar, members of the Congress, and government attorneys. Visiting scholars and journalists who make special arrangements can also use the library's resources.

Before coming to the court, Judith Gaskell worked for 20 years at the DePaul University College of Law. She is the tenth librarian of the Court and the third woman to hold that position. Gaskell has her law degree from DePaul and earned a Masters degree at the University of Chicago. She served as a reference librarian for the University of Chicago Law School before joining the staff at DePaul in 1983.

Running Mini Law Firms

Each of the justices has their own chambers and staff. Most have one or two secretaries, up to four law clerks, and an aide. The secretaries transcribe dictation, handle correspondence, and field telephone calls for the justice they serve. Rehnquist says the aide helps to circulate material to other chambers, makes copies, and helps in the preparations of his meals, as well as other things that make his life easier.

The clerks serve for just one year and research and write memos or draft opinions for the justices. We'll be looking more closely at the work of the law clerks in the next chapter.

The chambers for each justice is a series of offices. Location is based on seniority, which probably doesn't surprise you given the traditions of the Court we've already discussed. The chief justice's chambers are right next to the justices' conference room. The chief justice's chambers are always the same no matter who is sitting in that seat.

Just the Facts

Rehnquist writes in his book that the second floor offices had better views than the first floor ones, so that even when the first opportunity came for him to move to the first floor, he passed it up. Rehnquist finally moved to the first floor when he took over as chief justice in 1986.

When a senior associate justice leaves the Court, his or her chambers can be claimed by any justice, but the winner will be the most senior justice that claims the spot. In 1935 when the new Supreme Court building opened, each justice had three offices—one for himself, one for his law clerk, and one for the reception area in which the secretary and messenger sat. All nine of the justices were located on the first floor of the building.

As the number of law clerks gradually increased to today's maximum of four, the three-room suites were not large enough, and by 1972 the junior justices moved up to the second floor so the senior justices could have more space on the first floor.

Court Curator

The office of the curator was established by Congress in 1974. This office is responsible for the Court's historical papers and possessions. The curator also develops educational programs for the public about the Court's history and collections.

The Court's collections include antique furnishings, archives of documents, photographs, cartoons, and other memorabilia. More than 700,000 people visit the Court each year, and the curator provides courtroom lectures to about 600 of these visitors each day. The curator also develops films and historical exhibits, which are open to the public on the ground floor.

Public Information Officer

The position of public information officer (PIO) was created in 1935 to answer questions from the public, facilitate news coverage of the Court, and distribute information about the Court and the justices. This office is responsible for releasing Court opinions to the press as soon as they are announced in an open Court session.

The office also manages a bulletin board that posts any Court orders, Court session schedules and conferences, and changes in Court procedures. The PIO is responsible for managing the press room, which houses carrels for several major news organizations that cover the Court on a regular basis.

Any press person who wants access to the Court must contact the PIO for credentials. In addition to press releases and other information releases for the Court, the PIO also prepares the employee newsletter, *The Docket Sheet*.

Now that you've learned about the key staff people of the Court, we'll take a look at the way you might be able to get a temporary one-year position at the Court.

The Least You Need to Know

◆ The Supreme Court has a relatively small staff of only about 400 people, compared to the thousands that serve in the other two branches of government—the legislative and executive.

◆ The highest ranking staff person is the administrative assistant to the chief justice, who assists the chief justice with not only the running of the Court, but also with his other responsibilities outside the Supreme Court.

◆ Case filings are received and coordinated by the clerk of the Court, who distributes filings to the chambers of the justices, manages the Court docket, swears in members to the Supreme Court bar, and serves as liaison with the legal community.

◆ Public contact with the Court is made through the public information officer, who also manages relations with the press.

Chapter 11

Clerking on the Court

In This Chapter

- On the road to clerking
- Being a fellow
- Working as an intern
- Serving as a marshal's aide

Working as a law clerk to a Supreme Court justice is the fulfillment of a long-term dream for many newly minted lawyers, but it's an assignment not easy to get. A lawyer's future can be set with recommendations and opportunities that will help him or her succeed professionally throughout their career.

In this chapter we'll explore how one gets appointed as a law clerk and what the work entails. Law clerks work for a Supreme Court justice for one year.

There are other temporary one-year assignments college students and lawyers can get if they'd like to experience life at the Supreme Court including fellowships, internships, and work as marshal's aides. We'll review how to get those spots as well.

Choosing the Clerking Path

For someone who wants to work as a Supreme Court law clerk, he or she will likely have to start planning that path even before entering law school. That's because most of the law clerks chosen by Supreme Court justices rank in the top 10 percent of the top 10 law schools (in alphabetical order)—Columbia, Duke, Harvard, New York University, Stanford, University of California at Berkeley, University of Chicago, University of Michigan, University of Pennsylvania, and Yale.

Also, you are more likely to be successful if you are a white male. In fact, according to an NAACP study released in 1998, in the 200 years since hiring clerks, the Supreme Court has never hired a Native American. The NAACP president said in 1998 of the 394 clerks hired by the current justices during their tenures, only seven were black.

> **Supreme Sayings**
>
> NAACP President Kweisi Mfume said in 1998 the Supreme Court sent out the message that "people of color need not apply" for the "influential clerkships." He added, "People of good will understand this hypocrisy must end on the Supreme Court. If the Court were a private company, it would have been found guilty long ago of racial discrimination."

The NAACP found that 24.3 percent of law clerks were women, 4.5 percent were Asian American, 1.8 percent were black, 1 percent were Hispanic, and all the rest were white men. About 40 percent of all law clerks come from Harvard and Yale.

Today the numbers may be slightly improved. After the NAACP study was released, there were protests and a Congressional hearing. In 1999, of the 35 law clerks hired, five were minorities, including two blacks and three Asian Americans. There has not been follow-up study since 1998.

Chief Justice Rehnquist responded by letter to the Congress after hearings on the diversity of law clerks. In his response he said:

"Each of us is satisfied that no person is excluded from consideration for a clerkship because of race, religion, gender, nationality, or for any other impermissible reason. Each justice of course acts independently in deciding whom to employ as law clerks …

"We agree the statistics set forth in your letter identify concerns which all of us share, but you must realize that many factors entirely unrelated to the hiring of law clerks are responsible for this situation. We select clerks who have very strong academic backgrounds, and have previously successful law clerk experience, most often in the federal courts. As the demographic makeup of this pool changes, it seems entirely likely that the underrepresentation of minorities … will also change."

During this controversy, the public broadcasting show *NewsHour* interviewed five former law clerks. Three were professors of law—John Yoo now at the University of California at Berkeley who clerked for Justice Clarence Thomas, Neal Katyal now at Georgetown who clerked for Justice Stephen Breyer, and Sheryll Cashin also at Georgetown, who clerked for Justice Thurgood Marshall. Two of the interviewees are in private practice—Ted Cruz who clerked for Chief Justice William Rehnquist and Kathryn Bradley who clerked for Justice Byron White. Four of the five interviewed agreed that more diversity was needed in the hiring of law clerks for the Court.

Sheryll Cashin did the best job of summarizing the reasons more diversity was needed. "I think diversity among the law clerks is imperative or critical for three reasons: First, I think it would improve the quality of judging among Supreme Court justices. Supreme Court justices decide decisions that affect a broad array of people but they live very insular lives. And I would feel more confident about them seriously engaging in a diverse array of intellectual perspectives if they're personally confronted with people who represent different walks of life. Second the Supreme Court clerk's credential is an opportunity, an incredible opportunity, paid for by U.S. taxpayers, and I think it's only right and just that a broader array of people get a shot at that. And then finally and most importantly I think the public, the American public, would have more confidence in the institution if a broader array of people served the justices there."

While four of the five agreed with Sheryll, they also agreed the root of the problem was not necessarily one of discrimination by the justices, but rather a problem with the law school educational system. In reality few minorities attend the top 10 law schools, so they are just not in the pool used by the justices from which to select candidates.

Kathryn Bradley, who did not attend one of those top 10 schools but attended the University of Maryland said, "in practical experience the Court does not look in at all the pool out there. It's looking at a limited body of applicants drawn from a much broader potential set of people who are perfectly qualified to serve at the court .... I came from an atypical experience not only from being at the University of Maryland, but I'd also had a district court experience in a federal court for two years prior to coming to Justice White, as opposed to the typical path through an appellate clerkship."

> **Just the Facts**
>
> Neal Katyal, a former Supreme Court clerk, believes one must look at the state of today's legal system to find the core of the problem of diversity. He said only 3 percent of minorities are partners in the 250 top law firms and 94 percent of the judges are white. Change needs to start at the law school level.

John Yoo was the former clerk who spoke out against diversity. He said, "I think diversity would be a terrible thing at the Court. What the NAACP wants is to make the judiciary representative of the people as a whole or of the political system, and that's exactly what we don't want the judiciary to be. We want the justices to be impartial, separated from society, so they can stand up for individuals when the government oppresses their Constitutional rights."

So what is the actual pool from which most Supreme Court justices select their law clerks? Ideally if you want to serve as a law clerk you must attend one of the top 10 law schools, achieve academically so you are in the top 10 percent of your class and serve for at least a year as a law clerk with an appellate circuit court judge who has close ties to a Supreme Court justice. This pool totals about 150 to 200 people each year. Success comes to those who have made the right contacts as well as to those who have a bit of luck. Most clerks are suggested to a Supreme Court justice by an appellate judge or a law school professor who served as a clerk themselves.

Justices hire three or four law clerks each year, who serve on the court for one year. If every justice hires four law clerks, that means 36 is the greatest number of law clerks that can serve on the court in one year. Retired justices also get one clerk per year.

Clerk's Duties

Let's assume you've chosen the right path and actually have been offered a spot as a Supreme Court law clerk. What will your day be like? To discuss the life of a law clerk, I'll be using information from Chief Justice Rehnquist, who wrote about his experiences as a law clerk to Supreme Court Justice Robert Jackson in 1952, and Edward Lazarus, who served as a law clerk to Supreme Court Justice Harry Blackmun from 1988 to 1989 and wrote about his experiences in the book, *Closed Chambers: The Rise, Fall, and Future of the Modern Supreme Court.*

Court Connotations

Petitions for certiorari are documents filed by the losing party in a law suit asking the Supreme Court to review a decision of a lower court. Certiorari is a Latin word that means "to be informed of, or to be made certain in regard to."

One thing that is certain for every law clerk is that you will spend lots of time at the Court. Today law clerks work about 90 hours per week. They start their year in July, when most of the justices are away for the summer. Orientation and training is received primarily from the prior year's clerks. Most law clerks won't get to meet the other justices of the Court until they return in September, but all will have interviewed with the justice they will serve.

A good deal of any law clerk's time is spent reviewing the approximately 7,000 requests for Supreme Court review (called *petitions for certiorari* or certs) and the rest is spent writing memos, researching, and drafting opinions for the justice they serve. During the summer months, reviewing cert petitions fills all their time. By the end of the summer, approximately 1,000 cases are waiting for review by the justices.

As I discussed in Chapter 2, four of the nine justices must vote in favor of reviewing a case in order for the Court to decide to put it on the docket. The cert petitions and related filings are what the justices use to determine whether to take a case.

The justices have formed a cert pool to facilitate the workload of handling the petitions. The petitions are divvied up among the law clerks by the clerk of the Court. The law clerk assigned a particular case writes a cert memo and circulates the memo to the other justices and their clerks. In today's court, only Justice Stevens does not participate in the pool.

The cert pool memo summarizes the trial, the opinion from the court of appeals, the reasons for requesting Supreme Court review set out by the petitioner and the reasons review is not needed set out by the winning party. Then a recommendation is made as to whether the petition for cert should be granted or denied. If granted, the case will be heard by the Supreme Court. If denied the lower court ruling will stand.

Lazarus writes in his book *Closed Chambers* that Wednesday became the first day of the week for the clerks. That was when the paid petitions for cert were delivered to their desk. You may remember from the last chapter that the clerk of the Court separates the petitions between people who can afford to pay and people who cannot afford to pay. On Thursdays the larger pile from people who cannot afford to pay are delivered. While the petitions from the paying group are neatly typed and presented according to court rules, the group that cannot afford to pay are sometimes even handwritten and illegible.

> **Supreme Sayings**
>
> "This 'pool memo' summarizes a case and assesses whether it is 'certiworthy'—that is whether it raises a sufficiently important and controversial issue to merit the Supreme Court's attention. Although the justices do not follow the pool memo recommendations slavishly, in practice they carry great weight."
>
> —Edward Lazarus in his book *Closed Chambers*

A clerk's workload for the week is heavily dependent on the types of petitions he or she receives. Most of the petitions are for cases that clearly do not raise issues for the Court and a pool memo can be quickly written in a few hours. Cases that could potentially be granted cert require much more work and could take days of research.

No matter how long the clerk needs to finish the pool memo, it must be done by 10 A.M. the next Wednesday, so it can be circulated among the offices before the justices meet to discuss the cases being considered for cert. The chief justice's office manages the cert pool and will circulate a list of late pool memos at the Friday meeting, which will earn the late clerk the wrath of justice he or she serves. During the summer months the schedule is not as tight, since the justices are not around to meet.

In addition to the cert petitions, the Court also receives a steady stream of emergency applications that most often seek a stay of a lower court ruling (in other words, a petitioner is seeking to block the ruling of the lower court). Many of these emergency petitions seek a stay of execution in capital cases. Each justice is assigned to handle the emergency applications for one or two circuits. A person seeking a stay would apply to the justice of his or her circuit. The supervising justice can order the stay, but more commonly will refer the case to the entire Court if a stay seems warranted. Law clerks also assist the justice with reviewing these emergency applications.

For cases that have been granted cert and are ready to be heard, the law clerk writes a bench memo, to help the justice prepare for the oral arguments. After oral arguments, any cases assigned to the justice for writing are divvied up among the three or four law clerks in that justice's office. Each justice usually allows his or her law clerks to decide how to divvy up the work.

Supreme Sayings

"Juggling these daunting assignments seven days a week for weeks on end produces a mind-numbing exhaustion and also exacts a physical toll. Longtime staffers around the building would joke about the 'Blackmun diet,' the workaholic's method for shedding pounds. Clerks invented remarkable routines for keeping themselves sharp; one, late at night during the winter months, propped open the security gates on the Court's main floor so that he could run circuits around the building."

—Edward Lazarus in his book *Closed Chambers*

The law clerk assigned to the case will meet with the justice after the case conference, find out the decisions made at conference and get directions from his or her justice regarding what additional research is needed and how to write the decision. The law clerk will research the critical issues and then draft a decision for review. The justice will review, edit, and sometimes even rewrite the clerk's draft before circulating it to the other justices.

When the court finishes hearing new cases in April, the rest of the law clerk's term is spent on assisting with the drafting of opinions, as well as the continuing cert work. When law clerks finish their year of service in July after the last case decision is announced, they stay around for a few days to train the next crop of law clerks.

Getting a Fellowship

Each year the Supreme Court also offers four one-year fellowships. Fellows serve at the Supreme Court, the Federal Judicial Center, the Administrative office of the United States Courts, and the United States Sentencing Commission.

Competition is stiff and the applicants must have:

♦ at least one post-graduate degree;

♦ two or more years of professional experience; and

♦ multidisciplinary training and experience, including familiarity with the judicial process.

The chief justice appoints a panel to select the fellows. To give you an idea of the qualifications needed, I'm including the backgrounds of the fellows selected for 2003-2004:

Linda Bishai, who is a Supreme Court Fellow at the Federal Judicial Center, is on leave from her post as an assistant professor of International Law and International Relations at the University of Maryland. Her degrees include a B.A. in History and Literature from Harvard University, a J.D. from Georgetown University Law Center, an L.L.M. from the University of Stockholm, and a Ph.D. in International Relations from the London School of Economics (LSE). She has lectured on international law and politics at Stockholm University, the LSE, and Brunel University. In 2001, she guest lectured on diversity and international relations for the Southeast Europe Youth Leadership Institute, a summer program sponsored by the U.S. Department of State and other organizations to bring gifted high school students from Eastern Europe to the United States. Prior to teaching, Bishai practiced law at Edwards & Angell Law Firm in Providence, Rhode Island.

Scott N. Carlson, who is the Supreme Court Fellow at the United States Sentencing Commission, is on leave from his post as program director for Central and Eastern Europe and Judicial Reform for the American Bar Association. His degrees include a B.A. in English from the University of Alabama at Birmingham, a J.D. from the University of Georgia, and a Master of Laws in International and Comparative Law from Georgetown University. Prior to joining the Central and Eurasian Law Initiative, where he worked to promote the rule of law and human rights, he was a legal adviser to the Organization for Security and Cooperation in Europe (OSCE) in Albania. Between 1989-1995, he was an attorney for the U.S. Department of Treasury, and in 1995, he served as a resident tax advisor for the Treasury Tax Advisory Program in Tirana, Albania, where he assisted the International Monetary Fund and Albanian

Ministry of Finance with the review of regulations and implementation of a value-added tax. He received the Fulbright Scholar Award in Albania for 1997-1998, and in 1997, he was a research scholar at the University of Michigan.

Matthew S. Duchesne, who will be the Supreme Court Fellow serving at the Court, is on leave from his position as an associate at law firm Jones Day in Washington, D.C. There he prepares appellate briefs for cases under review in the Supreme Court of the United States, and federal and state appellate courts, and he works on issues involving international and comparative law, particularly as they relate to investor-state arbitration under the North America Free Trade Agreement (NAFTA). His degrees include a B.A. in Political Science from Miami University in Ohio, an M.A. in Public Administration from the University of North Carolina at Chapel Hill, and a J.D. from the University of North Carolina at Chapel Hill School of Law. Prior to joining Jones Day, Duchesne was a judicial clerk for Judge Richard L. Nygaard of the United States Court of Appeals for the Third Circuit. In 1994, Duchesne joined the Corporate Response Group in Washington, D.C., where he assisted government and private clients to develop and test crisis management and communication procedures to deal with catastrophic events. Beginning in 1991 he was a management analyst for the United States Office of Government Ethics where he evaluated ethics programs throughout the executive branch and participated in the investigation of allegations of ethics violations by government officials.

Steven S. Gensler, who will be the Supreme Court Fellow at the Administrative Office of the United States Courts, is on leave from his position as an associate professor at the University of Oklahoma College of Law. His degrees include a B.S. in Biology from the University of Illinois, and a J.D. from the University of Illinois College of Law. He specializes in civil procedure, alternative dispute resolution, federal courts, and conflicts of law. Gensler clerked for Judge Deanell Reece Tacha of the United States Court of Appeals for the Tenth Circuit, and for Judge Kathryn H. Vratil of the United States District Court for the District of Kansas. He also worked as an associate for Michael, Best & Friedrich LLP in their Labor and Employment Department and as a litigation associate with Reinhart, Boerner, Van Deuren, Norris & Rieselbach.

As you can see, fellows selected are already well established professionally. The work they do depends upon their assignment. For example, the fellow at the Supreme Court helps with long-term projects as well as day-to-day administrative tasks. He supervises two judicial interns (more about that position in the section that follows).

Projects can include:

♦ researching and providing background information for the chief justice's speeches and reports;

- preparing analytical reports on legal and managerial issues;

- providing assistance to other Court offices;

- assisting with branch seminars and committees; and

- developing programs designed to enhance the public understanding of the federal judiciary and the Supreme Court.

If you are interested in applying for a fellowship, you can find complete details at www.fellows.supremecourtus.gov/index.html.

Supreme Sayings

"Since its inception, the Fellows Program has offered a unique opportunity for exceptional individuals to contribute to the administration of justice at the national level. ... Our Fellows have a tradition of bringing creativity and fresh insights to projects that have had a lasting impact on the federal courts. ... Our need for motivated individuals who want to make a difference is as important today as it was when the Program began."

—Chief Justice William Rehnquist in a letter to fellow applicants

Getting an Internship

Only two people are selected each year to serve as judicial interns at the Supreme Court, positions which are open to advanced undergraduates and graduating seniors who are interested in law, management or social sciences. These positions were established in 1972 and assist the chief justice with fulfilling his nonjudicial responsibilities. Interns do not work on cases pending before the Court.

Intern responsibilities include:

- summarizing news articles,

- preparing memoranda and correspondence,

- conducting background research for speeches, and

- reviewing legislation on the federal judicial system.

Because only two positions are offered each year, competition is stiff. For more details about this opportunity go to www.supremecourtus.gov/publicinfo/jiprogram.pdf.

Working as a Marshal's Aide

If you are not successful in getting an internship, there is one other way to work at the court—as a marshal's aide. Before 1973, these aides were high school freshman. Today these positions are filled primarily with prelaw undergraduates or night law-school students.

When the court is in session, marshal's aides wait behind the bench and run messages between the justices or to other parts of courts. They also serve any need of the justices, including getting water from the fountain or getting reference material from the library.

If you want to apply for this position, contact the marshal's office at the Supreme Court of the United States, Washington, D.C. 20543.

Now that we reviewed how the Court operates, we'll be taking a look at the key Court precedents that are in place today, the critical cases that built these precedents, and how these precedents impact our country's laws.

The Least You Need to Know

- The cream of the crop of today's top law schools are eligible to serve as law clerks for Supreme Court justices. Success in getting the position is a combination of merit, contacts, and luck.

- Law professionals who would like to spend a year at the court can apply for one of four fellowships available each year.

- Two lucky college students are picked each year to serve as judicial interns.

- If all else fails and you'd still like to spend a year at the Court, you can apply for a spot as a marshal's aide.

Part 4

Forming Government Rights

From the day the court opened there were struggles about who would be more powerful—the states or the federal government. In this part, we'll look at some of those battles and how they are still being fought today as we elect our leaders, decide on taxes, educate our kids, and determine our property rights.

Chapter 12

Electing Our Leaders

In This Chapter

- ◆ Counting chads and election machinery
- ◆ Avoiding discrimination when establishing districts
- ◆ Setting rules for advertising and campaign funding
- ◆ Limiting party participation

State governments have the responsibility for running elections and setting the rules, even when electing federal officials. That doesn't mean they have free reign—they must still be sure that the rules and procedures mandated do not conflict with the Constitution.

While the Supreme Court does hesitate to get involved in these state decisions, there have been numerous cases heard by the Court over the years. Many involve redistricting, campaign financing, and equal access to public airwaves. There have also been cases to prevent last minute party switching.

In recent years, the most controversial election case was *Bush* v. *Gore*, which involved ballot counting problems in Florida. In this chapter, I'll review recent court rulings regarding state-run election provisions.

Election Machinery That Works

Most of us watched horrified as the fiasco unfolded in Florida while votes were being counted during the 2000 presidential election. News media first reported Gore the winner, switched to too close to call, then declared Bush the winner, then switched back to too close to call. I remember staying up all night amazed at the mess that was unfolding. Finally when all votes were in, the race was too close to call and an automatic recount was needed.

Florida was ripe for the kind of problems we witnessed. There were no statewide rules for how votes should be counted if a recount was necessary. The Florida law only states that a vote should be counted if clear "voter intent" could be discerned. Some counties believed that meant if a recount is needed all votes should be inspected manually, while others just checked their numbers, and still others ran the ballots through the counting machines one more time. Each county's election supervisor had the power to determine how the recount should be conducted. When the automatic recount was complete only 537 votes separated the two out of about 6 million votes cast.

Not only were there no rules about how to count votes, there were different types of voting mechanisms available in different counties. Some used paper ballots, some used optical-scanning equipment to count votes, some used punch cards, and some used lever machines. Even the ballots themselves looked different in every county. In fact, the butterfly ballot designed in Palm Beach County became the laughing stock of the nation when many voters became confused by the design and claimed they voted for the wrong person. Others voted twice when they realized they made a mistake.

Some speculate that Al Gore lost 20,000 votes because of the confusion surrounding this ballot, but since both parties had seen the design before the election and it was designed by a Democratic election supervisor, Gore decided not to take the case to court.

What Gore did decide to challenge was vote counts in three heavily Democratic counties (Miami Dade, Broward, and Palm Beach County) that used punch card machines, hoping to pick up enough votes to win the state and ultimately the presidency.

The vote study done after the election by a consortium of newspapers showed he would have been better off asking for a statewide recount. The study determined that, based on the prevailing statewide standard, Gore would have won the state. In fact, he would have won in five out of nine possible vote-counting scenarios studied, but would have lost based on the strategy of just recounting the three counties.

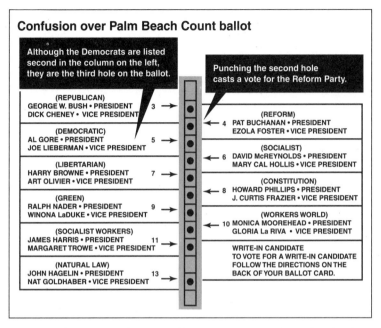

The butterfly ballot in Florida was the most controversial one after the election, but a challenge to this ballot did not make it to the Supreme Court.

Thousands of votes had been discarded in the counties Gore picked because of problems with the punch card machines. The media had a field day showing election workers holding up punch cards to the light trying to determine voter intent on uncounted ballots.

Just to be sure you understand what was being questioned, when a voter hits the hole on a punch card for the chosen candidate a piece of the card, called a chad, is supposed to be discharged. Sometimes these chads are not fully discharged because of either voter error or machine problems. In fact, in Miami it was discovered after the election that the punch card machines in some areas had not be cleaned for eight years and the voters had difficulty dislodging the chads.

Just the Facts

Statewide it was finally determined that approximately 180,000 votes went uncounted in Florida for several different reasons, according to a million-dollar project done by the National Opinion Research Center after the election. This study was paid for by a consortium of newspapers that included *The New York Times, Washington Post, Palm Beach Post, St. Petersburg Times*, Dow Jones & Co., Sentinel Co., Tribune Co., and the Associated Press.

In defending his recount request, Gore's legal team found a statement in the 1982 patent application for the Votomatic punchcard machine that backed up his claim about machine problems:

> "If chips are permitted to accumulate … this can interfere with the punching operations, … and occasionally, it has been observed that a partially punched chip has been left hanging on the card resulting in the machine becoming so clogged with chips as to prevent a clean punching operation. Incompletely punched cards can cause serious errors to occur in data processing operations utilizing such cards."

Nine types of errors were found in the counties that used punch card ballots as they held up the uncounted cards to the light:

1. Some ballots that were properly punched were not counted because of machine error.

2. Some ballots could not be punched all the way because of machine problems.

3. Some ballots were punched all the way but the voter failed to notice that the chad was still attached on one corner.

4. Some ballots were punched all the way but the chad was still attached on two corners.

5. Some ballots were punched all the way but the chad was only detached at one corner.

6. Some ballots only had a pin prick that could be seen when held up to the light, but no corner had been detached.

7. Some ballots had only dimpled chads. In other words there was an indentation but no light could be seen when holding up the card.

8. Some voters wrote a name on the card rather than punching through the chad, which probably indicated some problem using the punchcard machine.

9. Some voted for two candidates, which invalidated the vote. This was more common in Palm Beach County because of the butterfly ballot.

The Bush legal team filed a case in Florida's court system to stop the vote count, which made it all the way to the Florida Supreme Court. The Florida Supreme Court ordered a manual recount of all votes statewide and extended the deadline for certifying the election results by 12 days. The United States Supreme Court vacated that decision and sent the case back to the Florida Supreme Court for clarification of its decision.

The Supreme Court found that the Florida Supreme Court had violated Article II of the U.S. Constitution by changing the law enacted by the Florida legislature.

This decision amazed almost all Court watchers because the Florida Supreme Court did what has been done by courts throughout U.S. judiciary history. It found that two parts of Florida election laws passed by the state contradicted each other and tried to fix the problem. One part of Florida election law said that a candidate could challenge the vote in a county if there was an "error in the vote tabulation which could affect the outcome of the election." Another part of the law mandated that results be submitted within a week of the election. This deadline made it impossible to do a recount in the specified time. The Florida Supreme Court tried to solve this problem by extending the deadline.

> **Living Laws**
>
> Fixing an inconsistency in the law is a very traditional role for the courts when laws passed by the legislature contradict each other. In fact, the precedent for this was set by Chief Justice John Marshall in *Marbury v. Madison* (which we discussed in Chapter 4) when he wrote for the court, "if two laws conflict with each other, the courts must decide on the operation of each."

In asking for clarification, the United States Supreme Court sent a mixed message. It found that there were problems in the lack of uniform vote counting standards, but questioned the right of the Florida Supreme Court to fix the problem. The United States Supreme Court gave the message that only the legislature could fix the problem. Since there wasn't enough time for that, the Florida Supreme Court's hands were tied. When the Florida Supreme Court ordered the recount to be restarted, it ruled that the standard established by the Florida legislature must be used:

> "In tabulating the ballots and in making a determination of what is a 'legal' vote, the standards to be employed is that established by the Legislature in our Election Code, which is that the vote shall be counted as a 'legal' vote if there is 'clear indication of the intent of the voter.'"

Following what it thought was the advice of the United States Supreme Court, the Florida Supreme Court did not try to rewrite legislation by changing the standards set by the Florida legislature. The vote count was restarted at 4 P.M. on December 8 and promptly halted at 2:40 P.M. the next day by the United States Supreme Court on the basis of another legal issue not even raised in the initial request for clarification—the question of equal protection. By stopping the vote count the Supreme Court decided the Florida election and ultimately who would be president.

The *equal protection* question had been raised by the Bush legal team in its original filing, but had been ignored by the United States Supreme Court in its request for clarification. Some think this was a trap for the Florida Supreme Court.

In an unsigned opinion the United States Supreme Court ruled:

> "Upon due consideration of the difficulties identified to this point, it is obvious that the recount cannot be conducted in compliance with the requirements of equal protection and due process without substantial additional work. It would require not only the adoption (after opportunity for argument) of adequate statewide standards for determining what is a legal vote, and practicable procedures to implement them, but also orderly judicial review of any disputed matters that might arise. ... Seven Justices of the Court agree that there are constitutional problems with the recount ordered by the Florida Supreme Court that demand a remedy."

In its final decision, the United States Supreme Court said the Florida justices did have "the power to assure uniformity" and if they had there would be no equal-protection problem. The trap was set by the suggestion in the first ruling that warned against tampering with Florida election law.

Court Connotations

The **equal protection** clause of the Constitution states, "No state shall make or enforce any law which shall abridge the privileges or immunities of citizens of the United States; nor shall any state deprive any person of life, liberty, or property, without due process of law; nor deny to any person within its jurisdiction the equal protection of the laws." This is most commonly used in cases involving the death penalty. To use this clause, there must be proof that someone is being harmed by not receiving equal protection under law.

Outrage over the ruling was widespread. While it's logical to assume supporters of Gore would blast the United States Supreme Court ruling, the bigger surprise came from the number of conservatives who supported Bush that denigrated the decision. Here are a few compiled by Alan Dershowitz in his book about the case, *Supreme Injustice*:

◆ Robert Bork (who didn't get confirmed for a seat on the Court) said, "the per curiam opinion joined by five justices does have major problems" and it "endorsed a new and possibly damaging rationale."

◆ Bush supporter Richard Epstein (University of Chicago Law School) called the majority's ruling a "weird equal-protection theory" and the broadest "equal-protection test known to man." He said, "this equal-protection dog [would bark] only once."

◆ John Dilulo wrote in the conservative *Weekly Standard*, "the arguments that ended the battle and 'gave' Bush the Presidency are constitutionally disingenuous at best."

◆ Michael McConnell wrote in *The Wall Street Journal* that the failure to seek a proper recount denied George Bush the "clarity of victory that he must surely desire" and that this "means, unfortunately that Mr. Bush will take office under conditions of continued uncertainty."

History will probably place this ruling among those that live in infamy that we've already discussed—*Dred Scott* v. *Sandford* and the *Lochner* v. *New York* (Chapter 7). Even the justices who voted in favor of stopping the vote count wanted to limit the precedent set. The ruling limits its use as a precedent with this phrase, "Our consideration is limited to the present circumstances, for the problem of equal protection in election processes generally presents many complexities."

Many asked when all this was over if the justices would have ruled the same way if Gore had been in the lead at the same point in the vote count. Would they still have stopped the count? We'll never know, but few doubt politics played a hand in this decision.

Remapping Districts

Voting districts are mapped by each state every 10 years after the completion of a U.S. Census. These district maps draw the boundaries for voting in districts for the U.S. House of Representatives as well as for districts in state legislatures.

Voting districts are supposed to be as equal as possible in number of voters per representative. After a census count, in most states these lines need to be redrawn to reflect any population changes. States whose population is increasing may end up with more seats in the U.S. House of Representatives, while states that are losing population could lose seats in the House. The final total always needs to be 435, which is the number of Constitutionally mandated seats in the House. The Senate has 100 seats or two per state.

Games are played by politicians when designing the districts as they try to build districts that will be most beneficial to electing someone of their own party. In each state house, the party in control tries to draw districts that will give them the greatest number of safe seats—seats in which someone of their own party has the best chance of being elected. The party not in control will attempt to prevent this and if the new district map is questionable may even challenge it in state court.

> **Just the Facts** _____
>
> Texas went through a very visible battle over redistricting its Congressional seats in 2003. Democratic legislatures fled the state twice to prevent a vote on a new district map. Texas law requires a quorum for any voting to take place in its legislature. By fleeing the state the Democrats prevented a vote they knew they would lose. Traditionally redistricting is only done after a 10-year census, but Texas Republicans are trying to do one sooner. Challenges to this redistricting attempt will probably be taken to the courts and possibly even the United States Supreme Court.

Department of Commerce v. United States House

Redistricting issues are usually left to the state courts, but occasionally the United States Supreme Court does get involved if a question of constitutionality is raised. One case that directly impacted how the census data would be collected was decided by the Supreme Court on January 25, 1999, in *Department of Commerce* v. *United States House.*

In this case the House of Representatives and a group of individual taxpayers challenged the administration's plan for using statistical sampling in the 2000 census to supplement the more traditional procedure of trying to reach every household. As we discussed, this directly impacts how the nation's population is counted and how the seats in Congress will be divided among the states.

The Constitution's Census Clause authorizes Congress to direct an "actual Enumeration" of the American public every 10 years to provide a basis for apportioning Congressional representation among the states. The Congress delegated this responsibility to the Department of Commerce. Commerce wanted to supplement the traditional count with statistical sampling techniques in 2000 because it was widely known that minority populations were undercounted.

The House took the position that the use of sampling is barred by both the Constitution and the Census Act. The Supreme Court ruled the Census Act did prohibit "the proposed uses of statistical sampling in calculating the population for purposes of apportionment" and therefore did not need to rule on the constitutional question presented. Statistical sampling was barred from use and the Commerce Department conducted the census in the traditional manner.

City of Mobile v. Bolden

Another recent election dispute settled by the Supreme Court involved charges of discrimination in *City of Mobile* v. *Bolden*. William Bolden brought the case as a class action on behalf of himself and other residents of the city of Mobile, Alabama. He argued that the practice of electing city commissioners at-large unfairly diluted the voting strength of black citizens. In many cities commissioners are elected by district rather than at-large without specified district boundaries, so they represent a specific portion of the city. In most cities there are predominantly white neighborhoods and predominately black neighborhoods. In cities where commissioners represent districts there is a greater chance the black neighborhoods will be represented by someone sympathetic to their views.

Both the district court and the U.S. Court of Appeals for the Fifth District sided with Bolden. The district court ruled that the at-large electoral system violated the *Fifteenth Amendment* and discriminated against Negroes in violation of the equal protection clause of the Fourteenth Amendment. Bolden wanted the at-large electoral system to be changed to one of representative districts. The lower courts agreed.

Court Connotations

The **Fifteenth Amendment** prohibits denying the right to vote on the grounds of race, color, or previous conditions of servitude.

The Supreme Court overturned the lower courts on April 22, 1980, saying the Fifteenth Amendment did not entail "the right to have Negro candidates elected." It ruled the primary purpose of that amendment was to prevent citizens from being denied the freedom to vote because of discrimination. It also ruled the Fourteenth Amendment did not make multimember legislative districts unconstitutional, but would violate the equal protection clause of the Fourteen Amendment if they were "conceived or operated as a purposeful device to further racial … discrimination."

Mahan v. Howell

The most recent key reapportionment case decided by the Supreme Court is *Mahan* v. *Howell* in February 1973. Henry Howell challenged a redistricting plan passed by the Virginia legislature in 1971. The legislature had reapportioned the seats for its House of Representatives and provided for 100 representatives in 52 districts with each House member representing an average of 46,485 constituents.

Howell based his challenge on the variance in district sizes. The difference between the largest district and the smallest district was a difference of 16.4 percent. The ideal is considered to be about 4 percent. Howell said these deviations were too large to satisfy the principle of "one person, one vote" and unconstitutionally violated the equal protection clause of the Fourteenth Amendment. The district court agreed with Howell and drew up its own lines to reduce the percentage variation to about 10 percent.

> **Living Laws**
>
> The Supreme Court ruled in *Mahan* v. *Howell* that state legislative reapportionment is "given wider constitutional latitude" than for reapportionment of U.S Congressional seats to facilitate representation on local political issues.

The Supreme Court overturned the lower court ruling saying that the plan was constitutional under the equal protection clause, which requires a state to make an "honest and good faith effort" to constrict districts of equal population. The Supreme Court ruled that some deviations from the equal population principle are valid if based on legitimate considerations of a "rational state policy" and facilitates "enactment of statutes of purely local concern and preserves for the voters in the political subdivisions a voice in the state legislature on local matters."

Paying for Campaigns

Campaign financing laws can be another critical issue that frequently makes it to the Supreme Court. In fact, a major case whose ruling was announced December 10, 2003, the Supreme Court upheld two key components of the McCain-Feingold Bipartisan Campaign Reform Act of 2001, which was ruled at least partially unconstitutional in a convoluted decision by the federal district court earlier in the year. The Supreme Court heard that case in September 2003. The December ruling was decided on a split decision of 5 to 4 and upheld provisions that restricted "soft money" donations and advertising placed with this money just before elections. Prior to this law, major corporations, labor unions, and wealthy individuals could write a large check without limits to campaigns using what was known as "soft money" contributions. McCain-Feingold restricted these donations and the Court upheld those restrictions. Challengers to the law claimed this was a violation of the free speech provisions of the First Amendment.

The Supreme Court also ruled that the law's provisions that restrict the use of "soft money" 30 days before a primary and 60 days before a national election are constitutional. In writing for the majority, Justices Stevens and O'Connor said:

> "Just as troubling to a functioning democracy as classic quid pro quo corruption is the danger that officeholders will decide issues not on the merits or the desires of their constituencies, but according to the wishes of those who have

made large financial contributions valued by the officeholder. Even if it occurs only occasionally, the potential for such undue influence is manifest. And unlike straight cash-for-votes transactions, such corruption is neither easily detected nor practical to criminalize. The best means of prevention is to identify and to remove the temptation. The evidence set forth above, which is but a sampling of the reams of disquieting evidence contained in the record, convincingly demonstrates that soft-money contributions to political parties carry with them just such temptation."

Prior to this case, the most recent landmark ruling on campaign financing was *Buckley* v. *Valeo* in 1976. In an attempt to clean up the mess after the Watergate affair, Congress passed a law to deal with corruption in political campaigns by restricting financial contributions to candidates and how the money raised is spent. The Federal Election Campaign Act of 1971 included among its provisions an attempt to limit the amount of money an individual could contribute to a single campaign to $1,000 and a total of $25,000 to all federal candidates. Candidates and their immediate families were limited to contributions of $50,000 for presidential and vice presidential candidates, $35,000 for Senate candidates and $25,000 for House candidates. The act also required the reporting of contributions above $100. Contributions above $5,000 had to be reported within 48 hours of receipt. The act also created the *Federal Election Commission.*

Court Connotations

The **Federal Election Commission** administers and enforces the Federal Election Campaign Act (FECA)—the statute that governs the financing of federal elections. Its duties include the disclosure of campaign finance information and the enforcement of the FECA related to limits and prohibitions on contributions. It also oversees the public funding of presidential elections.

In addition to the contribution limits, the law also specified spending limits. The class action suit was brought to question whether the First Amendments guarantees of freedom of speech and association were limited by this new law. The Supreme Court upheld the part of the law related to funding limits, but overturned the part of the law related to spending limits.

The Supreme Court found that restrictions on individual contributions to political campaigns and candidates did not violate the First Amendment because these limits enhanced the "integrity of our system of representative democracy" by guarding against unscrupulous practices. The provisions of the law that restricted independent expenditures in campaigns, the limits on expenditures by candidates from their own personal or family resources, and the limits on total campaign expenditures were found by the Court to violate the First Amendment. The Court held that these practices do not necessarily enhance the potential for corruption that individual contributions to candidates do. In addition, the Court found that restricting these expenses did not serve a government interest great enough to warrant a curtailment on free speech and association.

Getting the Word Out

Another key controversy during election time is how much space a candidate should receive in a newspaper, in outside advertising or on the airwaves. Two recent precedent-setting Supreme Court cases involving election visibility were *Lehman* v. *City of Shaker Heights* (1974), which involved advertising on buses, and *Miami Herald Publishing Co.* v. *Tornillo* (1974), which involved equal time in a newspaper.

Harry J. Lehman sued the city of Shaker Heights because he was denied advertising space on buses in the city's transit system. He wanted to advertise his campaign on the buses, but his ads were refused by the city. Lehman said that since the city allowed other types of advertising on city buses, political advertising should also be allowed and his rights of freedom of speech and equal protection were being violated by the city's refusal to accept his ads. The Ohio Supreme Court found that the city's refusal to accept campaign advertising did not violate a candidate's free speech rights (First Amendment) or equal protection rights (Fourteenth Amendment). Lehman took it to the United States Supreme Court.

Living Laws
The precedent set in the *Lehman* decision has been used by the courts to decide cases involving persons who want to use government property for expressive activity in violation of rules that restrict or prohibit such activity. The Court has ruled that a site owned by the government is a traditional forum only if by long tradition or government mandate it is devoted to assembly and debate.

The United States Supreme Court upheld the Ohio Supreme Court's decision and concluded that car card space on a city transit system is not a First Amendment forum. The Court found:

> "The city consciously has limited access to its transit system advertising space in order to minimize chances of abuse, the appearance of favoritism, and the risk of imposing upon a captive audience. These are reasonable legislative objectives advanced by the city in a proprietary capacity. In these circumstances, there is no First or Fourteenth Amendment violation."

The case of *Miami Herald Publishing Co.* v. *Tornillo* involved the right of a candidate to respond to editorials critical of the candidate. This case was based on a Florida law that granted political candidates the "right of reply" to answer criticism and attacks by a newspaper and made it a misdemeanor for the newspaper to fail to comply.

The Florida Circuit Court found the statute unconstitutional because it infringed on freedom of the press and dismissed the case. Tornillo appealed the case to the Florida Supreme Court, which ruled that the statue did not violate freedom of the press guarantees and remanded the case back to the circuit court for further proceedings. The Florida Supreme Court decision was appealed to the United States Supreme Court.

The United States Supreme Court held that the statute does violate the First Amendment's guarantee of a free press. In a unanimous decision the Court ruled:

> "Even if a newspaper would face no additional costs to comply with a compulsory access law and would not be forced to forgo publication of news or opinion by the inclusion of a reply, the Florida statute fails to clear the barriers of the First Amendment because of its intrusion into the function of editors. A newspaper is more than a passive receptacle or conduit for news, comment, and advertising. The choice of material to go into a newspaper, and the decisions made as to limitations on the size and content of the paper, and treatment of public issues and public officials—whether fair or unfair—constitute the exercise of editorial control and judgment. It has yet to be demonstrated how governmental regulation of this crucial process can be exercised consistent with First Amendment guarantees of a free press as they have evolved to this time. Accordingly, the judgment of the Supreme Court of Florida is reversed."

Switching Parties

Last minute party switching to impact a primary election is another problem that has been dealt with in the courts. In a 1973 precedent-setting case, *Rosario* v. *Rockefeller*, the Supreme Court ruled that states could set lengthy time restrictions related to party affiliation to prevent last minute party switching.

New York State's requirement for a voter to register the party of his or her choice 30 days before a general election in order to vote in the next primary election was challenged as unconstitutional because it deprived voters of the right under the First and Fourteenth Amendments to associate with the party of their choice. The law creates the longest lead time in the country for declaring a party because it means prospective voters must register their party about eight months before a presidential primary and 11 months before a nonpresidential one.

The state claimed the primary purpose of this statute is to prevent last minute party switching and deter "raiding" by opposing party members. In a split 5 to 4 decision, the United States Supreme Court held that the law was constitutional. Justice Stewart wrote the opinion for the Court, which was signed by Burger, White, Blackmun, and Rehnquist. Justice Powell wrote the dissent, which was signed by Douglas, Brennan, and Marshall.

In the majority opinion, Stewart wrote:

> "It is true that the period between the enrollment deadline and the next primary election is lengthy. But that period is not an arbitrary time limit unconnected to any important state goal. The purpose of New York's delayed-enrollment scheme, we are told, is to inhibit party 'raiding,' whereby voters in sympathy with one party designate themselves as voters of another party so as to influence or determine the results of the other party's primary. This purpose is accomplished, the Court of Appeals found, not only by requiring party enrollment several months in advance of the primary, on the theory that 'long-range planning in politics is quite difficult,' but also by requiring enrollment prior to a general election … "

> "[T]he notion of raiding, its potential disruptive impact, and its advantages to one side are not likely to be as apparent to the majority of enrolled voters, nor to receive as close attention from the professional politician just prior to a November general election, when concerns are elsewhere, as would be true during the 'primary season,' which, for the country as a whole, runs from early February until the end of June. Few persons have the effrontery or the foresight to enroll as, say, "Republicans" so that they can vote in a primary some seven months hence, when they full well intend to vote "Democratic" in only a few weeks. And it would be the rare politician who could successfully urge his constituents to vote for him or his party in the upcoming general election while, at the same time, urging a cross-over enrollment for the purpose of upsetting the opposite party's primary. Yet the operation of section 186 requires such deliberate inconsistencies if large-scale raiding were to be effective in New York. Because of the statute, it is all but impossible for any group to engage in raiding."

The Supreme Court found that "New York did not prohibit the petitioners from voting in the 1972 primary election or from associating with the political party of their choice. It merely imposed a legitimate time limitation on their enrollment, which they chose to disregard."

In his dissent Justice Powell wrote:

> "The importance or significance of any such interest cannot be determined in a vacuum, but, rather, in the context of the means advanced by the State to protect it and the constitutionally sensitive activity it operates to impede. The state

interest here is hardly substantial enough to sustain the presumption, upon which the statute appears to be based, that most persons who change or declare party affiliation nearer than 8 to 11 months to a party primary do so with intent to raid that primary. Any such presumption assumes a willingness to manipulate the system which is not likely to be widespread.

"Political parties in this country traditionally have been characterized by a fluidity and overlap of philosophy and membership. And citizens generally declare or alter party affiliation for reasons quite unconnected with any premeditated intention to disrupt or frustrate the plans of a party with which they are not in sympathy. Citizens customarily choose a party and vote in its primary simply because it presents candidates and issues more responsive to their immediate concerns and aspirations. Such candidates or issues often are not apparent eight to 11 months before a primary. That a citizen should be absolutely precluded so far in advance from voting in a party primary in response to a sympathetic candidate, a new or meaningful issue, or changing party philosophies in his State, runs contrary to the fundamental rights of personal choice and expression which voting in this country was designed to serve.

"Whatever state interest exists for preventing cross-overs from one party to another is appreciably lessened where, as in the case of petitioners, there has been no previous affiliation with any political party. The danger of voters in sympathy with one party "raiding" another party is insubstantial where the voter has made no prior party commitment at all. Certainly, the danger falls short of the overriding state interest needed to justify denying petitioners, so far in advance, the right to declare an initial party affiliation and vote in the party primary of their choice."

As you can see, even though elections are state-controlled activities, the United States Supreme Court steps in when Constitutional questions arise. In the next chapter, we'll explore the role of the Supreme Court in taxation issues.

The Least You Need to Know

- The U.S. Supreme Court essentially decided the 2000 presidential election by halting the vote re-count in Florida in a decision that has been widely criticized by both liberals and conservatives.

- Setting district boundaries for the U.S House of Representatives has a stricter set of requirements than those for representatives to state legislatures. The United States Supreme Court has ruled that states can consider the importance of local issues when setting boundaries for state representatives.

◆ Limitations on individual campaign contributions, as well as some limitations on campaign spending for advertising just prior to an election, are permitted.

◆ Freedom of the press to decide editorially what will be printed in the newspaper is of greater importance than the right of a candidate to reply to critical editorials.

◆ Local governments can restrict political advertising on government-run transportation.

◆ State governments can set time limits for registering your choice of party in order to participate in a primary election.

Chapter 13

Taxing the Populace

In This Chapter

- ◆ Taxing waiters' tips
- ◆ Gambling taxes
- ◆ Indian nations and tax burdens
- ◆ Avoiding taxes by mail

As we discussed in Chapter 7, the Constitution did not allow for a federal income tax unless it was apportioned to the states. All that changed in 1913 with the ratification of the Sixteenth Amendment.

Today most tax cases involving federal laws are settled in the U.S. Tax Courts, but occasionally the Supreme Court will decide to hear a case if there is a question of constitutionality that needs to be decided. The Supreme Court also gets involved in tax disputes relating to state tax issues that cross state boundaries.

In this chapter, we'll review some of the recent Supreme Court tax decisions that include topics such as taxes on tips, gaming taxes, and sales taxes.

Taxes on Employee's Tip Income

A controversy over collecting taxes for Social Security and Medicare sent shockwaves through the restaurant industry after the Supreme Court ruled in favor of the Internal Revenue Service's (IRS) position in *Fior D'Italia, Inc.* v. *United States* on June 17, 2002. The case started when the IRS billed Fior d'Italia, a restaurant based in San Francisco, for $23,262 in unpaid Social Security and Medicare payroll taxes for tips that its employees allegedly failed to report in 1991 and 1992. The IRS based its case on the restaurant's own records.

The restaurant sued the IRS, claiming it had no legal authority to bill the restaurant for these taxes until the IRS had first determined which employees had actually under-reported tips. Both a federal court and a federal appeals court ruled in the restaurant's favor, so the government took the case to the Supreme Court, which accepted it on January 11, 2002. While the 9th Circuit Court of Appeals ruled in Fior d'Italia's favor, four other Circuit Courts sided with the IRS in similar restaurant cases. Circuit courts siding with the IRS were the 7th Circuit (Illinois), 11th Circuit (Florida and Alabama), and Federal Circuit (Washington, D.C.).

The National Restaurant Association (NRA) contributed $100,000 to Fior d'Italia's legal battle and filed a friend-of-the-court brief to help the restaurant take the case all the way to the Supreme Court. If the restaurant lost the case, NRA vowed to take the fight to Congress because it does not believe restaurants should be forced into the role of "tip police." This battle is now at Congress' doorstep.

Supreme Sayings

"For more than five years, Fior d'Italia has single-handedly fought the IRS through the judicial system. Small businesses like this are the cornerstone of the restaurant industry …. To have the IRS continue to exert pressure on a single operator, and casually extract funds without performing a thorough audit of employees' records, is unconscionable."

—Bill Hyde, chairman of the NRA's Save American Free Enterprise (SAFE) Fund in the trade publication *Restaurants USA* in January 2002

Let's look at how the IRS calculated the tax bill in question. The IRS used the restaurant's charge card data and calculated that credit card customers tipped at the rate of 14.49 percent in 1991 and 14.29 percent in 1992. The IRS then used these averages to estimate tips generated by cash sales received by the restaurant's employees. Using those assumptions the IRS concluded that the restaurant should have reported total tips of $772,100 over the two year period rather than the $468,026 that was reported.

The difference of $304,000 was used to calculate the $23,262 based on the tax of 7.65 percent due for Social Security and Medicare.

The restaurant claimed this was not an accurate calculation because the tips on cash sales did not average the same amount as on credit sales. In most cases cash tips are lower than credit card tips, the restaurant stated in its brief. In addition, the restaurant claimed that many of the tips on credit card sales also included cash back to customers, which is done as a service to their customers if requested.

Justice Steven Breyer wrote the 6-3 opinion for the Supreme Court. He was joined by Chief Justice William Rehnquist and Associate Justices John Paul Stevens, Sandra Day O'Connor, Anthony M. Kennedy and Ruth Bader Ginsburg. In his opinion, Breyer comments directly on the restaurant's claim that the IRS method of calculating tips is unreasonable:

> "Fior D'Italia adds that these potential errors can make an enormous difference to a restaurant, for restaurant profits are often low, while the tax is high …. Indeed, the restaurant must pay this tax on the basis of amounts that the restaurant itself cannot control, for the restaurant's customers, not the restaurant itself, determine the level of tips. Fior D'Italia concludes that the IRS should avoid these problems by resting its assessment upon individual calculations of employee tip earnings, and argues that the IRS' failure to do so will always result in an overstatement of tax liability, rendering any assessment that results from aggregate estimates unreasonable and outside the limits of any delegated IRS authority.

> "In our view, these considerations do not show that the IRS' aggregate estimating method falls outside the bounds of what is reasonable. It bears repeating that in this litigation, Fior D'Italia stipulated that it would not challenge the particular IRS calculation as inaccurate. Absent such a stipulation, a taxpayer would remain free to present evidence that an assessment is inaccurate in a particular case. And we do not accept Fior D'Italia's claim that restaurants are unable to do so—that they "simply do not have the information to dispute" the IRS assessment. Why does a restaurant owner not know, or why is that owner unable to find out: how many busboys or other personnel work for only a day or two—thereby likely earning less than $20 in tips; how many employees were likely to have earned more than $55,000 or so in 1992; how much less cash-paying customers tip; how often they "stiff" waiters or ask for a cash refund; and whether the restaurant owner deducts a credit card charge of, say 3 percent, from employee tips? After all, the restaurant need not prove these matters with precision. It need only demonstrate that use of the aggregate method in the particular case has likely produced an inaccurate result. And in doing so, it may well be able to convince a judge to insist upon a more accurate formula.

Living Laws

The Internal Revenue Service can use aggregate estimates based on credit card receipts to determine the total tips at a restaurant. If tips are underreported, the IRS can bill the restaurant for Social Security and Medicare taxes based on its aggregate estimates.

"Nor has Fior D'Italia convinced us that individualized employee assessments will inevitably lead to a more "reasonable" assessment of employer liability than an aggregate estimate. After all, individual audits will be plagued by some of the same inaccuracies Fior D'Italia attributes to the aggregate estimation method, because they are, of course, *based on estimates themselves* .... Consequently, we cannot find that the aggregate method is, as a general matter, so unreasonable as to violate the law."

Associate Justice Souter wrote the dissenting opinion and was joined by Associate Justices Scalia and Thomas. He believes the majority erred in its opinion and does not think the IRS is carrying out the intent of Congress. Souter states:

"In fact, the only real advantage to the IRS seems to be that the threat of audit, litigation, and immediate liability may well force employers to assume the job of monitoring their employees' tips to ensure accurate reporting. But if that explanation for the Government's practice makes sense of it, it also flips the Government from the frying pan into the fire. Congress has previously stymied every attempt the IRS has made to impose such a burden on employers. In the days when employers were responsible only for withholding the employee's share of the FICA tax, the IRS attempted to force employers to include tip income on W-2 forms; this effort was blocked when Congress modified [tax code] to exclude tip income expressly from the W-2 requirements .... Finally, when the IRS developed its Tip Reporting Alternative Commitment (TRAC) program .... Congress forbade the IRS from "threaten[ing] to audit any taxpayer in an attempt to coerce the taxpayer" into participating .... And although the use of a threatened aggregate estimate (after an audit) to induce monitoring of employee tips may not technically run afoul of that statute, it is difficult to imagine that Congress would allow the aggregation practice as a lever on employers, when it forbade the use of an audit for the same purpose."

For the time being the majority opinion stands and the IRS can use the aggregate method questioned in the Fior d'Italia case until Congress passes a law to stop it. Legal experts for the restaurant industry believe this ruling has the potential to devastate small restaurants because the IRS can go back as far as 1988, which is the first year employers were liable for Social Security and Medicare taxes on all employee tips. "With restaurant profit margins around 3 to 5 percent, this could potentially put a number of restaurants out of business," according to Peter Kilgore, senior vice president and general counsel for the NRA.

Gambling Taxes Collected at Indian Reservations

Companies that run gaming operations must pay federal wagering excise and occupational taxes. State-sponsored gambling activities are exempt from these taxes. The Chickasaw Nation wanted that state exemption as well and filed a case in federal court. The court of appeals rejected that claim and the Chickasaw Nation took the case to the Supreme Court in 2001.

This case was based on the Indian Gaming Regulatory Act, which permits and governs gambling operations on Indian reservations. The Chickasaw Nation believed this act was written in such a way to exempt Indian nations from taxes that state governments don't have to pay.

> ### Just the Facts
>
> The Indian Gaming Regulatory Act was passed in 1988 to govern Indian gaming. There are three classes of gaming specified in the act. Class I is traditional Indian social gaming for minimal prizes, which is exclusively regulated by tribal governments. Class II are common games of chance, such as bingo. Tribal governments are responsible for regulating this class with oversight by the National Indian Gaming Commission. Class III includes all games not in Class I or II, such as slot machines, black jack, craps and roulette, and is fully regulated by the commission.

The Indians based their claim on a technicality that involved certain wording in parenthetical reference. The Supreme Court ruled that the language outside the parenthesis was unambiguous and related only to the reporting and withholding of taxes.

In the majority opinion announced on November 27, 2001, the Supreme Court declared this a drafting mistake and said it could "find no comparable instance in which Congress legislated an exemption through a parenthetical numerical cross-reference."

Associate Justice Sandra Day O'Connor dissented in this case in support of the Indian Nations and she was joined by Souter. In her dissent, she said:

> "Exempting Nations from federal gaming taxation in the same manner as States preserves the Nations' sovereignty and avoids giving state gaming a competitive advantage that would interfere with the Nations' ability to raise revenue in this manner. Because nothing in the text, legislative history, or underlying policies … clearly resolves the contradiction inherent in the section, it is appropriate to turn to canons of statutory construction. The Nations urge the Court to rely upon the Indian canon, that 'statutes are to be construed liberally in favor of the

Indians, with ambiguous provisions interpreted to their benefit.' … In this case, because Congress has chosen gaming as a means of enabling the Nations to achieve self-sufficiency, the Indian canon rightly dictates that Congress should be presumed to have intended the Nations to receive more, rather than less, revenue from this enterprise."

Indian nations were not granted exemption and must pay the same taxes as other non-governmental gambling operations.

Sales Taxes on Mail Orders

Many of us enjoy the benefits of ordering by mail from out of state companies so we can avoid paying state taxes. Numerous states have tried to require companies to collect sales or use taxes on products sold to its residents through the mail, in print, and on radio or television, but so far have been stopped by the courts. Some states, such as Connecticut, put the burden on its citizens who order from out of state to report these purchases and pay the taxes on them directly to the state.

North Dakota passed a law in 1987 requiring out-of-state mail-order houses to collect and pay a use tax on goods purchased for use in the state. Quill Corporation refused to comply and the state of North Dakota took them to state court. The trial court ruled in Quill's favor and found that based on Supreme Court precedent in a 1969 case (*National Bellas Hess, Inc.* v. *Department of Revenue of Ill.*) the law created an unconstitutional burden on interstate commerce based on the Fourteenth Amendment's due process clause. In addition the Supreme Court found it conflicted with the *commerce clause* because, "The very purpose of the Commerce Clause was to ensure a national economy free from such unjustifiable local entanglements. Under the Constitution, this is a domain where Congress alone has the power of regulation and control."

Court Connotations

The **Commerce Clause** is in Article I of the Constitution and gives the federal government the right "To regulate commerce with foreign Nations, and among the several States, and with the Indian Tribes."

States can only require companies to collect taxes if the company has a physical presence in the state. The North Dakota State Supreme Court reversed this decision based on the ruling in another precedent setting case, *Complete Auto Transit Inc.* v. *Brady* decided in 1977, which loosened up the rules for physical presence within the state.

The Quill Corporation appealed the State Supreme Court's ruling to the United States Supreme Court. Quill based its case on the fact that it is a Delaware corporation with offices and warehouses in Illinois, California, and Georgia. None of its employees work or live in North Dakota and it owns no tangible property in the state. Quill's only activity in North Dakota was to sell office equipment and supplies through catalogs and flyers, advertisements in national magazines, and telephone calls. At the time Quill argued the case before the Supreme Court, Quill's annual sales volume was $1 million to about 3,000 customers in the state.

The United States Supreme Court reversed the decision of the North Dakota Supreme Court. Justice Steven said in the opinion he wrote for the Court that the commerce clause was not influenced "so much by concerns about fairness for the individual defendant as by structural concerns about the effects of state regulation on the national economy. Under the Articles of Confederation, State taxes and duties hindered and suppressed interstate commerce; the Framers intended the Commerce Clause as a cure for these structural ills."

Although it agreed with the North Dakota State Supreme Court that cases subsequent to *Bellas Hess* adopted a more flexible "presence requirement," this did compel the United States Supreme Court to "reject the rule that *Bellas Hess* established in the area of sales and use taxes." The Court went on to rule:

> "This aspect of our decision is made easier by the fact that the underlying issue is not only one that Congress may be better qualified to resolve, but also one that Congress has the ultimate power to resolve. No matter how we evaluate the burdens that use taxes impose on interstate commerce, Congress remains free to disagree with our conclusions .... Indeed, in recent years Congress has considered legislation that would "overrule" the *Bellas Hess* rule. Its decision not to take action in this direction may, of course, have been dictated by respect for our holding in *Bellas Hess* that the Due Process Clause prohibits States from imposing such taxes, but today we have put that problem to rest. Accordingly, Congress is now free to decide whether, when, and to what extent the States may burden interstate mail order concerns with a duty to collect use taxes."

The Supreme Court threw the issue of who should collect sales and use taxes on interstate commerce back into the lap of Congress. The issue has heated up even more in recent years because of the massive increase in interstate sales thanks to the growth of sales using the Internet. You can probably bet some legislation will find its way into state and federal legislatures soon.

While the United States Supreme Court may not take very many tax cases, whenever they do, it can have a significant impact in many state houses. This ruling overturned numerous state laws.

Now that you have an idea of the types of tax cases the Supreme Court heard recently, we'll take a look at how the Court has ruled on laws affecting your property ownership.

The Least You Need to Know

- Employees whose income is partially earned through tips must report that income. If employees underreport that income their employers may still have to pay Social Security and Medicare taxes on the unreported income.

- Indian nations do not receive the same tax exemptions as state governments who run gambling operations.

- For now at least, many of us can avoid state sales and use taxes if we buy from companies that do not have a physical presence in our state.

Chapter 14

Deciding Property Rights

In This Chapter

- ◆ Taking your property
- ◆ Stalling development legally
- ◆ Protecting your copyrights
- ◆ Granting your patent rights
- ◆ Trading on trademarks

Your home is your castle and your rights to it are strongly protected in the Fifth Amendment to the Constitution, which states your private property cannot be "taken for public use without just compensation." The key issue questioned in cases brought before the Court over the years is what constitutes a "taking."

Your land or home is not the only property that get special attention in the Constitution. Legislation for patents, trademarks and copyrights fall under Section 1 of the Constitution, known as the enumerated powers clause, which gives Congress the power to make laws to "promote the progress of science and the useful arts."

Let's review the recent Court cases that impact your property rights, whether it involves your tangible (land or home) or intangible (copyrights, patents, and trademarks) property.

Protecting Land and Home

Most of the time when you see a story about a government entity "taking" someone's property it relates to the construction of a new road or for other public needs. In these cases, there is clear legal precedent that for the purposes of the public good, governments can "take" an owner's property provided they are offered just compensation. Many people who lose their homes to a new roadway or other public project, probably do not believe they have been given "just compensation." Most states have a formula for compensation that has long been established through case law.

These types of takings are physical takings, in which the government acquires property for its own use. A second, less clearly defined type of taking is a *regulatory taking*. These types of takings involve regulations that prevent landowners from developing their property.

Court Connotations

Regulatory taking or inverse condemnation means the government has regulated the use of a property to so great an extent that it no longer has an economically beneficial use for the owner—essentially condemning the land. When this happens the property may be consider "taken" without just compensation. Court cases filed on this issue generally involve denied wetlands permits, denied coastal development permits, denied zoning variances, and other denied development applications.

Supreme Sayings

"… while property may be regulated to a certain extent, if the regulation goes too far it will be recognized as a taking."

—Associate Justice Oliver Wendell Holmes in his opinion for the court in the precedent-setting "takings" case *Pennsylvania Coal Co.* v. *Mahon* in 1922

Case law surrounding regulatory taking and development planning is not as well formulated. Cases that made it all the way to U.S. Supreme Court in recent years relate primarily to attempts by state and local governments to control development along coastlines or in wetlands or regulatory taking. Even temporary building moratoria (or freezes) raised questions that made it to the Court.

I'm going to review three recent rulings. The oldest, *Lucas* v. *South Carolina Coast*, decided in 1992, involves the South Carolina coastline. *Palazzolo* v.

Rhode Island, decided in 2001, involves development in Rhode Island wetlands. *Tahoe-Sierra Preservation Council, Inc. et al.* v. *Tahoe Regional Planning Agency et al.* involves temporary moratoria to halt construction for planning purposes.

Mandating Coastline Protection

David Lucas purchased two residential lots in 1986 on a South Carolina barrier island for $975,000. At the time he purchased the property, it was legal to build a single-family house on each of the lots with no special permits required.

Two years after he purchased the property, the state of South Carolina passed the Beachfront Management Act, which mandated that the South Carolina Coastal Council set a baseline for development along the seashore. Any property nearer the water than that baseline could not be developed. The baseline set made it impossible for David Lucas to develop his property.

Lucas filed suit in state court claiming the baseline and its construction ban effected a "taking" of his property without just compensation, which was in violation of the Fifth Amendment to the Constitution. The state trial court ruled in favor of Lucas and ordered the state to pay him $1 million for his land. The South Carolina Supreme Court reversed that decision and said it was not a taking. In its ruling, the State Supreme Court said that preventing beach erosion was a valid exercise of police power "to prevent serious public harm," so it did not require compensation.

> ### Just the Facts
>
> *Pennsylvania Coal Co.* v. *Mahon*, decided by the court in 1922, is the landmark case that states there are limits to a government's claim of exercising police power. In writing the opinion for the court Justice Holmes found that government's power to redefine the range of interest in a property was constrained by constitutional limits. He found that if the government could take property unrestrained without compensation under the guise of police power, "the natural tendency of human nature [would be] to extend the qualification more and more until at last private property disappear[ed]."

Lucas appealed the South Carolina State Supreme Court's decisions to the United States Supreme Court, which ruled in Lucas' favor. Justice Scalia wrote in his opinion for the Court:

> "We think, in short, that there are good reasons for our frequently expressed belief that when the owner of real property has been called upon to sacrifice *all* economically beneficial uses in the name of the common good, that is, to leave

his property economically idle, he has suffered a taking …. The trial court found Lucas's two beachfront lots to have been rendered valueless by respondent's enforcement of the coastal zone construction ban."

Justices Stevens and Blackmun wrote separate dissents to this opinion. Justice Souter stated that the writ in this case should not even have been granted. In his dissent, Stevens said:

"In addition to lacking support in past decisions, the Court's new rule is wholly arbitrary. A landowner whose property is diminished in value 95 percent recovers nothing, while an owner whose property is diminished 100 percent recovers the land's full value. The case at hand illustrates this arbitrariness well. The Beachfront Management Act not only prohibited the building of new dwellings in certain areas, it also prohibited the rebuilding of houses that were "destroyed beyond repair by natural causes or by fire." … Thus, if the homes adjacent to Lucas' lot were destroyed by a hurricane one day after the Act took effect, the owners would not be able to rebuild, nor would they be assured recovery. Under the Court's categorical approach, Lucas (who has lost the opportunity to build) recovers, while his neighbors (who have lost *both* the opportunity to build *and* their homes) do not recover."

Justice Blackmun wrote is his dissent that the decision was made before all the facts were in and the United States Supreme Court accepted a case that was not ready for decision:

"The Beachfront Management Act includes a finding by the South Carolina General Assembly that the beach/dune system serves the purpose of 'protect[ing] life and property by serving as a storm barrier which dissipates wave energy and contributes to shoreline stability in an economical and effective manner.' … The General Assembly also found that 'development unwisely has been sited too close to the [beach/dune] system. This type of development has jeopardized the stability of the beach/dune system, accelerated erosion, and endangered adjacent property.'

"If the state legislature is correct that the prohibition on building in front of the setback line prevents serious harm, then, under this Court's prior cases, the Act is constitutional …. Long ago it was recognized that all property in this country is held under the implied obligation that the owner's use of it shall not be injurious to the community, and the Takings Clause did not transform that principle to one that requires compensation whenever the State asserts its power to enforce it.

"Petitioner never challenged the legislature's findings that a building ban was necessary to protect property and life. Nor did he contend that the threatened harm was not sufficiently serious to make building a house in a particular location a "harmful" use, that the legislature had not made sufficient findings, or that the legislature was motivated by anything other than a desire to minimize damage to coastal areas. Indeed, petitioner objected at trial that evidence as to the purposes of the setback requirement was irrelevant …. Nothing in the record undermines the General Assembly's assessment that prohibitions on building in front of the setback line are necessary to protect people and property from storms, high tides, and beach erosion. Because that legislative determination cannot be disregarded in the absence of such evidence … and because its determination of harm to life and property from building is sufficient to prohibit that use under this Court's cases, the South Carolina Supreme Court correctly found no taking."

As this case was working its way through the courts, some thought it would be a landmark ruling to strengthen private property rights, but it failed because new questions were raised about regulatory taking. This case only protected property rights in situations where regulation permanently denied all possible uses of the land. The Court continued to define the issue of regulatory taking, as shown in the next two cases.

Saving Wetlands

Anthony Palazzolo owned waterfront property on the Rhode Island coast. Most of that property was salt marsh, which was subject to tidal flooding. The land was purchased by a corporation in which Palazzolo was a sole owner in 1959. When the corporation failed to pay income taxes, the property passed to Palazzolo. The change of title occurred after the Rhode Island Resources Management Council was created and regulations were adopted to protect and greatly limit development of Rhode Island's coastal wetlands.

Palazzolo filed suit in state court claiming that the state's wetlands regulations had "taken" his property without compensation in violation of the Fifth and Fourteen Amendments because he was denied "all economically beneficial use" of his property. The state courts denied his claim for three reasons:

1. the claim was not ripe (he had not exhausted all development options);

2. the regulations predated his ownership of the land; and

3. there was evidence that part of the land could still be developed, so it was not 100 percent unusable.

The Supreme Court disagreed with the state court's ruling and decided (on a split 5 to 4 vote) in favor of Palazzolo. The majority opinion was written by Justice Kennedy, but there were two concurring opinions, two dissenting opinions, and one opinion concurring on some issues and dissenting on others. Joining Kennedy were Rehnquist, O'Connor, Scalia, and Thomas. Justices O'Connor and Scalia wrote concurring opinions. Justice Ginsburg wrote a dissenting opinion that was joined by Souter and Breyer. Breyer also wrote an additional dissenting opinion. Justice Stevens wrote an opinion that partially concurred and partially dissented. Kennedy wrote for the majority:

> "the State Supreme Court erred in finding petitioner's claims were unripe and in ruling that acquisition of title after the effective date of the regulations barred the takings claims. The court did not err in finding that petitioner failed to establish a deprivation of all economic value, for it is undisputed that the parcel retains significant worth for construction of a residence."

The case was remanded back to Rhode Island's state courts to decide whether or not the land was 100 percent "taken." Testimony during the case indicated that the uplands portion of the property was worth $200,000. If Palazzolo is granted a permit to build on that portion of the land it does not meet that test of being 100 percent taken. The decision on the uplands portion of the land was still making its way through the state courts at the time of this writing.

Living Laws
Palazzolo established the precedent that a "takings" claim can be made on property that came into your possession after a regulation that limits development of that property—thereby protecting heirs to your property. Also a property owner does not need to go through countless rounds of repetitive land use review processes before filing suit.

One key precedent set in this case was that an owner who gained title to property after a development regulation became law still had the right to claim a taking without compensation. The state tried to argue Palazzolo had no claim because ownership was transferred to him after the new regulations were in place. This is particularly important to heirs, who now clearly have the right to challenge laws that limit the fair use and value of land they have inherited. The second key precedent is that the Court ruled a landowner "need not go through countless rounds of repetitive land use review processes with other agencies just to prove that the claim was 'ripe.'"

Justice Ginsburg in her dissent did not believe this case was ripe for decision because a final development decision had not yet been made by the state agency. She wrote:

> "Although Palazzolo submitted several applications to develop his property, those applications uniformly sought permission to fill most or all of the wetlands

portion of the property. None aimed to develop only the uplands. Upon denial of the last of Palazzolo's applications, Palazzolo filed suit claiming that Rhode Island had taken his property by refusing 'to allow any development.'

"As the Rhode Island Supreme Court saw the case, Palazzolo's claim was not ripe for several reasons, among them, that Palazzolo had not sought permission for 'development only of the upland portion of the parcel' …. The Rhode Island court emphasized the undisputed evidence in the record that it would be possible to build at least one single-family home on the existing upland area, with no need for additional fill …. I would reject Palazzolo's bait-and-switch ploy and affirm the judgment of the Rhode Island Supreme Court."

Moratoria that temporarily take away "all economically beneficial uses" of a property do not enjoy the same protections against "taking" as permanent regulations. This issue was clarified in the next case we'll review, *Tahoe-Sierra Preservation Council, Inc. et al* v. *Tahoe Regional Planning*.

Stalling Lake Development

California and Nevada sought to preserve the beauty of Lake Tahoe, which they believed was threatened by development. To preserve the lake they formed the Tahoe Regional Planning Compact and created the Tahoe Regional Planning Agency (TRPA) in 1972. When the TRPA failed to limit new residential development, the two states formed a new compact in 1980 that required the agency to develop standards for water quality, air quality, and vegetation conservation. Once developed, the TRPA was required to adopt a regional plan to achieve those standards. The states also directed the TRPA to place a moratorium (freeze) on development until implementing the plan.

Two moratoria ended up stopping all development over a 32-month period while the TRPA put together its comprehensive land-use plans. The property owners filed a series of suits in federal district court claiming that these moratoria were a taking of their property without compensation. The district court sided with the owners that the moratoria did constitute a taking based on the rules set forth in *Lucas* v. *South Carolina Coastal Council*.

TRPA appealed the district court decision to the 9th Circuit Court, which sided with the TRPA, saying the moratoria only had a temporary impact on the landowners, so it was not a taking. The 9th Circuit Court went on to say that *Lucas* was not an appropriate precedent because, in the current case, there was not a permanent denial of all productive use of the land.

The U.S. Supreme Court sided with the TRPA in a 6 to 3 decision on April 23, 2002. Justice Stevens wrote the majority opinion and was joined by Justices O'Connor, Kennedy, Souter, Ginsburg, and Breyer. Chief Justice Rehnquist wrote the dissent and was joined by Justices Scalia and Thomas. Justice Thomas also wrote a separate dissent that was joined by Justice Scalia.

In the majority opinion, Stevens wrote:

> "Moratoria are an essential tool of successful development. The interest in informed decision-making counsels against adopting a *per se* rule that would treat such interim measures as takings regardless of the planners' good faith, the landowners' reasonable expectations, or the moratorium's actual impact on property values. The financial constraints of compensating property owners during a moratorium may force officials to rush through the planning process or abandon the practice altogether. And the interest in protecting the decisional process is even stronger when an agency is developing a regional plan than when it is considering a permit for a single parcel. Here, TRPA obtained the benefit of comments and criticisms from interested parties during its deliberations, but a categorical rule tied to the deliberations' length would likely create added pressure on decision-makers to quickly resolve land-use questions, disadvantaging landowners and interest groups less organized or familiar with the planning process. Moreover, with a temporary development ban, there is less risk that individual landowners will be singled out to bear a special burden that should be shared by the public as a whole. It may be true that a moratorium lasting more than one year should be viewed with special skepticism, but the District Court found that the instant delay was not unreasonable. The restriction's duration is one factor for a court to consider in appraising regulatory takings claims, but with respect to that factor, the temptation to adopt *per se rules* in either direction must be resisted."

Court Connotations

A **per se rule** is a rule set by judges after long experience with certain practices that are common in a given market condition. Once set, the per se rule helps to avoid expensive litigation in areas that a clear rule of law has been set. Before this per se rule is set, cases are determined on a rule of reason that looks at the specific issues of the case before the judge.

Chief Justice Rehnquist in his dissent questioned the length of time for these particular moratoria. He believed the decision-making process took too long in this case. Rehnquist wrote:

"Because the prohibition on development of nearly six years in this case cannot be said to resemble any 'implied limitation' of state property law, it is a taking that requires compensation .... Lake Tahoe is a national treasure and I do not doubt that respondent's efforts at preventing further degradation of the lake were made in good faith in furtherance of the public interest. But, as is the case with most governmental action that furthers the public interest, the Constitution requires that the costs and burdens be borne by the public at large, not by a few targeted citizens."

At least for now, temporary moratoria are not considered takings, but it is likely that more cases will make it to the court until a per se rule is established for moratoria.

Protecting Patents, Copyrights and Trademarks

So far we have been talking about tangible property—things you can touch. Some people have intangible property rights that have no physical characteristics, such as *copyrights*, *patents*, and *trademarks*.

Court Connotations

Copyrights are legal rights granted to an author, composer, playwright, publisher, or distributor to exclusive publication, production, sale, or distribution of a literary, musical, dramatic, or artistic work.

Patents are legal rights granted to the creator of an invention for the sole right to make, use, and sell that invention for a set period of time.

Trademarks are legal rights granted to a company for a name, symbol, or other device identifying a product, officially registered and legally restricted to the use of the owner or manufacturer.

All three of these property rights are protected under Section I of the Constitution in the enumerated powers clause, which grants Congress the power to enact laws for purposes including the creation of money or the promotion of science and the arts.

Copyrights for Freelancers

Copyright law is well established, but the introduction of new electronic media and the Internet have raised questions about the actual rights newspapers and magazines hold versus the rights the original authors of the materials hold, if the authors are freelance writers hired as independent contractors.

Many publications print articles by staff writers as well as freelance writers. Freelance writers sign contracts as independent contractors, which spell out how a publisher can use the work. Most of the older contracts were written before computerized databases were a major source of income.

Freelance authors filed suit to stop print publications from putting their articles in computerized databases without compensation. The print and electronic publishers won a judgment in district court stating that these articles were part of the original collective work to which the authors first contributed, so therefore they were not owed additional compensation. The Court of Appeals disagreed and ruled in favor of the freelance authors.

The New York Times, Newsday, and *Time* appealed the case to the Supreme Court in a case titled, *New York Times Co., Inc. et al.* v. *Tasini et al.* The case was argued before the Supreme Court on March 28, 2001. The court ruled in favor of the freelancers on June 25 in a 7 to 2 opinion written by Justice Ginsburg in which she says, "the databases reproduce and distribute articles standing alone and not in context, not 'as part of that particular collective work' to which the author contributed, 'as part of … any revision' thereof, or 'as part of … any later collective work in the same series.' Both the print publishers and the electronic publishers, we rule, have infringed the copyrights of the freelance authors."

In answer to the publisher's warnings that this ruling would have devastating consequences for the public, Ginsburg went on to say:

> "The Publishers' warning that a ruling for the Authors will have 'devastating' consequences, punching gaping holes in the electronic record of history, is unavailing. It hardly follows from this decision that an injunction against the inclusion of these Articles in the Databases (much less all freelance articles in any databases) must issue. The Authors and Publishers may enter into an agreement allowing continued electronic reproduction of the Authors' works; they, and if necessary the courts and Congress, may draw on numerous models for distributing copyrighted works and remunerating authors for their distribution. In any event, speculation about future harms is no basis for this Court to shrink authorial rights created by Congress."

The Supreme Court sent the case back to the district court to decide on the best remedy in the case. In his dissent, which was joined by Justice Breyer, Justice Stevens wrote:

"Because it is likely that Congress did not consider the question raised by this case when drafting [the legislation], because I think the District Court's reading of that provision is reasonable and consistent with the statute's purposes, and because the principal goals of copyright policy are better served by that reading, I would reverse the judgment of the Court of Appeals. The majority is correct that we cannot know in advance the effects of today's decision on the comprehensiveness of electronic databases. We can be fairly certain, however, that it will provide little, if any, benefit to either authors or readers."

The full impact of the decision on the public is not yet known, since the decision is only two years old. Contracts for freelance writers have been adjusted to fix this void. Most authors must sign over electronic rights to get a freelance contract today.

Patents for Biotechs

As science enters new realms, inventors seek patents for their inventions. Sometimes a company that sells a patented product questions whether a patent should have been granted. Such was the case in *J.E.M. Ag Supply, Inc.* v. *Pioneer Hi-Bred International, Inc.*

Pioneer Hi-Bred International is a biotechnology firm that holds 17 patents for the manufacture, use, and sale of its hybrid corn seed products under section 101 of the patent law. Pioneer sells its patented hybrid seeds under a label license agreement that allows for the production of grain and feed. J.E.M. Ag Supply, doing business as Farm Advantage, bought the patented seeds from Pioneer in bags bearing the license agreement and then resold the bags.

Pioneer filed suit claiming Farm Advantage had infringed on its patent. Farm Advantage responded that the patent was invalid because sexually reproducing plants, such as Pioneer's corn plants, were not patentable. Farm Advantage claimed that the Plant Patent Act (PPA) of 1930 and the Plant Variety Protection Act (PVPA) protected plant life from being patented. The district court sided with Pioneer and stated that neither the PPA or PVPA removed plants from patent rights. The federal circuit court agreed, and J.E.M. took the case to the Supreme Court.

Just the Facts

There are currently over 1.2 million patents in force in the United States. These patents give the owners an exclusive right to produce and sell the product. Without patent protection, the inventor of a new product would risk losing all that he or she spent developing the product if no property rights were granted, because anyone could duplicate the product without paying for the right to use it.

In a 6 to 2 opinion the Supreme Court affirmed the local court rulings. Justice Thomas wrote the majority decision and was joined by Rehnquist, Scalia, Kennedy, Souter and Ginsburg. In his opinion, Thomas wrote:

> "Denying patent protection under section 101 simply because such coverage was thought technologically infeasible in 1930, however, would be inconsistent with the forward-looking perspective of the utility patent statute."

Justice Stevens wrote a dissenting opinion and was joined by Breyer. O'Connor did not participate in the consideration of this case. Justice Stevens did not think the patent process applied to plants. He wrote:

> "Those who write statutes seek to solve human problems. Fidelity to their aims requires us to approach an interpretive problem not as if it were a purely logical game, like a Rubik's Cube, but as an effort to divine human intent that underlies the statute. Here that effort calls not for an appeal to canons, but for an analysis of language, structure, history, and purpose. Those factors make clear that the Utility Patent Statute does not apply to plants."

If the Congress did not intend for the patent act to include newly invented plants, it would now have to update the patent statute to clarify intent.

Trademark for Sex Shop

Trademark cases tend to get a lot more publicity because they usually involve some well-known marketing identification that is being used by a less well-known commercial entity. Victoria's Secret, known for its lingerie sold in stores and by catalog, thought its brand name was being harmed by a small local sex shop called "Victor's Secret." The shop's owner, Victor Moseley, contended that the name was chosen because he wanted to keep his business secret from his former employer when he first opened the store with his wife.

The case started in 1998 when Victor Moseley and his wife Cathy opened "Victor's Secret" as an adult store in Kentucky. Victoria's Secret asked them to cease and desist using their trademark, so the Moseleys changed the name to "Victor's Little Secret." Victoria's Secret still was not satisfied and filed a suit claiming its trademark was being harmed by the store.

Victoria's Secret won the case in district court. The Moseleys challenged the ruling in the 6th Circuit Court, saying that Victoria's Secret had failed to prove it sustained any economic harm. The circuit court ruled it was not necessary to prove economic harm, so the Moseleys took the case to the Supreme Court in a case titled, *Moseley et al., dba Victor's Little Secret* v. *V Secret Catalogue, Inc., et al.*

The Supreme Court ruled unanimously on March 4, 2003, in favor of the Moseleys. Writing the majority opinion, Justice Stevens said:

> "There is a complete absence of evidence of any lessening of the VICTORIA'S SECRET mark's capacity to identify and distinguish goods or services sold in Victoria's Secret stores or advertised in its catalogs."

The Supreme Court did not offer companies any clear guidelines for proving harm though, so this issue is likely to make its way to the Court again to settle the issue of proof.

Protecting private property rights is a long-standing tradition in this country, and protecting these rights sometimes falls in direct opposition to the needs of society. As land for development becomes more and more scarce, issues involving development will continue to wind their way through the courts and likely again be brought to the doorstep of the Supreme Court until a rule is perfected that clearly gives the lower courts a precedent to follow.

Property rights involving copyrights and patents also will be continually questioned as new technologies are invented and used. No doubt future cases will involve new inventions that find new ways to use people's property that raise questions of who owns what rights.

In the next chapter, we'll explore Supreme Court decisions that impacted the education of our children.

The Least You Need to Know

- Your home or land can only be taken by the government if you receive just compensation. The law is not as clear if the government places regulations on the use of that land.

- Copyrights are granted to companies, writers, and other artists for their original works. Copyright holders must be compensated for the use of their copyrighted works.

- Patents are granted to inventors for their inventions. Anyone who uses those patented inventions must compensate the owner of the patents.

- Trademarks are identities that have been carefully developed by a company for marketing purposes. These trademarks are frequently defended in courts if someone uses them without permission.

Educating Our Kids

In This Chapter

- ◆ Becoming disciplinarians
- ◆ Finding drugs
- ◆ Stopping sexual harassment
- ◆ Testing separation of church and state

Too often today we turn on the television and hear a horror story about a shooting at school, drugs found in the schoolyard, or children being sexually assaulted by trusted adults. Sending your child to school seems much riskier today than it was 30 years ago.

School cases that made it to the Supreme Court seek to improve conditions. Issues include proper methods of punishment, drug testing, and sexual harassment. In addition, in recent years the Court has ruled a number of times on the topic of religion in the schools. Let's explore significant school cases that have made it all the way to the Supreme Court.

Punishing Students

Schools always struggle with the issue of how to appropriately discipline students to maintain control in the school. Paddling is still used in 22 states, while suspensions are more common in others. Both methods have been challenged in cases brought to the Supreme Court. We'll review two of them: *Ingraham* v. *Wright*, which looks at rules for paddling, and *Goss* v. *Lopez*, which sets rules for suspensions.

Getting Spanked

James Ingraham and Roosevelt Andrews were students at Charles R. Drew Junior High School in Dade County, Florida, when they filed suit in U.S. district court in 1971 complaining about a disciplinary paddling they received at the school. Florida law does allow teachers to paddle students provided they consult first with the principal and that the punishment is not "degrading or severe." Florida actually specifies the length and width of the paddle and mandates that all blows are to the student's buttocks. Evidence in court showed that the paddling was exceptionally harsh. In fact one of the boys was unable to attend school for 11 days and the other lost use of his arm for one week.

Just the Facts

In 2003, two-thirds of Florida school districts still spank students. There is a move though toward using suspensions as the preferred mode of discipline. About 11,000 Florida students were paddled in 2003, according to the Florida Department of Education. Most schools that still use the paddle are in small, rural counties. Larger, urban counties opt instead to either send students home or use "in-school" suspensions, where the students are segregated from their classmates. Twenty-two states allow teachers to paddle students.

Ingraham and Andrews accused school officials of inflicting punishment that was in violation of the cruel and unusual provision of the Eighth Amendment to the Constitution and said they did not receive due process for their actions.

The district court dismissed the case because it found that there was no constitutional basis for relief. The circuit court agreed with the district court, so it was appealed to the Supreme Court.

The Supreme Court agreed with the lower courts and found:

◆ The cruel and unusual punishments clause of the Eighth Amendment does not apply to disciplinary corporal punishment in public schools. This Amendment is clearly designed to protect someone convicted of a crime.

♦ There is no need to extend the Eighth Amendment protections to public school disciplinary practices because there are significant safeguards in place in the community if school officials go too far.

♦ The due process clause of the Fourteenth Amendment does not require notice and hearing prior to the imposition of corporal punishment in the schools provided there are procedural safeguards in place that minimize the risk of wrongful punishment and provide for resolution of disputes.

Justice Powell wrote in his opinion for the court announced on April 9, 1977:

"The use of corporal punishment in this country as a means of disciplining schoolchildren dates back to the colonial period. It has survived the transformation of primary and secondary education from the colonials' reliance on optional private arrangements to our present system of compulsory education and dependence on public schools. Despite the general abandonment of corporal punishment as a means of punishing criminal offenders, the practice continues to play a role in the public education of schoolchildren in most parts of the country. Professional and public opinion is sharply divided on the practice, and has been for more than a century. Yet we can discern no trend toward its elimination …. An examination of the history of the Amendment and the decisions of this Court construing the proscription against cruel and unusual punishment confirms that it was designed to protect those convicted of crimes. We adhere to this longstanding limitation, and hold that the Eighth Amendment does not apply to the paddling of children as a means of maintaining discipline in public schools."

Suspending Students

Many schools choose to suspend students rather than paddle them today. You may be surprised to learn that the Supreme Court actually ruled that suspension can raise a constitutional question.

In February and March 1971 there was a period of unrest in which many students were suspended from schools in Columbus, Ohio. Nine of these students filed suit in district court claiming they had been suspended from public school for up to 10 days without a hearing. They said these suspensions violated the due process clause of the Fourteenth Amendment because they were deprived their rights to an education without a hearing of any kind. Students also asked that references to these suspensions be removed from their student records.

Six of the students attended Marion-Franklin High School and were suspended for disruptive or disobedient conduct because of a demonstration in the high school auditorium. None of the students was given a hearing to determine the facts, but each was offered the opportunity to attend a conference with their parents after being suspended to discuss the student's future.

The named plaintiff, Dwight Lopez, testified that 75 students were suspended from his junior high, Central High. He said he was not a party to the destructive conduct in the lunchroom, but was only an innocent bystander. There was no evidence in the court record from the school administrators that questioned Lopez's testimony. Lopez was never given a hearing.

School officials contended there was no constitutional right to an education at public expense and that the due process clause did not protect against expulsions. The Supreme Court disagreed in a split 5 to 4 decision. Justices White, Douglas, Brennan, Stewart and Marshall were in the majority. In delivering the opinion for the Court on January 22, 1975, Justice White wrote:

> "The Fourteenth Amendment forbids the State to deprive any person of life, liberty, or property without due process of law. Protected interests in property are normally 'not created by the Constitution. Rather, they are created and their dimensions are defined' by an independent source such as state statutes or rules entitling the citizen to certain benefits .... Here, on the basis of state law, appellees plainly had legitimate claims of entitlement to a public education. Ohio Rev Code ... direct local authorities to provide a free education to all residents between five and 21 years of age, and a compulsory-attendance law requires attendance for a school year of not less than 32 weeks. It is true that ... the Code permits school principals to suspend students for up to 10 days; but suspensions may not be imposed without any grounds whatsoever. All of the schools had their own rules specifying the grounds for expulsion or suspension. Having chosen to extend the right to an education to people of appellees' class generally, Ohio may not withdraw that right on grounds of misconduct, absent fundamentally fair procedures to determine whether the misconduct has occurred. Although Ohio may not be constitutionally obligated to establish and maintain a public school system, it has nevertheless done so and has required its children to attend. Those young people do not 'shed their constitutional rights' at the schoolhouse door. ... The Fourteenth Amendment, as now applied to the States, protects the citizen against the State itself and all of its creatures—Boards of Education not excepted. The authority possessed by the State to prescribe and enforce standards of conduct in its schools although concededly very broad, must be exercised consistently with constitutional safeguards."

In its decision the Supreme Court held that a 10-day suspension is not *de minimis* and may not be imposed in complete disregard of the due process clause. The Court specified that due process requires a student be given oral or written notice of the charges against him or her. If he or she denies them, an explanation of the evidence authorities have must be presented and the student must be given a chance to present his or her version.

> **Court Connotations**
>
> **De minimis** is the Latin word for "of minimum importance" or "trifling." In law it refers to something or a difference that is so small or tiny that the law does not refer to it or consider it. For example in a contract deal, a $1 million error could be questioned legally, while a $10 error is de minimis.

This notice and hearing should precede the student's removal from the school and in most cases does almost immediately follow the misconduct before the student is removed from the school. In some cases where the student is so disruptive he or she must be removed from school property immediately, the notice and hearing can take place after removal as soon as practicable.

Sarita Sarvate, a reporter for Pacific News Service (PNS), learned close-up how this works when her son was suspended from school in 2002 and she wrote up her experiences for PNS. In her story, she described how she received a call from the principal saying her son had stolen a substitute teacher's sunglasses and there were witnesses to the crime. Her son insisted the sunglasses had fallen from the teacher's desk and when he picked them up the lenses popped out. The sunglasses were never found, but her son insisted he didn't take them.

Sarita Sarvate and her husband were in the principal's office the next day where they were shown the written notice of the charges as required by the Supreme Court. After trying to defend their son's position, her husband told the principal, "When the CEO of Enron lies, he is offered First Amendment protection. But when a child denies guilt, he doesn't get Miranda rights?" They asked for a hearing but were denied and were told an internal investigation had already been conducted. The written notice was all the proof they were going to get that their son had been judged, condemned, and given his sentence.

Sarvate raised numerous questions that many parents are probably still asking today about the suspension process:

- ◆ Why do our textbooks tell our children that a person is innocent until proven guilty? That a person accused of a crime has the right to a defense? At school, in real situations, they learn the opposite.

◆ Do our schools criminalize children unnecessarily? Does that lead some to such distrust of the world and loss of self-esteem that suspicion of misbehavior and even crime become a self-fulfilling prophecy?

The situation might actually be worse if Justice Powell's dissenting opinion had been the majority rule. Chief Justice Burger and Justices Blackmun and Rehnquist joined Powell's dissent. Powell wrote:

> "One of the more disturbing aspects of today's decision is its indiscriminate reliance upon the judiciary, and the adversary process, as the means of resolving many of the most routine problems arising in the classroom. In mandating due process procedures the Court misapprehends the reality of the normal teacher-pupil relationship. There is an ongoing relationship, one in which the teacher must occupy many roles—educator, adviser, friend, and, at times, parent-substitute. It is rarely adversary in nature except with respect to the chronically disruptive or insubordinate pupil whom the teacher must be free to discipline without frustrating formalities.

> "The Ohio statute, providing as it does for due notice both to parents and the Board, is compatible with the teacher-pupil relationship and the informal resolution of mistaken disciplinary action. We have relied for generations upon the experience, good faith and dedication of those who staff our public schools, and the nonadversary means of airing grievances that always have been available to pupils and their parents. One would have thought before today's opinion that this informal method of resolving differences was more compatible with the interests of all concerned than resort to any constitutionalized procedure, however blandly it may be defined by the Court."

Do you know your school's policies on punishment for your child? As a parent it's a good idea to understand exactly what the school can and cannot do before your child comes home after being tried and convicted for an action in school.

Testing for Drugs

Drug-free schools are a slogan you see in many communities. Working to keep them that way is a constant challenge for school administrations. Some schools conduct periodic drug testing for students. One such program at Tecumseh, Oklahoma School District requires all middle and high school students who want to participate in extracurricular activities to submit to urinalysis testing for drugs.

Two Tecumseh High School students and their parents sued the school saying this policy violated the students *Fourth Amendment* rights. The district court disagreed and ruled in favor of the school administrators.

The students and parents then appealed the case to the circuit court, which ruled in their favor and agreed the policy did violate the Fourth Amendment.

The board of education appealed the circuit court decision to the Supreme Court in the case *Board of Education* v. *Earls.* The case was decided on a split 5 to 4 decision. Justice Thomas wrote the opinion of the Court and was joined by Chief Justice Rehnquist, and Justices Scalia, Kennedy and Breyer. Justice O'Connor filed a dissent and was joined by Souter. Justice Ginsburg also wrote a dissent and was joined by Stevens, O'Connor and Souter.

> **Court Connotations**
>
> The **Fourth Amendment** states, "The right of the people to be secure in their persons, houses, papers, and effects, against unreasonable searches and seizures, shall not be violated, and no Warrants shall issue, but upon probable cause, supported by Oath or affirmation, and particularly describing the place to be searched, and the persons or things to be seized."

In the majority opinion announced June 27, 2002, Thomas wrote:

> "Tecumseh's Policy is a reasonable means of furthering the School District's important interest in preventing and deterring drug use among its schoolchildren and does not violate the Fourth Amendment .... In contrast to the criminal context, a probable cause finding is unnecessary in the public school context because it would unduly interfere with maintenance of the swift and informal disciplinary procedures that are needed. In the public school context, a search may be reasonable when supported by 'special needs' beyond the normal need for law enforcement. Because the 'reasonableness inquiry cannot disregard the schools' custodial and tutelary responsibility for children, a finding of individualized suspicion may not be necessary."

> **Supreme Sayings**
>
> "The ruling could not have come at a better time. *Monitoring the Future*, a national survey that tracks drug use among America's youth, reports that in 2001 more than half of all students had used illicit drugs by the time they finished high school. Moreover, the 2000 *National Household Survey on Drug Abuse* revealed that of the 4.5 million people age 12 and older who need drug treatment, 23 percent are teenagers.
>
> —John P. Walters, Director, Office of National Drug Control Policy in the Bush Administration

In deciding this case the majority used a precedent set in 1995—*Vernonia School Dist. 47J v. Acton*—in which a school district was granted the right to test all athletes for drugs because drug use could increase the risk of sports injury. In writing her dissent, Justice O'Connor did not believe the Tecumseh School District's drug testing program met the test:

> "Today, the Court relies upon *Vernonia* to permit a school district with a drug problem its superintendent repeatedly described as 'not ... major,' to test the urine of an academic team member solely by reason of her participation in a nonathletic, competitive extracurricular activity—participation associated with neither special dangers from, nor particular predilections for, drug use.

> "[T]he legality of a search of a student, this Court has instructed, 'should depend simply on the reasonableness, under all the circumstances, of the search.' ... The particular testing program upheld today is not reasonable, it is capricious, even perverse: Petitioners' policy targets for testing a student population least likely to be at risk from illicit drugs and their damaging effects ....

> "In this case ... Lindsay Earls and her parents allege that the School District handled personal information collected under the policy carelessly, with little regard for its confidentiality. Information about students' prescription drug use, they assert, was routinely viewed by Lindsay's choir teacher, who left files containing the information unlocked and unsealed, where others, including students, could see them; and test results were given out to all activity sponsors whether or not they had a clear 'need to know.' ... The policy requires that '[t]he medication list shall be submitted to the lab in a sealed and confidential envelope and shall not be viewed by district employees'.

> "In granting summary judgment to the School District, the District Court observed that the District's 'Policy expressly provides for confidentiality of test results, and the Court must assume that the confidentiality provisions will be honored.'"

Given how closely divided the court was on this issue, it is likely another case will wind its way to the Court in the future.

Dealing with Sexual Harassment

Sexual harassment makes the headlines almost daily as cases of abuse of children are reported in many communities. The most devastating reports in 2003 were those related to abuse by Catholic priests over many years and hidden by the church. Churches are not the only place an adult in authority can use that authority to sexually harass a child. Schools are another likely location and it does happen. *Gebser* v. *Lago Vista Independent School District* is one example that made it to the Supreme Court in 1998.

In 1991, Alida Gebser was first introduced to Frank Waldrop by his wife, who at the time was Gebser's eighth grade teacher. Her eighth grade teacher encouraged Gebser to participate in a Great Books discussion group led by her husband when she went to school at Lago Vista High School in Texas the next year.

Waldrop did end up being one of Gebser's teachers. Waldrop began making suggestive comments to Gebser when she was 13 years old. In the spring of 1992, Waldrop visited Gebser at her home when her parents were away. While there he started kissing and fondling her, which was the beginning of an approximately one and a half year relationship that included numerous acts of sexual intercourse. Waldrop's behavior was finally discovered in January 1993 when police caught the two engaged in sexual activity.

Gebser sued the school district in the United States district court for the western district of Texas claiming the school district violated her rights under *Title IX*. There were two parts to her claim:

1. Since Waldrop was employed by the school district, he acted as its agent, so the district was liable for his actions; and,

2. The school district failed to have an adequate sexual harassment policy that educates both students and faculty on the definition of sexual harassment and the reporting procedures in place to confront it.

> **Court Connotations**
>
> **Title IX** of the Educational Amendments of 1972 is the landmark legislation that bans sex discrimination in schools, whether it be in academics or athletics. Title IX states: "No person in the U.S. shall, on the basis of sex be excluded from participation in, or denied the benefits of, or be subjected to discrimination under any educational program or activity receiving federal aid."

The district court awarded summary judgment to the school without even letting the case go to trial. Gebser appealed the decision to the U.S. 5th Circuit Court, which affirmed the lower court's ruling. The circuit court found that in order for the district to be held liable there would have to be proof that another school employee knew about the improper relationship, someone who had the supervisory power to do something about it and didn't stop it.

Gebser then appealed her case to United States Supreme Court. The case was titled, *Gebser* v. *Lago Vista Independent School District*. She challenged the standard established by the 5th Circuit because she said a school district should be liable if it received constructive notice (if the school district knew or should have known of the behavior) of the harassment and failed to have "effective complaint and investigative procedures." She also claimed that students, as a result of the teacher-student relationship, do not separate the authority wielded by teachers from the authority held by the school district. Hence, the school district is indirectly responsible for its teacher's behavior.

The school district disagreed and asked the Supreme Court to uphold the lower courts' holdings, saying the school district should not have liability for acts that occurred beyond its knowledge. Furthermore, the school district opposed expanding the definition of an agent to include all teachers. It argued that, in essence, a school district would be liable "in virtually every case in which a teacher harasses, seduces or sexually abuses a student," thereby creating an unduly burdensome strict liability standard. The school district also expressed that such expansion would inhibit healthy student-teacher relationships for fear of future repercussions.

Just the Facts

Friend of the Court briefs were submitted on Gebser's behalf by the National Women's Law Center (joined by American Association of University Women, California Women's Law Center, Center for Women Policy Studies, Clearinghouse on Women's Issues, Connecticut Women's Education and Legal Fund, Inc., Equal Rights Advocates, National Association for Girls and Women in Sport, National Coalition for Sex Equity in Education, National Organization for Women Legal Defense and Education Fund, Southern Coalition for Educational Equity, Wider Opportunities for Women, Women Employed, Women's Law Project, Women's Legal Defense Fund and Y.W.C.A.), National Education Association, and United States government. Briefs for the school district were submitted by the National School Boards Association, Kentucky School Boards Association, Texas Association of School Boards Legal Assistance Fund, and American Insurance Association.

The Supreme Court affirmed the lower courts' rulings on a split 5 to 4 vote. The majority opinion was written by Justice O'Connor and joined by Chief Justice Rehnquist and Justices Scalia, Kennedy, and Thomas. Justice Stevens wrote a dissenting opinion signed by Souter, Ginsburg, and Breyer. Justice Ginsburg also filed a dissenting opinion signed by Souter and Breyer.

The majority established an actual notice standard of review for teacher-student sexual harassment cases where monetary damages are requested. The Court declined to address Waldrop's actions as those of an agent for the school district since, "Title IX contains no [reference] to an educational institution's 'agents,' and so does not expressly call for application of agency principles." The Court held that it would "frustrate the purposes" of Title IX to permit an award of damages where the school district itself was never notified of the misconduct. In fact, the Court did not find the teacher's knowledge of his wrongful behavior to be relevant to this liability analysis. Justice O'Connor wrote in the opinion released June 22, 1998:

> "Title IX contains important clues that this was Congress' intent. Title IX's express means of enforcement requires actual notice to officials of the funding recipient and an opportunity for voluntary compliance before administrative enforcement proceedings can commence. The presumable purpose is to avoid diverting education funding from beneficial uses where a recipient who is unaware of discrimination in its programs is willing to institute prompt corrective measures. Allowing recovery of damages based on principles of … constructive notice in cases of teacher-student sexual harassment would be at odds with that basic objective, as liability would attach even though the district had no actual knowledge of the teacher's conduct and no opportunity to take action to end the harassment …. Lago Vista's alleged failure to comply with federal regulations requiring it to promulgate and publicize an effective policy and grievance procedure for sexual harassment claims does not establish the requisite actual notice and deliberate indifference, and the failure to promulgate a grievance procedure does not itself constitute discrimination in violation of Title IX."

> **Supreme Sayings**
>
> "The Court has created a veritable 'smoking gun' requirement for harassment suits, forcing the victim to prove that the school district knew of the teacher's actions and consciously ignored them. This places a heavy burden upon the victim, especially when faced with a district who may have been sympathetic to the student's concerns, yet refused action upon them."
>
> —From the website of the National Organization for Women

Justice Stevens wrote in his dissent:

> "During her freshman and sophomore years of high school, petitioner Alida Star Gebser was repeatedly subjected to sexual abuse by her teacher, Frank Waldrop, whom she had met in the eighth grade when she joined his high school book discussion group. Waldrop's conduct was surely intentional and it occurred during, and as a part of, a curriculum activity in which he wielded authority over Gebser that had been delegated to him by respondent. Moreover, it is undisputed that the activity was subsidized, in part, with federal moneys.

"The Court nevertheless holds that the law does not provide a damages remedy for the Title IX violation alleged in this case because no official of the school district with 'authority to institute corrective measures on the district's behalf' had actual notice of Waldrop's misconduct .... That holding is at odds with settled principles of agency law, under which the district is responsible for Waldrop's misconduct because 'he was aided in accomplishing the tort by the existence of the agency relation.' ... This case presents a paradigmatic example of a tort that was made possible, that was effected, and that was repeated over a prolonged period because of the powerful influence that Waldrop had over Gebser by reason of the authority that his employer, the school district, had delegated to him. As a secondary school teacher, Waldrop exercised even greater authority and control over his students than employers and supervisors exercise over their employees. His gross misuse of that authority allowed him to abuse his young student's trust."

The case definitely threw it back in the laps of parents to be certain their children were not being abused in the schools.

Legalizing School Vouchers

The Bush Administration is a big proponent of school vouchers. The door was at least partially opened for vouchers after a 2002 Supreme Court ruling in *Zelman* v. *Simmons-Harris*.

Opponents of school vouchers believe they will force citizens—Christians, Jews, Muslims, and atheists—to pay for religious indoctrination of school children at schools with narrow parochial agendas. Estimates are that 80 percent of vouchers will be used in schools whose central mission is religious training. Religion permeates these schools in the classroom, the lunchroom, even on the athletic fields. Channeling public money in this direction, opponents believe, flies in the face of the constitutional mandate of separation of church and state.

The *Zelman* v. *Simmons-Harris* case did not give a green light for all school vouchers programs, only ones designed in a similar way to the Cleveland School District's voucher program. The Court ruled a legal voucher program must:

◆ Be a part of a wider program of multiple educational options including magnet schools and after-school tutorial assistance,

◆ Offer parents a real choice between religious and nonreligious education,

◆ Not only address private schools, but ensure benefits go to schools regardless of whether they are public or private, religious or not.

Zelman v. *Simmons-Harris* also was narrowly decided on a split 5 to 4 decision. Chief Justice Rehnquist wrote the opinion for the court with Justices O'Connor, Scalia, Kennedy, and Thomas joining. Justice O'Connor also wrote a concurring opinion joined by Thomas. Souter filed a dissenting opinion joined by Stevens, Ginsburg and Breyer. Stevens filed his own dissenting opinion and Breyer filed a dissenting opinion joined by Stevens and Souter.

Chief Justice Rehnquist wrote in the opinion announced by the Court on June 27, 2002:

> "Because the program was enacted for the valid secular purpose of providing educational assistance to poor children in a demonstrably failing public school system, the question is whether the program nonetheless has the forbidden effect of advancing or inhibiting religion …. This Court's jurisprudence makes clear that a government aid program is not readily subject to challenge under the Establishment Clause if it is neutral with respect to religion and provides assistance directly to a broad class of citizens who, in turn, direct government aid to religious schools wholly as a result of their own genuine and independent private choice."

In his dissent, Souter wrote:

> "The Court's majority holds that the Establishment Clause is no bar to Ohio's payment of tuition at private religious elementary and middle schools under a scheme that systematically provides tax money to support the schools' religious missions. The occasion for the legislation thus upheld is the condition of public education in the city of Cleveland. The record indicates that the schools are failing to serve their objective, and the vouchers in issue here are said to be needed to provide adequate alternatives to them. If there were an excuse for giving short shrift to the Establishment Clause, it would probably apply here. But there is no excuse. Constitutional limitations are placed on government to preserve constitutional values in hard cases, like these ….

> "Today, however, the majority holds that the Establishment Clause is not offended by Ohio's Pilot Project Scholarship Program, under which students may be eligible to receive as much as $2,250 in the form of tuition vouchers transferable to religious schools. In the city of Cleveland the overwhelming proportion of large appropriations for voucher money must be spent on religious schools if it is to be spent at all, and will be spent in amounts that cover almost all of tuition. The money will thus pay for eligible students' instruction not only in secular subjects but in religion as well, in schools that can fairly be characterized as founded to teach religious doctrine and to imbue teaching in all subjects with a religious dimension. Public tax money will pay at a systemic level for teaching the covenant with Israel and Mosaic law in Jewish schools, the primacy of the Apostle Peter and

the Papacy in Catholic schools, the truth of reformed Christianity in Protestant schools, and the revelation to the Prophet in Muslim schools, to speak only of major religious groupings in the Republic."

The battle for school vouchers is far from over. The next round will probably be fought at either state legislatures or in the U.S. Congress as proponents try to develop voucher systems that meet the tests set by the majority in this case.

As you can see, the Supreme Court plays a major role in key education decisions that affect your child and how your child is treated inside the schools. In the next chapter, we'll look at the issue of sharing power between state and federal governments.

The Least You Need to Know

◆ Schools can spank kids as long as strict guidelines are in place. Spanking comes with fewer restrictions than suspending a child from school.

◆ Schools do have the right to test all children for drugs.

◆ Schools cannot be held responsible for the sexual harassment of a child unless a school officer who had the supervisory power to stop it knew it was happening and didn't stop it.

◆ School vouchers can pass the test of separation of church and state if narrowly designed to include both public and private schools, as well as religious and nonreligious schools.

Chapter 16

Separating Government Powers

In This Chapter

- ◆ Battle for power
- ◆ Striking down gun control
- ◆ Granting family leave
- ◆ Keeping states out of the bedroom

Today states' rights arguments are a battle cry heard primarily from the right wing of society that believes in weakening federal power. The major battles supporting a strong federal government were won during the time of the Marshall Court, as we discussed in Chapter 4.

During various times between the Marshall Court and the Rehnquist Court, the ebbs and flows of court politics did revitalize the state's right cause, but there hasn't been much interest shown by the Supreme Court in defending states' rights since the battle over the New Deal legislation in the 1930s, as we discussed in Chapter 7. Most believe the lines in today's battleground were redrawn in 1995 when the Supreme Court struck down the federal Gun Free School Zones Act in *United States* v. *Lopez*, which we'll discuss in this chapter.

Numerous cases since *Lopez* have shown the Rehnquist Court's preference for states' rights over federal control, but the winds seemed to be shifting again with two shocking cases whose rulings were announced at the end of the Court's 2003 term—*Nevada Department of Human Resources* v. *Hibbs* (involving the Family Medical Leave Act) and *Lawrence* v. *Texas* (striking down the Texas Sodomy Law).

In this chapter, I'll review the constitutional issues at stake in states' rights cases. Then I'll discuss several recent key Supreme Court decisions.

Who's in Control—the States or the Federal Government?

Two Constitutional amendments are used when deciding whether states' rights should prevail or if a strong federal government is more important—the Eleventh Amendment and the Fourteenth Amendment.

The Eleventh Amendment states, "The Judicial power of the United States shall not be construed to extend to any suit in law or equity, commenced or prosecuted against one of the United States by Citizens of another State, or by Citizens or Subjects of any Foreign State." This amendment primarily has been used to grant states immunity from being sued.

The portion of the Fourteenth Amendment that limits the Eleventh Amendment states, "No State shall make or enforce any law which shall abridge the privileges or immunities of citizens of the United States; nor shall any State deprive any person of life, liberty, or property, without due process of law; nor deny to any person within its jurisdiction the equal protection of the laws."

All cases in which states' rights is a critical part of the issues to be decided involve at least one and more likely both of these amendments. When the Supreme Court struck down the gun control law in 1995, states' rights proponents believed the Court had the majority it needed to move more aggressively in support of states' rights.

They were correct for about eight years and enjoyed watching the court grant states immunity from discrimination laws and other federal laws that impinged on state sovereignty. In fact, in a 2000 policy paper developed by Michael Greve for the American Enterprise Institute he declared:

> "The Fair Labor Standards Act, a New Deal war horse, was held effectively unenforceable against state governments a year ago. This past year, in *Kimel* v. *Board of Regents*, the Court placed state employers beyond the reach of lawsuits for damages under the Age Discrimination in Employment Act. The Family

and Medical Leave Act is likewise unenforceable. Next year, in a case that the Supreme Court has already agreed to hear, core provisions of the Americans with Disabilities Act may well meet the same fate. Only civil rights statutes at the heart of the Fourteenth Amendment—those dealing with race discrimination—will probably remain intact."

His analysis was partially correct. State's were granted immunity from the Americans with Disabilities Act in cases related to hiring practices such as the *Board of Trustees of the University of Alabama* v. *Garrett, Patricia*. We'll delve more deeply into that case in Chapter 18. He was wrong about the Family and Medical Leave Act, which was upheld in a 2003 case *Nevada Department of Human Resources* v. *Hibbs* (I'll call it *Hibbs* for short from this point on), which I'll describe in greater detail in a later section.

From the time of the New Deal legislation victory, the Supreme Court supported Congress's authority to regulate interstate commerce and gave Congress just about free reign to establish federal mandates that states must accept. Rehnquist's Court decided to challenge that, believing states as sovereign powers don't have to obey some federal mandates.

Supreme Sayings

"Rehnquist's problem here was that he shouldn't have even started exempting state governments from laws that all the state's citizens must obey. He saw the doctrine going places that made him unhappy, and he needed an exit strategy. When the Supreme Court needs to back down or turn around it often resorts to desperate distinctions as a way to hide retreat."

—Michael Kinsley, *Washington Post* columnist and editor of MSN's *Slate, in a Washington Post column on May 30, 2003*

Greve wrote that in order for the Supreme Court to continue on its states' rights path it needed a strong constituency for its version of federalism. The only such constituency that Greve could find was what Republican strategist Grover Norquist calls the "Leave-Us-Alone" coalition, which is made up of socially conservative, populist constituencies, such as gun owners, home schoolers and school choice groups, property-rights advocates, and religious organizations.

The Bush Administration certainly panders to this constituency, which gave the Supreme Court a friend in the White House. But, that friend even disserted the Court before the *Hibbs* ruling, which I'll discuss in a later section.

We don't know for sure whether the Court is ready to shift away from its states' rights course permanently or if the cases decided in 2003 were an aberration until the Court's next session, which began October 2003. During that term the Court will hear another key states' rights case, *Tennessee* v. *Lane*, which looks at whether a state must obey a provision in the Americans for Disabilities Act that guarantees people access to public buildings. While the Court ruled states did not have to provide equal protection rights for people with disabilities in regards to state hiring, the *Tennessee* v. *Lane* case looks at a different aspect—the Constitutional guarantee of due process.

> **Just the Facts** _____
>
> The *Tennessee* v. *Lane* case involves two people who were unable to access the state's courtrooms because courtrooms were not wheelchair accessible. George Lane, one of the plaintiffs, crawled up two flights of stairs for his arraignment on a misdemeanor traffic violation. He was arrested and jailed on a "failure to appear" violation when he refused to crawl up the steps a second time for a pretrial hearing.

Now let's take a look at the case that started the recent state's right trend— *U.S.* v. *Alfonso Lopez*.

Killing Gun Control

Alfonso Lopez arrived at Edison High School in San Antonio Texas carrying a concealed .38 caliber handgun with five bullets on March 10, 1992. School authorities received an anonymous tip about the gun and after confronting Lopez, he admitted he was carrying the weapon.

> **Just the Facts** _____
>
> The Gun-Free School Zones Act of 1990 prohibits "any individual knowingly to possess a firearm at a place that [he] knows ... is a school zone." The act was passed by Congress in 1990 because of growing public concerns about violence, particularly gun violence, in the nation's schools.

Lopez was arrested and charged under Texas law with possession of a firearm on school premises. The next day, state charges were dismissed after federal agents decided to charge Lopez with a violation of the Gun Free School Zones Act of 1990.

Lopez's attorneys moved to dismiss the federal indictment on the ground that it was "unconstitutional as it is beyond the power of Congress to legislate control over our public schools." The district court denied the motion, concluding the act was "a constitutional exercise of Congress's well defined power to regulate activities in and affecting commerce, and the 'business' of elementary, middle and high schools ... affects interstate commerce." Lopez waived his right to a jury trial. The district court conducted a *bench trial*, found him guilty and sentenced him to six months' imprisonment and two years' supervised release.

Lopez appealed the conviction based on the claim that Congress had exceeded its legislative powers under the commerce clause. The 5th Circuit Court agreed with Lopez and reversed his conviction. The Supreme Court decided to hear the case and affirmed the 5th Circuit Court's ruling and declared the Gun Free School Zones Act of 1990 unconstitutional.

> **Court Connotations**
>
> **Bench trial** is a trial without a jury. The judge determines all questions of law and tries the defendant.

The Court's ruling on April 26, 1995 was a split 5 to 4 decision. Chief Justice Rehnquist wrote the opinion for the Court and was joined by Justices O'Connor, Scalia, Kennedy and Thomas. Rehnquist wrote:

> "The possession of a gun in a local school zone is in no sense an economic activity that might, through repetition elsewhere, substantially affect any sort of interstate commerce. Respondent was a local student at a local school; there is no indication that he had recently moved in interstate commerce, and there is no requirement that his possession of the firearm have any concrete tie to interstate commerce.
>
> "To uphold the Government's contentions here, we would have to pile inference upon inference in a manner that would bid fair to convert congressional authority under the Commerce Clause to a general police power of the sort retained by the States."

Justice Breyer's dissent was joined by Justices Ginsburg, Souter, and Stevens. In his dissent Breyer wrote:

> "Having found that guns in schools significantly undermine the quality of education in our Nation's classrooms, Congress could also have found, given the effect of education upon interstate and foreign commerce, that gun-related violence in and around schools is a commercial, as well as a human, problem. Education, although far more than a matter of economics, has long been inextricably intertwined with the Nation's economy. ... In recent years the link between secondary education and business has strengthened, becoming both more direct and more important. Scholars on the subject report that technological changes and innovations in management techniques have altered the nature of the workplace so that more jobs now demand greater educational skills."

The Supreme Court's ruling did not stand for long. Congress passed a slightly revised bill called the Gun-Free School Zones Amendments Act of 1995, which is still on the books. The new law's revisions were widely considered to be cosmetic changes.

The revised school gun law included the requirement that the Government prove the firearms had moved in interstate commerce or "the possession of such firearm otherwise affects interstate or foreign commerce." This requirement rarely hurts the government's case since the vast majority of firearms do move in interstate commerce before being purchased.

Supporting Family Leave

The Supreme Court softened its stance on state immunity from discrimination suits when it ruled in favor of a Nevada state employee, William Hibbs. Hibbs sued the Nevada Department of Human Resources when he was denied 12 weeks leave under the *Family and Medical Leave Act of 1993* (FMLA) to care for his wife, who was recovering from neck surgery and other injuries related to a car accident.

Hibbs first asked for the leave in April and May of 1997 and was granted the right to use that leave intermittently as needed between May and December 1997. Hibbs used it as needed until August 5, 1997, after which he did not return to work. In October 1997 the state informed him he had exhausted his FMLA leave and that he must report to work by November 12, 1997. When Hibbs did not return to work on that date he was fired.

Court Connotations

The **Family and Medical Leave Act of 1993 (FMLA)** entitles an eligible employee to take up to 12 work weeks of unpaid leave annually for the onset of a "serious health condition" by the employee's spouse or other family-related medical needs. The act is most frequently used by women after giving birth to a child or by person to care for elderly parents or children.

Hibbs sued the state in district court seeking damages. The district court ruled in favor of the state on the grounds that it was protected by the Eleventh Amendment from being sued and that Hibbs' Fourteenth Amendment rights had not been violated. Hibbs appealed to the 9th Circuit Court, which reversed the district court. The state then appealed the case to the Supreme Court.

Most expected the Supreme Court would continue on its path of protecting states' rights and were surprised by the Court's May 27, 2003, upholding the 9th Circuit Court and ruling in favor of Hibbs against the state. Chief Justice Rehnquist wrote the 6 to 3 opinion of the court and was joined by Justices O'Connor, Ginsburg, Breyer, and Souter. In addition

Souter filed a concurring opinion that was joined by Ginsburg and Breyer. Stevens filed a separate concurring opinion. The dissenting opinion was written by Kennedy, who was joined by Scalia and Thomas. Scalia also wrote his own dissenting opinion.

Supreme Sayings

"Millions of state workers will now have full protection under the Family and Medical Leave Act, giving them greater ability to balance their work lives against crises at home. The decision also promotes sexual equality because family care has often fallen on women.

But the Supreme Court is still wrongly discriminating among kinds of discrimination. Because it is sympathetic to gender-based claims, it has held that states are not immune to suits like the one at issue yesterday. But in the case of age and disability, about which the court has been more skeptical, states can discriminate without fear of being sued for damages.

This makes no sense."

—*The New York Times* editorial on May 28, 2003

In writing for the Court, Rehnquist said:

"The FMLA aims to protect the right to be free from gender-based discrimination in the workplace. We have held that statutory classifications that distinguish between males and females are subject to heightened scrutiny. ... For a gender-based classification to withstand such scrutiny, it must 'serv[e] important governmental objectives,' and 'the discriminatory means employed [must be] substantially related to the achievement of those objectives.' ... The State's justification for such a classification 'must not rely on overbroad generalizations about the different talents, capacities, or preferences of males and females.' ...

"Stereotypes about women's domestic roles are reinforced by parallel stereotypes presuming a lack of domestic responsibilities for men. Because employers continued to regard the family as the woman's domain, they often denied men similar accommodations or discouraged them from taking leave. These mutually reinforcing stereotypes created a self-fulfilling cycle of discrimination that forced women to continue to assume the role of primary family caregiver, and fostered employers' stereotypical views about women's commitment to work and their value as employees. Those perceptions, in turn, Congress reasoned, lead to subtle discrimination that may be difficult to detect on a case-by-case basis ...

"By creating an across-the-board, routine employment benefit for all eligible employees, Congress sought to ensure that family-care leave would no longer be stigmatized as an inordinate drain on the workplace caused by female employees, and that employers could not evade leave obligations simply by hiring men. By setting a minimum standard of family leave for *all* eligible employees, irrespective of gender, the FMLA attacks the formerly state-sanctioned stereotype that only women are responsible for family caregiving, thereby reducing employers' incentives to engage in discrimination by basing hiring and promotion decisions on stereotypes."

In his dissent, Justice Kennedy supported the right of states to design their own benefits plans:

"If Congress had been concerned about different treatment of men and women with respect to family leave, a congruent remedy would have sought to ensure the benefits of any leave program enacted by a State are available to men and women on an equal basis. Instead, the Act imposes, across the board, a requirement that States grant a minimum of 12 weeks of leave per year … This requirement may represent Congress' considered judgment as to the optimal balance between the family obligations of workers and the interests of employers, and the States may decide to follow these guidelines in designing their own family leave benefits. It does not follow, however, that if the States choose to enact a different benefit scheme, they should be deemed to engage in unconstitutional conduct and forced to open their treasuries to private suits for damages.

"Well before the federal enactment, Nevada not only provided its employees, on a gender-neutral basis, with an option of requesting up to one year of unpaid leave, but also permitted, subject to approval and other conditions, leaves of absence in excess of one year … To be sure, the Nevada scheme did not track that devised by the Act in all respects. The provision of unpaid leave was discretionary and subject to a possible reporting requirement … A congruent remedy to any discriminatory exercise of discretion, however, is the requirement that the grant of leave be administered on a gender-equal basis, not the displacement of the State's scheme by a federal one. The scheme enacted by the Act does not respect the States' autonomous power to design their own social benefits regime."

I would bet most companies would also like to be exempt from the FMLA, so they could design their own "social benefits regime." In fact, before the FMLA was passed into law, President George Bush, Sr. vetoed it twice calling it a "costly government mandate" that would result in lost jobs, reduce worker benefits and American productivity, and make it difficult to compete internationally. After Bill Clinton took office, the FMLA was the first major piece of legislation enacted during his administration.

Interestingly the current President George Bush asked his Justice Department to write a brief in support of *Hibbs*. In the brief, Bush's Justice Department wrote, "This nation has a lengthy and regrettable history of discrimination on the basis of gender. For generations, state laws and conduct relegated women to a position of social, cultural, economic, and political inferiority."

Another even more shocking ruling by the Supreme Court during its 2003 session is the next case I'll discuss, *Lawrence* v. *Texas*.

> **Living Laws**
>
> Today you are entitled to up to 12 weeks family medical leave to take care of a family member. Your employer must have a job waiting for you when you return to work after this leave.

Accepting Homosexuality

Two men, John Geddes Lawrence and Tyron Garner, were charged with a misdemeanor on a sex charge in 1998. They were each fined $200 and forced to spend a night in jail.

The case started when a neighbor called in a fake distress call saying someone was "going crazy" in Lawrence's Texas apartment. When the police pushed open the door, they found Lawrence and Garner engaging in sodomy, which was illegal in Texas. In fact, until the ruling in *Lawrence* v. *Texas*, 13 states had sodomy laws and four of them prohibited oral and anal sex between same-sex couples. These four states were Texas, Kansas, Oklahoma, and Missouri. The other nine states ban consensual sodomy for all citizens—Alabama, Florida, Idaho, Louisiana, Mississippi, North Carolina, South Carolina, Utah, and Virginia.

This case was not the first time the Supreme Court ruled on the legality of sodomy laws. In 1986, a precedent-setting ruling in *Bowers* v. *Harwick* upheld a Georgia anti-sodomy law that was similar to the Texas law just struck down.

> **Just the Facts**
>
> *Bowers* v. *Harwick* involved the arrest of Harwick, who was charged with violating Georgia's sodomy law when he was caught engaging in a sexual act with another male in his bedroom in August 1982. Only three of the current justices were on the Court at the time—Chief Justice Rehnquist and Justices O'Connor and Stevens. Stevens dissented with the ruling. At that time, 24 states had anti-sodomy laws on the books.

Texas defended its sodomy law because it protected the state's interest in marriage and child-rearing. The state said in its defense of the law that homosexual sodomy had "nothing to do with marriage or conception or parenthood and it is not on a par with these sacred choices."

The greatest fears of proponents of the Texas sodomy laws, and similar laws in other states, is that without these laws the country will head down the path of legalizing same-sex marriages. Opponents believe sexual relations in the privacy of one's home should not be the subject of legislation.

Justice Kennedy wrote the 6 to 3 opinion for the court and was joined by Justices Breyer, Ginsburg, Souter, and Stevens. Justice O'Connor wrote a separate concurring opinion. Justice Scalia wrote a dissenting opinion, which was joined by Chief Justice Rehnquist and Justice Thomas.

In his opinion for the Court, Justice Kennedy wrote:

> "Liberty protects the person from unwarranted government intrusions into a dwelling or other private places. In our tradition the State is not omnipresent in the home. And there are other spheres of our lives and existence, outside the home, where the State should not be a dominant presence. Freedom extends beyond spatial bounds. Liberty presumes an autonomy of self that includes freedom of thought, belief, expression, and certain intimate conduct."

Justice Scalia, who believes this ruling will end all rights of the states to enact laws based on morality, wrote in his dissent:

> "*Bowers* held, first, that criminal prohibitions of homosexual sodomy are not subject to heightened scrutiny because they do not implicate a 'fundamental right' under the Due Process Clause … Noting that '[p]roscriptions against that conduct have ancient roots,' … that '[s]odomy was a criminal offense at common law and was forbidden by the laws of the original 13 States when they ratified the Bill of Rights,' … and that many States had retained their bans on sodomy … *Bowers* concluded that a right to engage in homosexual sodomy was not 'deeply rooted in this Nation's history and tradition.' …

> "The Texas statute undeniably seeks to further the belief of its citizens that certain forms of sexual behavior are "immoral and unacceptable.' … the same interest furthered by criminal laws against fornication, bigamy, adultery, adult incest, bestiality, and obscenity. *Bowers* held that this *was* a legitimate state interest. The Court today reaches the opposite conclusion. The Texas statute, it says, 'furthers *no legitimate state interest* which can justify its intrusion into the personal and private life of the individual' … The Court embraces instead Justice

Stevens' declaration in his *Bowers* dissent, that 'the fact that the governing majority in a State has traditionally viewed a particular practice as immoral is not a sufficient reason for upholding a law prohibiting the practice.' ... This effectively decrees the end of all morals legislation. If, as the Court asserts, the promotion of majoritarian sexual morality is not even a *legitimate* state interest, none of the above-mentioned laws can survive rational-basis review."

No one knows what's next after this ruling. Moves are certainly being made in Congress to introduce a new constitutional amendment to respond to the Court's ruling. At a July 2, 2003 press conference at the White House, President Bush was asked if a new "federal constitutional amendment that would define marriage as a union between a man and a woman" was needed. In response, Bush said, "I don't know if it's necessary yet. Let's let the lawyers look at the full ramifications of the recent Supreme Court hearing. What I do support is the notion that marriage is between a man and a woman."

Deal Hudson, the editor of the Catholic magazine *Crisis*, says that "*Lawrence* is a devastating decision, worse than most people think—and for reasons that haven't fully dawned on them yet. This is without question the most damaging decision handed down by the courts since *Roe* v. *Wade*—one that will have even more far-reaching effects than its predecessor." He believes that the ruling leaves the states with no defense against homosexual marriage and could lead to the removal of legal restrictions on other kinds of sexual behavior and could be used to strike down euthanasia restrictions. He says all these laws could, "fall like dominoes."

Only time will tell if Hudson's dire predictions come true. This case obviously involved not only states' rights, but also individual rights, which we'll discuss further in our next section starting with a chapter on laws that deal with control of our bodies.

The Least You Need to Know

- ◆ Cases involving states' rights deal with two aspects of the Constitution—the Eleventh and Fourteenth Amendments.

- ◆ Anyone who carries a gun onto school property can be charged with violating federal law.

- ◆ States are immune from suits involving age or disability discrimination, but can be sued if discrimination involves family medical leave.

- ◆ Anti-sodomy laws were struck down in the 2003 *Lawrence* v. *Texas* Supreme Court ruling. It will probably be years before we know the full impact of that ruling.

Part 5

Assembling a Social Structure

You may think that government takes too great a role in controlling our lives. In this part, we'll explore the Supreme Court decisions that control what we can do with our bodies. We'll also see how the Court's decisions impact who gets hired or accepted at colleges, as well as, review what's been done to protect our privacy and what is in place to protect our freedoms.

17

Controlling Our Bodies

In This Chapter

- ◆ Restricting abortion
- ◆ Regulating end-of-life decisions
- ◆ Testing for drugs
- ◆ Saying no to marijuana

Most of us think of the abortion issue when someone talks about court cases that involve control of our bodies. Whether you are male or female, you probably have very strong feelings about legalized abortion.

But that is not the only issue that has come before the Supreme Court relating to who gets to say what you or the government can do to your body. Drug testing, euthanasia, and the legalization of medical marijuana are all issues that have been the subject of recent cases decided by the Supreme Court.

In this chapter, I'll review the key cases that control what you can or cannot do to your body, as well as what the government can or cannot do to your body.

Limiting Abortion Rights

Since abortion was legalized in 1973 by the Supreme Court in its opinion on *Roe* v. *Wade*, state governments have been trying to limit its impact by drafting laws that control access to abortions. The most recent battles have centered around the controversial "partial-birth abortion" procedure.

Just the Facts

Partial-birth abortions, also known as D&X method, are performed in the second or third trimesters of pregnancy. While the procedures are rarely used, the anti-abortion forces have used graphic pictures to build a strong case against them. Laws to ban this late-term abortion procedure have passed in at least 25 states including Alabama, Alaska, Arizona, Arkansas, Florida, Georgia, Illinois, Indiana, Kansas, Louisiana, Michigan, Missouri, Mississippi, Montana, Nebraska, New Jersey, Ohio, Oklahoma, Rhode Island, South Carolina, South Dakota, Tennessee, Utah, Virginia and Wisconsin. Federal legislation passed Congress in October 2003 and President Bush signed it. A court challenge is expected because the law does not include an exception if the mother's life is in danger.

Many of the partial-birth abortion bills have been struck down in the courts. One case made it all the way to the Supreme Court—*Stenberg* v. *Carhart* in 2000.

Leroy Carhart, a Nebraska physician, filed suit in district court challenging the Nebraska law prohibiting "partial-birth abortion" unless the procedure was necessary to save the mother's life was unconstitutional. The law broadly defined "partial-birth abortion" as a procedure in which a doctor "partially delivers vaginally a living unborn child before killing … the child." The law goes on to define killing the child to mean "intentionally delivering into the vagina a living unborn child, or a substantial portion thereof, for the purpose of performing a procedure that the [abortionist] knows will kill the … child and does kill the … child." This description could also fit a more common procedure called D&E.

Any doctor who performed this type of abortion could be charged with a felony and could have his or her license to practice medicine automatically revoked if convicted. Carhart said the law was unconstitutionally vague and placed an undue burden on both doctors and patients seeking abortion. The district court agreed with Carhart and ruled the law unconstitutional. The 8th Circuit Court agreed, so the state of Nebraska took the case to the Supreme Court.

The Supreme Court's 5 to 4 ruling was so convoluted that you almost need a roadmap to follow the opinion with its concurrences and dissents. Justice Breyer wrote the Court's opinion and was joined by Justices Ginsburg, O'Connor, Souter, and Stevens. Stevens wrote a concurring opinion and was joined by Ginsburg. Ginsburg wrote a concurring opinion and was joined by Stevens. O'Connor also wrote her own concurring opinion. The dissenting side wasn't any clearer. Chief Justice Rehnquist wrote his own dissent, as did Justice Scalia. Justice Kennedy wrote a dissent opinion and was joined by Rehnquist. Justice Thomas wrote a dissenting opinion and was joined by Rehnquist and Scalia. Probably safe to say there wasn't much agreement in the case conference for this one.

Basically what all the mess showed is that the court is not ready to overturn *Roe* v. *Wade* with its current membership and the key reason for that is the belief that any law that bans abortion after a fetus is viable must include a health exemption.

Justice Breyer wrote in the Court's opinion:

> "The upshot is a District Court finding that D&X obviates health risks in certain circumstances, a highly plausible record-based explanation of why that might be so, a division of medical opinion over whether D&X is generally safer, and an absence of controlled medical studies that would help answer these medical questions. Given these circumstances, the Court believes the law requires a health exception. ... Doctors often differ in their estimation of comparative health risks and appropriate treatment. And ... 'appropriate medical judgment' must embody the judicial need to tolerate responsible differences of medical opinion. For another thing, the division of medical opinion signals uncertainty. If those who believe that D&X is a safer abortion method in certain circumstances turn out to be right, the absence of a health exception will place women at an unnecessary risk. If they are wrong, the exception will simply turn out to have been unnecessary."

Breyer also wrote that the law did not clearly differentiate between the D&X procedure and the more common D&E procedure. Therefore he concluded that, "In sum, because all those who perform abortion procedures using the D&E method must fear prosecution, conviction, and imprisonment, the Nebraska law imposes an undue burden upon a woman's right to make an abortion decision."

Living Laws
Any state or federal abortion law that does not provide an exception for a case in which a woman's health is threatened would likely be held unconstitutional if heard by the current makeup of Supreme Court justices.

This problem of legal definition is found in most of the state laws, so many are being challenged if they haven't already been challenged. At the time of this writing, the U.S. Congress was still working on drafting legislation that could pass both Houses this year and meet the limitations set by the Supreme Court's ruling. Conflicting bills passed both Houses and lawmakers were in conference hashing out a final bill at the time of this writing.

Since Justice Thomas attracted the most joiners, I'll quote from his dissenting opinion. He wrote:

> "I will assume, for the sake of discussion, that the category of women whose conduct Nebraska's partial-birth abortion statute might affect includes any woman who wishes to obtain a safe abortion after 16 weeks' gestation. I will also assume (although I doubt it is true) that, of these women, every one would be willing to use the partial-birth abortion procedure if so advised by her doctor. Indisputably, there is no "large fraction" of these women who would face a substantial obstacle to obtaining a safe abortion because of their inability to use this particular procedure. In fact, it is not clear that *any* woman would be deprived of a safe abortion by her inability to obtain a partial-birth abortion. More medically sophisticated minds than ours have searched and failed to identify a single circumstance (let alone a large fraction) in which partial-birth abortion is required. … And so today we are told that 30 States are prohibited from banning one rarely used form of abortion that they believe to border on infanticide. It is clear that the Constitution does not compel this result."

No doubt more cases dealing with the subject of abortion will find their way to the Supreme Court. The battle lines have been drawn and there is no sign the war is over.

Denying the Right to Die

Can a person seek assistance to die from a physician if they are terminally or seriously ill? That all depends on the state you live in. So far the Supreme Court has ruled that states can ban assisted suicide. Two cases decided June 26, 1997, upheld bans on physician-assisted suicide. One involved a law in New York state and the second involved a Washington state law.

Dr. Harold Glucksberg challenged the Washington state law along with four other physicians and a nonprofit organization that counsels individuals contemplating physician-assisted suicide. The state of Washington criminalizes the promotion of suicide attempts by those who "knowingly cause or aid another person to attempt suicide." The district court ruled in favor of Glucksberg and the 9th Circuit Court agreed, so Washington state took the case to the Supreme Court.

Just the Facts

The state of Oregon is the only state that provides for legalized assisted suicide. The Oregon Death with Dignity Act was passed in 2001. The state tracks the number of prescriptions written for lethal does of medication. In 2001, 44 prescriptions were written, which was an increase from 24 prescriptions in 1998, 33 in 1999, and 39 in 2000. Ninety-four percent of patients in Oregon that request assistance from their physicians for suicide say it is because of loss of autonomy. Other major reasons are the inability to participate in activities that make life enjoyable (76 percent) or the loss of control of bodily functions (53 percent).

Dr. Timothy Quill challenged the constitutionality of New York state's ban on physician-assisted suicide in district court. New York does allow a patient to refuse lifesaving treatment, but makes it a crime for a doctor to help patients commit or attempt suicide, even if the patient is terminally ill or in great pain. The district court ruled in the state's favor, but the 2nd Circuit Court overturned that ruling, so the state of New York appealed to the Supreme Court.

The Supreme Court ruled unanimously that states had the right to prohibit assisted suicide. Chief Justice Rehnquist wrote the opinion for the court and was joined by Justices Kennedy, O'Connor, Scalia, and Thomas. Justice O'Connor also wrote a concurring opinion and was joined by Ginsburg and Breyer in part. Additional concurring opinions were filed individually by Stevens, Souter, Ginsburg, and Breyer.

Rehnquist wrote in his opinion for the Court in *Washington* v. *Glucksberg*:

> "More specifically, for over 700 years, the Anglo-American common law tradition has punished or otherwise disapproved of both suicide and assisting suicide ... Though deeply rooted, the States' assisted suicide bans have in recent years been reexamined and, generally, reaffirmed. Because of advances in medicine and technology, Americans today are increasingly likely to die in institutions, from chronic illnesses. ... Public concern and democratic action are therefore sharply focused on how best to protect dignity and independence at the end of life, with the result that there have been many significant changes in state laws and in the attitudes these laws reflect. Many States, for example, now permit 'living wills,' surrogate health care decision-making, and the withdrawal or refusal of life sustaining medical treatment. ... Attitudes toward suicide itself have changed ... but our laws have consistently condemned, and continue to prohibit, assisting suicide. Despite changes in medical technology and notwithstanding an increased emphasis on the importance of end-of-life decision-making, we have not retreated from this prohibition."

Rehnquist's opinion for *Vacco* v. *Quill* cites the *Glucksberg* ruling for full legal interpretation, so I won't quote from that here. While the Court ruled that a state could ban assisted suicide it also invited continued debate on the subject:

> "Throughout the Nation, Americans are engaged in an earnest and profound debate about the morality, legality, and practicality of physician-assisted suicide. Our holding permits this debate to continue, as it should in a democratic society."

The debate about assisted suicide is continuing at the ballot box and in state legislatures. California and Michigan have laws on the books regarding end-of-life care. In fact California requires physicians to take classes in pain management and end-of-life care as part of getting their licenses.

Supreme Sayings

"… we must be wary of those who are too willing to end the lives of the elderly and the ill. If we ever decide that a poor quality of life justifies ending that life, we have taken a step down a slippery slope that places all of us in danger. There is a difference between allowing nature to take its course and actively assisting death."
—C. Everett Koop, M.D., former Surgeon General of the United States

Using Marijuana

One way that states are trying to help patients deal with pain and other difficulties faced when seriously or terminally ill is by permitting the use of marijuana for medicinal purposes. This choice is in direct conflict with the federal government's attempts to control illegal drugs.

President Bush ordered the U.S. Justice Department to step up enforcement efforts in states that enacted laws that permit doctors to recommend marijuana. These states include Alaska, Arizona, California, Colorado, Hawaii, Maine, Nevada, Oregon, and Washington. So far only one case has made it all the way to the Supreme Court—*United States* v. *Oakland Cannabis Buyers Cooperative*. This case did not involve a physician, but instead involved a cooperative where people bought the prescribed marijuana or cannabis.

The cooperative is a not-for-profit organization that operates in downtown Oakland. Its medical director is a physician and there are registered nurses on staff during business hours. In order to become a member of the cooperative a patient must have a written statement from a treating physician that states marijuana therapy will help and must submit to a screening interview. If accepted the patient will receive an identification card that allows him or her to obtain marijuana from the cooperative.

In January 1998, the United States government sued the cooperative and its executive director, Jeffrey Jones, in district court seeking to stop the cooperative from distributing marijuana. Even though the cooperative's activities are legal in California, distributing and manufacturing of marijuana, a controlled substance, violates the federal Controlled Substances Act. The district court granted a preliminary injunction to stop the cooperative.

The cooperative did not appeal the injunction, but instead continued to violate the law by distributing marijuana. The U.S. government then initiated contempt proceedings against the cooperative. The cooperative contended that marijuana is the only drug that can alleviate the pain and other debilitating symptoms of the cooperative's patients. The district court didn't buy that argument, found the cooperative in contempt and gave the U.S. Marshal the power to seize the cooperative's premises. The cooperative filed a motion to modify the injunction to permit distributions that were medically necessary, which was rejected by the district court. The cooperative appealed the case to the 9th Circuit Court, which ruled the district court should have weighted the "public interest" and considered "factors such as the serious harm in depriving patients of marijuana." The district court then modified its injunction to incorporate the medically necessary defense.

Supreme Sayings

National Review Senior Editor Richard Brookhiser, who used marijuana to cope with the agony of chemotherapy during his bout with cancer, wrote, "My support for medical marijuana is not a contradiction of my principles, but an extension of them. I am for law and order, but crime has to be fought intelligently, and the law disgraces itself when it harasses the sick. I support the Christian Coalition and supported the moral majority, but carrying your moral beliefs to unjust ends is not moral, it is philistine. More importantly, I believe in getting government off people's backs. We should include the backs of sick people trying to help themselves."

The U.S. government then appealed to the Supreme Court questioning the circuit court's ruling that medical necessity is a legally cognizable defense to violations of the Controlled Substances Act. The Court ruled unanimously to overturn the circuit court and decided there was no medical necessity exception to the Controlled Substances Act's prohibitions on manufacturing and distributing marijuana. Justice Thomas wrote the opinion for the Court and was joined by Chief Justice Rehnquist and Justices Kennedy, O'Connor and Scalia. Justice Stevens filed a concurring opinion and was joined by Justices Ginsburg and Souter. Justice Breyer did not participate in this case.

Justice Thomas wrote for the Court on May 14, 2001:

> "Because that Act classifies marijuana as a Schedule I controlled substance, it provides only one express exception to the prohibitions on manufacturing and distributing the drug: Government-approved research projects. The Cooperative's contention that a common-law medical necessity defense should be written into the Act is rejected. There is an open question whether federal courts ever have authority to recognize a necessity defense not provided by statute. But that question need not be answered to resolve the issue presented here, for the terms of the Controlled Substances Act leave no doubt that the medical necessity defense is unavailable."

In an attempt to fix this problem Congressman Barney Frank (D-Massachusetts) introduced a bill in 2001 and again on May 22, 2003, called the "States Rights to Medical Marijuana Act." This bill moves marijuana from the Schedule I of the Controlled Sub-stances Act to Schedule II, which allows more flexibility. It also allows:

- ◆ Physicians to prescribe marijuana for medical use;

- ◆ Patients to obtain and use marijuana based on a prescription or recommendation by a physician for medical use;

- ◆ Pharmacies to obtain and hold marijuana for the prescription or recommendation of marijuana by a physician for medical use under applicable state law.

Similar changes would also be made to the Federal Food, Drug and Cosmetic Act with this bill. The bill is currently sitting in the House Committee on Energy and Commerce. While it languishes there, doctors around the country are being threatened with loss of licenses for prescribing medical marijuana.

Just the Facts

As part of a U.S. Justice Department effort to punish clinic directors who provide medical marijuana, the president of the Los Angles Cannabis Resource Center, Scott Imler, faces a maximum of 20 years in prison and a fine of up to $500,000 after accepting a plea bargain in July 2003 on federal charges of maintaining a drug establishment. The final sentence will probably be less severe. Sentencing was set for November 24, 2003 at the time of this writing.

In October 2003, the Supreme Court decided not to take a related case involving whether doctors could inform patients about the use of medical marijuana. By not taking the case the Supreme Court let stand a lower court ruling that doctors may not be investigated, threatened, or punished by federal regulators for recommending marijuana as a medical treatment for their patients.

This ruling allows doctors in the states that permit marijuana for medical uses to discuss this option freely with their patients without fear a losing of their license to prescribe drugs. As part of the war on drugs, the Bush Administration hoped to overturn these state laws. These hopes were dashed by the Court's decision not to take the case. Medical marijuana advocates hope to use this victory to encourage other states to pass similar laws.

Forcing Drug Tests

Another stage of the war on drugs placed pregnant women on the battlefield. In 1989 in Charleston, South Carolina, representatives of the City of Charleston Police Department, the Charleston County Solicitor's Office (the prosecutor), and the Medical University of South Carolina (MUSC), which is a public hospital, developed and implemented the Interagency Policy on Cocaine Abuse in Pregnancy. Pregnant women were forced to take drug tests if they came to the hospital to give birth and fell into one of these categories:

- no or minimal prenatal care
- unexplained pre-term labor
- birth defects or poor fetal growth
- separation of the placenta from the uterine wall
- history of drug or alcohol abuse
- intrauterine fetal death

At the early stages of the policy, women were immediately arrested after they or their newborns tested positive for cocaine. In 1990, an amnesty component was added to the program. Women who tested positive were given the option of entering a drug treatment program to avoid arrest. If they didn't complete the treatment program or tested positive for drugs a second time they were arrested.

In 1994, the Civil Rights Division of the U.S. Department of Health and Human Services investigated MUSC on the issue of whether the hospital had violated the civil rights of its African American patients during the implementation of this policy. Of the 30 women arrested under this policy, 29 were African American. MUSC dropped the program after this investigation.

> ### Supreme Sayings
>
> "In the past several years, the state has increasingly intruded into the lives of pregnant women, policing their conduct in the name of protecting fetuses. Pregnant women have been forced to undergo unwanted cesareans; they've been ordered to have their cervixes sewn up to prevent miscarriage; they've been incarcerated for consuming alcohol; and they've been detained, as in the case of one young woman, simply because she 'lack[ed] motivation or [the] ability to seek medical care.'"
>
> —From the article, "Court-Ordered Obstetrical Intervention," in a 1987 issue of the *New England Journal of Medicine*

Patients of MUSC who were arrested after testing positive for cocaine filed suit in district court challenging the policy on the basis that the warrantless and nonconsensual drug tests conducted for criminal investigatory purposes were unconstitutional searches. The district court instructed the jury to find for the petitioners unless they had consented to the searches. The jury found in favor of MUSC and the women appealed, arguing the evidence was not sufficient to support the jury's finding that the women consented to the tests.

The 4th Circuit Court found that the searches in question were reasonable based on the principle that "'special needs' may, in certain exceptional circumstances, justify a search policy designed to serve non-law enforcement ends." The 4th Circuit Court did not rule on the consent issue.

Living Laws

Pregnant women cannot be subjected to warrantless, suspicionless searches just because they are pregnant. Drug testing of a pregnant woman must be done either with her consent or a valid warrant.

In a 6 to 3 decision on March 21, 2001, the Supreme Court disagreed and held that, "A state hospital's performance of a diagnostic test to obtain evidence of a patient's criminal conduct for law enforcement purposes is an unreasonable search if the patient has not consented to the procedure. The interest in using the threat of criminal sanctions to deter pregnant women from using cocaine cannot justify a departure from the general rule that an official nonconsensual search is unconstitutional if not authorized by a valid warrant."

Justice Stevens wrote the opinion for the Court and was joined by Justices Breyer, Ginsburg, O'Connor and Souter. Justice Kennedy wrote a concurring opinion. Justice Scalia wrote a dissenting opinion and was joined by Chief Justice Rehnquist and Justice Thomas. In his opinion for the Court, Stevens wrote:

> "While the ultimate goal of the program may well have been to get the women in question into substance-abuse treatment and off of drugs, the immediate objective of the searches was to generate evidence *for law enforcement purposes* in order to reach that goal. The threat of law enforcement may ultimately have been intended as a means to an end, but the direct and primary purpose of MUSC's policy was to ensure the use of those means. In our opinion, this distinction is critical. Because law enforcement involvement always serves some broader social purpose or objective, under respondents' view, virtually any nonconsensual suspicionless search could be immunized under the special needs doctrine by defining the search solely in terms of its ultimate, rather than immediate, purpose. Such an approach is inconsistent with the *Fourth Amendment.* Given the primary purpose of the Charleston program, which was to use the threat of arrest and prosecution in order to force women into treatment, and given the extensive involvement of law enforcement officials at every stage of the policy, this case simply does not fit within the closely guarded category of 'special needs.'

> "The fact that positive test results were turned over to the police does not merely provide a basis for distinguishing our prior cases applying the 'special needs' balancing approach to the determination of drug use. It also provides an affirmative reason for enforcing the strictures of the Fourth Amendment. While state hospital employees, like other citizens, may have a duty to provide the police with evidence of criminal conduct that they inadvertently acquire in the course of routine treatment, when they undertake to obtain such evidence from their patients *for the specific purpose of incriminating those patients*, they have a special obligation to make sure that the patients are fully informed about their constitutional rights, as standards of knowing waiver require."

Court Connotations _____

The **Fourth Amendment** states, "The right of the people to be secure in their persons, houses, papers, and effects, against unreasonable searches and seizures, shall not be violated, and no warrants shall issue, but upon probable cause, supported by oath or affirmation, and particularly describing the place to be searched, and the persons or things to be seized." This amendment protects citizens from searches without a valid search warrant.

Justice Scalia wrote in his dissent:

> "As I indicated at the outset, it is not the function of this Court—at least not in Fourth Amendment cases—to weigh petitioners' privacy interest against the State's interest in meeting the crisis of 'crack babies' that developed in the late 1980s. I cannot refrain from observing, however, that the outcome of a wise weighing of those interests is by no means clear. The initial goal of the doctors and nurses who conducted cocaine-testing in this case was to refer pregnant drug addicts to treatment centers, and to prepare for necessary treatment of their possibly affected children. When the doctors and nurses agreed to the program providing test results to the police, they did so because (in addition to the fact that child abuse was required by law to be reported) they wanted to use the sanction of arrest as a strong incentive for their addicted patients to undertake drug-addiction treatment. And the police themselves used it for that benign purpose, as is shown by the fact that only 30 of 253 women testing positive for cocaine were ever arrested, and only 2 of those prosecuted. It would not be unreasonable to conclude that today's judgment, authorizing the assessment of damages against the county solicitor and individual doctors and nurses who participated in the program, proves once again that no good deed goes unpunished.

> "But as far as the Fourth Amendment is concerned: There was no unconsented search in this case. And if there was, it would have been validated by the special-needs doctrine. For these reasons, I respectfully dissent."

As you can see from the cases discussed in this chapter, the Supreme Court does get called upon to decide cases directly impacting our bodies and the type of medical care we receive. In the next chapter, we'll explore issues of discrimination and affirmative action.

The Least You Need to Know

- Since abortion was legalized with the Supreme Court decision in *Roe v. Wade*, numerous state laws have been passed to restrict access to abortion. In one recent case the Supreme Court struck down laws related to restricting partial-birth abortions.

- States can prevent doctors from helping you commit suicide, even if you are seriously or terminally ill.

- Clinics that provide marijuana for medical purposes can be charged with a felony in violation of the "Controlled Substances Act" even if they operate in a state in which medical marijuana is legal.

- Pregnant women cannot be tested for drugs without their consent or a valid search warrant.

Chapter **18**

Keeping Things Equal

In This Chapter

- ◆ Affirming admissions policies
- ◆ Denying policies by the numbers
- ◆ Determining states' ADA responsibilities
- ◆ Setting disability guidelines

Discrimination on the basis of disability is the most common type of equality case that makes it to the Supreme Court today. The passage of the Americans with Disabilities Act of 1990 (ADA) is the reason for the current influx of cases.

Another key equality issue, admissions policies at universities, faced new court scrutiny in 2003 as the Court announced a mixed decision on affirmative action. This was the Court's first major case revisiting the issue of affirmative action and college admissions since the landmark 1978 *Bakke* v. *Regents of the University of California*.

In this chapter, I'll review key recent cases related to affirmative action and disability rights.

Saying Yes to Affirmative Action, Sometimes

When the Supreme Court ruled in 2003 on affirmative action, it actually ruled on two cases. One involved the University of Michigan's law school affirmative action policy, which it upheld by a vote of 5 to 4—*Grutter* v. *Bollinger*. The other involved the University of Michigan's undergraduate affirmative action policy, which was struck down by a vote of 6 to 3—*Gratz* v. *Bollinger*.

These were the first major rulings on affirmative action involving university admissions since the landmark *Bakke* case. That decision involved the admissions policy at the University of California Medical School, which at the time reserved 16 out of its 100 seats for members of certain minority groups. Six separate decisions came out of that case and none of them got a majority. Four justices upheld the program on the grounds that the government can use race to remedy disadvantages caused by past racial prejudices. Four justices believed the admissions program should be struck down completely. Justice Powell was the swing vote. He wrote the opinion for the court that invalidated the University of California program, but left the door open for affirmative action programs provided their purpose is to "attain a diverse student body."

> **Supreme Sayings**
>
> The "nation's future depends upon leaders trained through wide exposure' to the ideas and mores of students as diverse as this Nation … [i]t is not an interest in simple ethnic diversity, in which a specified percentage of the student body is in effect guaranteed to be members of selected ethnic groups," that can justify using race. Rather, "[t]he diversity that furthers a compelling state interest encompasses a far broader array of qualifications and characteristics of which racial or ethnic origin is but a single though important element."
>
> —Former Supreme Court Justice Lewis Powell from the *Bakke* opinion

In both of the 2003 cases, the University argued its purpose was to attain a diverse student body. One program passed Supreme Court muster and the other did not. Let's look at each of these rulings and why the Court voted to allow one and not the other.

Constitutional Law School Admissions Policy—*Grutter* v. *Bollinger*

Barbara Grutter is a white woman who applied for admission to the University of Michigan law school in 1996 and was rejected. After investigating her rejection, she found that African Americans and other ethnic minority applicants who had lower overall admissions scores were accepted into the school in the same year.

The University of Michigan clearly states as part of its admissions policy that the highest possible score does not guarantee admission to the law school. Nor does a low score automatically disqualify an applicant. Instead, the admissions officials look beyond grades and test scores to other criteria that are considered important to the school's education objectives. These other variables include recommendations, quality of undergraduate institution, quality of applicant's essay, difficulty of undergraduate course selection, and other factors that help them to assess an "applicant's likely contributions to the intellectual and social life of the institution."

The university states its policy aspires to "achieve that diversity which has the potential to enrich everyone's education and thus make a law school class stronger than the sum of its parts." The policy did, however, reaffirm the Law School's longstanding commitment to "one particular type of diversity," that is, "racial and ethnic diversity with special preference to the inclusion of students from groups which have been historically discriminated against, like African-Americans, Hispanics and Native Americans, who without this commitment might not be represented in our student body in meaningful numbers."

Grutter believed this policy was illegal discrimination and filed suit against the university. Her suit was based on *Bakke*, which said that race and ethnicity could be taken into account, but quotas could not be used as part of an admissions policy. She believed the University of Michigan Law School affirmative action policy did use a quota system and therefore was unconstitutional.

The district court ruled in favor of Grutter, but the 6th Circuit Court of Appeals disagreed, so Grutter appealed to the Supreme Court. Since the *Bakke* decision was so convoluted and did not give universities a clear set of guidelines, the Supreme Court decided it was time to revisit the issue.

> ### Supreme Sayings
>
> "So why were universities, public and private, so happy about the decision? Part of the answer is that back in say, 1995, it looked as if an irresistibly powerful anti-affirmative-action wave might be sweeping the country. The decision provides what looks like a guarantee that affirmative action in admissions is now safe for another generation. Having it in writing—writing that has the force of law—is always a relief."
>
> —Nicholas Lehmann in writing an analysis for *The New York Times*

In 2003, Sandra Day O'Connor was the swing vote in support of the University of Michigan's Law School admissions policy. She said she hoped that one day affirmative action would no longer be needed in America, but believed it was still needed today.

The Court is still closely divided on the issue. It is another one of those decisions for which you need a roadmap. Justice O'Connor wrote the opinion for the Court and was joined by Breyer, Ginsburg, Souter, and Stevens. Scalia and Thomas also joined part of this decision. Ginsburg filed a concurring opinion and was joined by Breyer. Scalia filed an opinion that partially concurred, but also dissented to part of the opinion. Thomas also filed an opinion that concurred in part and dissented in part. Scalia and Thomas joined parts of each others opinions. Chief Justice Rehnquist filed a dissenting opinion, which was joined by Kennedy, Scalia, and Thomas. Kennedy filed another dissenting opinion. So while universities were given a clearer set of guidelines by O'Connor, you can see the Court is still strongly divided on this issue.

In her opinion, O'Connor wrote:

> "We have long recognized that, given the important purpose of public education and the expansive freedoms of speech and thought associated with the university environment, universities occupy a special niche in our constitutional tradition. ... In announcing the principle of student body diversity as a compelling state interest, Justice Powell invoked our cases recognizing a constitutional dimension, grounded in the First Amendment, of educational autonomy: 'The freedom of a university to make its own judgments as to education includes the selection of its student body.' From this premise, Justice Powell reasoned that by claiming 'the right to select those students who will contribute the most to the 'robust exchange of ideas,' a university 'seek[s] to achieve a goal that is of paramount importance in the fulfillment of its mission. ... Our conclusion that the Law School has a compelling interest in a diverse student body is informed by our view that attaining a diverse student body is at the heart of the Law School's proper institutional mission, and that 'good faith' on the part of a university is 'presumed' absent 'a showing to the contrary.'"

In addition to commenting on the importance of student body diversity, O'Connor also talked about the important role universities have in training future leaders:

> "In order to cultivate a set of leaders with legitimacy in the eyes of the citizenry, it is necessary that the path to leadership be visibly open to talented and qualified individuals of every race and ethnicity. All members of our heterogeneous society must have confidence in the openness and integrity of the educational institutions that provide this training. As we have recognized, law schools 'cannot be effective in isolation from the individuals and institutions with which the law interacts.' ... Access to legal education (and thus the legal profession) must be inclusive of talented and qualified individuals of every race and ethnicity, so that all members of our heterogeneous society may participate in the educational institutions that provide the training and education necessary to succeed in America."

In his dissent Justice Thomas strongly disagreed with these conclusions:

"It is uncontested that each year, the Law School admits a handful of blacks who would be admitted in the absence of racial discrimination ... Who can differentiate between those who belong and those who do not? The majority of blacks are admitted to the Law School because of discrimination, and because of this policy all are tarred as undeserving. This problem of stigma does not depend on determinacy as to whether those stigmatized are actually the 'beneficiaries' of racial discrimination. When blacks take positions in the highest places of government, industry, or academia, it is an open question today whether their skin color played a part in their advancement. The question itself is the stigma—because either racial discrimination did play a role, in which case the person may be deemed 'otherwise unqualified,' or it did not, in which case asking the question itself unfairly marks those blacks who would succeed without discrimination. Is this what the Court means by 'visibly open'?

> ### Living Laws
>
> Universities can use affirmative action policies that consider race as long as it is done qualitatively along with other considerations to achieve diversity in the student body. A purely quantitative evaluation, as the point system used in the undergraduate program at the University of Michigan discussed here, is a violation of the equal protection clause and cannot be used.

"Finally, the Court's disturbing reference to the importance of the country's law schools as training grounds meant to cultivate 'a set of leaders with legitimacy in the eyes of the citizenry,' through the use of racial discrimination deserves discussion. As noted earlier, the Court has soundly rejected the remedying of societal discrimination as a justification for governmental use of race ... For those who believe that every racial disproportionality in our society is caused by some kind of racial discrimination, there can be no distinction between remedying societal discrimination and erasing racial disproportionalities in the country's leadership caste. And if the lack of proportional racial representation among our leaders is not caused by societal discrimination, then 'fixing' it is even less of a pressing public necessity.

The Court's civics lesson presents yet another example of judicial selection of a theory of political representation based on skin color—an endeavor I have previously rejected .... The majority appears to believe that broader utopian goals justify the Law School's use of race, but '[t]he Equal Protection Clause commands the elimination of racial barriers, not their creation in order to satisfy our theory as to how society ought to be organized.'"

Unconstitutional Undergraduate Admissions Policy—*Gratz* v. *Bollinger*

Now that you understand what type of affirmative action policy is constitutional, let's briefly review the type of policy that the court ruled unconstitutional. Starting in 1995, the undergraduate program used a point system in which an applicant could score up to 150 points. Applicants that scored 100 to 150 were admitted, 90 to 99 were admitted or postponed, 75 to 89 were delayed or postponed and 74 and below were delayed or rejected.

Points were based on high school grade point average, standardized test scores, academic quality of an applicant's high school, strength or weakness of high school curriculum, in-state residency, alumni relationship, personal essay, and personal achievement or leadership. There was also a miscellaneous category that gave an applicant 20 points based upon membership in an underrepresented racial or ethnic minority group.

> **Just the Facts**
>
> Jennifer Gratz, a white female, applied for admission to the University of Michigan's College of Literature, Science, and the Arts (LSA) as a resident of Michigan in the fall of 1995. She was notified in January that a final decision on her application had been delayed until April. The University said that she was "well qualified," but "less competitive than the students who ha[d] been admitted on first review." In April she was rejected and instead enrolled at the University of Michigan at Dearborn. She graduated from there in the spring of 1999.

The university added one more layer to the process in 1999. Any applicant from an under-represented racial or ethic minority group that was awarded 20 points was flagged for additional review by an Admissions Review Committee (ARC) if the applicant proved to be academically able to succeed, had achieved a minimum selection index and possessed a quality or characteristic important to the University's composition of its freshman class. These included variables such as high class rank, unique life experiences, challenges, circumstances, interests or talents, socioeconomic disadvantage, and under-represented race, ethnicity, or geography. After reviewing "flagged" applications, the ARC determined whether to admit, defer, or deny each applicant.

The Supreme Court found that because the freshman admissions policy is not narrowly tailored to achieve diversity, it violates the equal protection clause. By automatically distributing 20 points, or one-fifth of the points needed to guarantee admission to every single "underrepresented minority" applicant just because of race, does not narrowly tailor the affirmative action policy to achieve educational diversity. This method does not provide individualized consideration as does the law school admissions policy, which the court upheld. The only consideration for the 20-point automatic distribution is the fact that the applicant is from an under-represented minority. The 20-point distribution has the effect of making "the factor of race … decisive" for virtually every minimally qualified under-represented minority applicant.

The additional flagging for individualized consideration, added in 1999, did not correct the problem, but instead emphasized the flaws of the University's system, the Court ruled. This individualized review is provided only after the points are automatically distributed, so it does not change the fact that the points "plus" are a decisive factor for virtually every minimally qualified under-represented minority applicant. The University claimed the volume of applications made it impractical for the type of individual review found constitutional under Grutter. The Court said the fact that an individualized review raised administrative challenges does not make the points system constitutional.

Chief Justice Rehnquist wrote the opinion for the 6 to 3 majority ruling and was joined by Justices Kennedy, O'Connor, Scalia, and Thomas. Justice Breyer concurred with Rehnquist in a separate opinion and also joined O'Connor in a concurring opinion that she wrote. Justice Stevens wrote a dissenting opinion and was joined by Justice Souter. Souter also wrote a dissenting opinion and was joined in part by Justice Ginsburg. Justice Ginsburg wrote another dissenting opinion, which was joined by Souter and Breyer in part.

Now let's move onto other forms of discrimination based on disability or age.

Which One Wins—States' Rights or ADA?

When it comes to monetary damages related to disabilities, the right of the states under the Eleventh Amendment to be immune from lawsuits takes precedence over *Title I of the Americans with Disabilities Act*, the Supreme Court ruled on February 21, 2001 in *University of Alabama* v. *Garrett*. Even though businesses can be sued if they don't make accommodations for the disabled, states are immune from monetary damages for the same reason.

Patricia Garrett was employed as the Director of Nursing, OB/Gyn/Neonatal Services, for the University of Alabama in Birmingham Hospital. In 1994, she was diagnosed with breast cancer and underwent a lumpectomy, radiation treatment, and chemotherapy. Her treatments required her to take substantial leave from work.

When she returned to work in July 1995, her supervisor told her she would have to give up her director position. Instead she was transferred to a lower-paying position as a nurse manager.

Garrett sued the state in district court seeking monetary damages based on the ADA. The district court ordered summary judgment because it did not believe the Congress had the right to take away the state's immunity to lawsuits based on the Eleventh Amendment. Garrett appealed the case to the 11th Circuit Court, which reversed the district court's ruling, so the state took the case to the Supreme Court.

The Supreme Court agreed with the district court and essentially said that there was not enough proof of a long history of state discrimination against the disabled to justify abrogating the state's claim to immunity, so states were given an immunity to being sued based on an ADA claim. In a 5 to 4 decision written by Chief Justice Rehnquist, who was joined by Justices Kennedy, O'Connor, Scalia and Thomas, the Court ruled:

Court Connotations

Title I of the Americans with Disabilities Act of 1990 (ADA) prohibits employers from "discriminat[ing] against a qualified individual with a disability because of th[at] disability ... in regard to ... terms, conditions, and privileges of employment." Employers must make reasonable accommodations for the employee with a disability.

"Congress made a general finding in the ADA that 'historically, society has tended to isolate and segregate individuals with disabilities, and, despite some improvements, such forms of discrimination against individuals with disabilities continue to be a serious and pervasive social problem.' ... The record assembled by Congress includes many instances to support such a finding. But the great majority of these incidents do not deal with the activities of States.

"Respondents in their brief cite half a dozen examples from the record that did involve States. A department head at the University of North Carolina refused to hire an applicant for the position of health administrator because he was blind; similarly, a student at a state university in South Dakota was denied an opportunity to practice teach because the dean at that time was convinced that blind people could not teach in public schools. A microfilmer at the Kansas Department of Transportation was fired because he had epilepsy; deaf workers at the University of Oklahoma were paid a lower salary than those who could hear. The Indiana State Personnel Office informed a woman with a concealed disability that she should not disclose it if she wished to obtain employment.

"Several of these incidents undoubtedly evidence an unwillingness on the part of state officials to make the sort of accommodations for the disabled required by the ADA ... these incidents taken together fall far short of even suggesting the pattern of unconstitutional discrimination on which legislation must be based."

Justice Breyer wrote the dissent and was joined by Justices Ginsburg, Souter, and Stevens. He found there was enough evidence collected by the Congress to justify mandating that the states comply with the ADA and lose their immunity from being sued. Breyer wrote:

> "The powerful evidence of discriminatory treatment throughout society in general, including discrimination by private persons and local governments, implicates state governments as well, for state agencies form part of that same larger society. There is no particular reason to believe that they are immune from the 'stereotypic assumptions' and pattern of 'purposeful unequal treatment' that Congress found prevalent ... there is no need to rest solely upon evidence of discrimination by local governments or general societal discrimination. There are roughly 300 examples of discrimination by state governments themselves in the legislative record ... I fail to see how this evidence 'fall[s] far short of even suggesting the pattern of unconstitutional discrimination on which legislation must be based.'"

> "The congressionally appointed task force collected numerous specific examples, provided by persons with disabilities themselves, of adverse, disparate treatment by state officials. They reveal, not what the Court describes as 'half a dozen' instances of discrimination, but hundreds of instances of adverse treatment at the hands of state officials—instances in which a person with a disability found it impossible to obtain a state job, to retain state employment, to use the public transportation that was readily available to others in order to get to work, or to obtain a public education, which is often a prerequisite to obtaining employment. State-imposed barriers also frequently made it difficult or impossible for people to vote, to enter a public building, to access important government services, such as calling for emergency assistance, and to find a place to live due to a pattern of irrational zoning decisions."

Even though the four-vote minority did believe there was enough evidence to justify Congress's decision to include the states under Title I of the ADA, the five-vote majority made it possible for states to avoid the sometimes costly accommodations businesses must provide, as well as risk getting sued.

Determining Who Is Disabled Under the ADA

Ever since the ADA was passed, the Supreme Court rulings have limited aspects of that law and the impact it has on both states and businesses. One such case is *Toyota Motor Mfg.* v. *Williams* decided on January 8, 2002.

Ella Williams developed carpal tunnel syndrome in her upper extremities. This condition involves painful muscle and tendon injuries that resulted from highly repetitive motions, such as would be required on a Toyota assembly line. Toyota reassigned Williams to other positions, which worked for three years, but then Toyota added some task that reawakened the pain of carpal tunnel syndrome. Williams and Toyota disagreed about what happened next, but ultimately Williams was fired.

The district court ruled that Williams was not disabled because carpal tunnel syndrome had not substantially limited any major life activity and said there was not evidence that Williams had a record of "substantially limiting impairment." The 6th Circuit Court reversed that decision because it found that Williams had demonstrated that her manual disability involved a class of manual activities that did affect her ability to perform tasks at work so some accommodation should have been made. The Supreme Court unanimously reversed the circuit court, finding that an impairment must be permanent or long-term.

Supreme Sayings

"This court seems determined to set a very strict test for deciding who is disabled. You are either not disabled enough to be covered by the ADA or you are too disabled to do the job. That is not what Congress intended. A worker in Williams' position is now faced with a Catch-22. At the same time they are trying to show how much the impairment affects their daily life, they are also trying to prove they are qualified for the job. By proving you're disabled, you can prove yourself out of a job."

—From the friend of the court brief submitted by the National Council on Disability

In writing the opinion of the Court, Justice O'Connor ruled:

"Given the large potential differences in the severity and duration of carpal tunnel syndrome, an individual's carpal tunnel syndrome diagnosis, on its own, does not indicate whether the individual has a disability within the meaning of the ADA."

Keeping things equal can be a difficult balance that frequently pits the Congress against the Court. Next we'll explore the issues of freedom guaranteed by the First Amendment.

The Least You Need to Know

- ◆ Universities can consider race as part of their admissions policies, but those policies must be based on qualitative rather than quantitative evaluations.

- ◆ States are immune from lawsuits seeking monetary damages based on the ADA.

- ◆ A person must be disabled permanently or long-term to recover damages based on the ADA.

Chapter **19**

Fighting for Freedoms

In This Chapter

- ◆ Phone tapping and the press
- ◆ Limiting child pornography on film
- ◆ Restricting pornography access in libraries
- ◆ When crosses can be burned

Guaranteeing everyone freedom of expression frequently means granting rights to people who protest in ways or speak about issues one finds offensive. Most cases involving the protection of First Amendment freedoms that make it all the way to the Supreme Court deal with issues a majority of the population find offensive.

The recent cases I'll review in this chapter are no different—cross burning and child pornography. These activities offend a large segment of the population, but the freedoms granted all persons under the First Amendment protect even those who offend.

Using Illegal Communication

Freedom of the press cases do not frequently make it to the Supreme Court today. The first major press-freedom case to be decided in a decade was *Bartnicki* v. *Vopper*, which was decided on May 21, 2001. The case involved an illegally intercepted communication that was used in press reports. The Supreme Court had to decide which took precedence—freedom of the press to use information or protection of the privacy of the persons' whose conversations were intercepted.

The case started when a Pennsylvania broadcaster named Frederick Vopper, known on the air as Fred Williams, was sued by two labor leaders for using an intercepted conversation in which it was suggested that union members go to the homes of school board members and "blow off their porches." This conversation took place between Gloria Bartnicki and Anthony Kane during heated labor negotiations between the teachers union and the school board. The conversation was intercepted by an unknown person and left in the mailbox of a local activist, Jack Yokum, who turned over a copy to Vopper.

Supreme Sayings

"In a democratic society privacy of communication is essential if citizens are to think and act creatively and constructively. Fear or suspicion that one's speech is being monitored by a stranger, even without the reality of such activity, can have a seriously inhibiting effect upon the willingness to voice critical and constructive ideas."

—From the report of the President's Commission on Law Enforcement and Administration of Justice, *The Challenge of Crime in a Free Society* in 1967

Bartnicki and Kane sued Vopper, Yokum, and the radio station that aired the conversation, asking the court to enforce federal and state laws against wiretapping and intercepting electronic communications by punishing the media personnel who used the intercepted conversation. The district court ruled in favor of Bartnicki and Kane, concluding that an individual who violates federal wiretapping laws by intentionally disclosing the contents of an electronic communication even though he or she knows or suspects the information was obtained illegally are not protected by the First Amendment.

The 3rd Circuit Court disagreed and found the wiretapping statutes invalid because they deterred significantly more speech than was necessary to protect private interests at stake. The Supreme Court in a 6 to 3 ruling found that the public's right to know takes precedence over privacy when publishing information vital to the public interest. Justice Stevens wrote the opinion for the Court and was joined by Justices Breyer, Ginsburg, Kennedy, O'Connor, and Souter. Chief Justice Rehnquist wrote the dissenting opinion and was joined by Scalia and Thomas. In writing the opinion for the Court, Stevens said:

"In considering that balance, we acknowledge that some intrusions on privacy are more offensive than others, and that the disclosure of the contents of a private conversation can be an even greater intrusion on privacy than the interception itself. As a result, there is a valid independent justification for prohibiting such disclosures by persons who lawfully obtained access to the contents of an illegally intercepted message, even if that prohibition does not play a significant role in preventing such interceptions from occurring in the first place.

"We need not decide whether that interest is strong enough [the related statute] … to disclosures of trade secrets or domestic gossip or other information of purely private concern … In other words, the outcome of the case does not turn on whether [this statute] may be enforced with respect to most violations of the statute without offending the First Amendment. The enforcement of that provision in this case, however, implicates the core purposes of the First Amendment because it imposes sanctions on the publication of truthful information of public concern.

"In this case, privacy concerns give way when balanced against the interest in publishing matters of public importance. As Warren and Brandeis stated in their classic law review article: 'The right of privacy does not prohibit any publication of matter which is of public or general interest.' … One of the costs associated with participation in public affairs is an attendant loss of privacy."

> ### Living Laws
>
> When balancing the issue of the public's need to know versus privacy, the Supreme Court believes the press freedoms need to be protected above the rights of privacy and that people involved in public affairs do lose some rights related to privacy.

In writing the dissent, Chief Justice Rehnquist disagreed and said:

"Technology now permits millions of important and confidential conversations to occur through a vast system of electronic networks. These advances, however, raise significant privacy concerns. We are placed in the uncomfortable position of not knowing who might have access to our personal and business e-mails, our medical and financial records, or our cordless and cellular telephone conversations. In an attempt to prevent some of the most egregious violations of privacy, the United States, the District of Columbia, and 40 States have enacted laws prohibiting the intentional interception and knowing disclosure of electronic communications. The Court holds that all of these statutes violate the First Amendment insofar as the illegally intercepted conversation touches upon a matter of 'public concern,' an amorphous concept that the Court does not even attempt to define. But the Court's decision diminishes, rather than enhances, the purposes of the First Amendment: chilling the speech of the millions of Americans who rely upon electronic technology to communicate each day."

Clearly this ruling will be revisited as new issues arise involving ever-evolving new technologies. Lee Levine who argued the case for Vopper said, "privacy is the battlefield for the future." We'll explore privacy issues more closely in the next chapter.

Protecting Pornography

Unless you are someone who either makes money from child pornography or enjoys viewing child pornography, you probably find protecting any aspect of that sleazy business abhorrent. In two recent cases, the Supreme Court tried to balance issues of free speech versus child protection laws. The first, decided on April 16, 2002, *Ashcroft* v. *Free Speech*, involved provisions of the *Child Pornography Prevention Act of 1996 (CPPA)*. The second, decided on June 23, 2003, *United States* v. *ALA*, involved provisions of the *Children's Internet Protection Act (CIPA)*, which was passed in December 2000.

> **Court Connotations** _____
>
> The **Child Pornography Prevention Act of 1996 (CPPA)** prohibits "any visual depiction, including any photograph, film, video, picture, or computer or computer-generated image" that appears to show a minor engaging in "sexually explicit conduct."
>
> The **Children's Internet Protection Act (CIPA)** addresses problems associated with the availability of Internet pornography in public libraries. In order for a library to receive federal assistance it must install software that blocks images that show obscenity or child pornography and prevent minors from accessing this material.

Both laws enjoy widespread public support, but raise freedom of speech questions. Let's look at the issues considered by the courts in these cases.

Child Pornography in Films

The Free Speech Coalition, which is an adult-entertainment trade association, filed suit in district court questioning two aspects of CPPA. The suit claimed that the terminology "appears to be" and "conveys the impression" used in defining pornography in the law was too overbroad and vague and could restrict the production and distribution of works that are protected by the First Amendment.

Congress, when it was considering the language for the law, was seeking to control new computer technology that allowed computer alteration of innocent images of real children or images created from scratch that simulated children posed in sexual acts. This law expanded existing bans on the more usual sort of child pornography. Congress believed that while no real children were harmed by the production of these computer-generated images, feeding the appetites of pedophiles or child molesters could harm real children.

The Free Speech Coalition said that while it opposes child pornography, the law could snare legitimate films and photographs produced by its members. The group did not challenge the part of the law that banned the use of identifiable children, but only the part that related to computer-altered sexual images.

A district court judge upheld the law, but the 9th Circuit Court overturned the lower court and ruled that the law did violate the Constitution's free speech guarantee. The U.S. government then appealed the decision to the Supreme Court in *Ashcroft* v. *Free Speech Coalition*. Both the Clinton and Bush administrations defended the law, saying it "helps to stamp out the market for child pornography involving real children."

In a 6 to 3 Supreme Court opinion announced on April 16, 2002, the Supreme Court ruled that the two phrases that the Free Speech Coalition questioned were overbroad and unconstitutional. The Court said that these aspects of the pornography definition in CPPA were inconsistent with previous Supreme Court rulings, which require a stricter definition of pornography. The Court also found that since the CPPA provisions related to computer-generated images prohibit speech that is not a crime and create no victims, they do not meet previously established precedents in that regard either.

Justice Kennedy wrote the Court's opinion and was joined by Justices Breyer, Ginsburg, Souter, and Stevens. Justice Thomas wrote a concurring opinion. Justice O'Connor wrote an opinion that concurred in part and dissented in part and was joined in part by Chief Justice Rehnquist and Justice Scalia. Chief Justice Rehnquist wrote the dissenting opinion and was joined by Scalia.

In writing for the majority, Justice Kennedy said:

> "As a general principle, the First Amendment bars the government from dictating what we see or read or speak or hear. The freedom of speech has its limits; it does not embrace certain categories of speech, including defamation, incitement, obscenity, and pornography produced with real children ... While these categories may be prohibited without violating the First Amendment, none of them includes the speech prohibited by the CPPA ... the CPPA is much more than a supplement to the existing federal prohibition on obscenity ... The materials

need not appeal to the prurient interest. Any depiction of sexually explicit activity, no matter how it is presented, is proscribed. The CPPA applies to a picture in a psychology manual, as well as a movie depicting the horrors of sexual abuse. It is not necessary, moreover, that the image be patently offensive. Pictures of what appear to be 17-year-olds engaging in sexually explicit activity do not in every case contravene community standards.

"The CPPA prohibits speech despite its serious literary, artistic, political, or scientific value. The statute proscribes the visual depiction of an idea—that of teenagers engaging in sexual activity—that is a fact of modern society and has been a theme in art and literature throughout the ages. Under the CPPA, images are prohibited so long as the persons appear to be under 18 years of age … This is higher than the legal age for marriage in many States, as well as the age at which persons may consent to sexual relations … It is, of course, undeniable that some youths engage in sexual activity before the legal age, either on their own inclination or because they are victims of sexual abuse.

"Both themes—teenage sexual activity and the sexual abuse of children—have inspired countless literary works. William Shakespeare created the most famous pair of teenage lovers, one of whom is just 13 years of age … In the drama, Shakespeare portrays the relationship as something splendid and innocent, but not juvenile. The work has inspired no less than 40 motion pictures, some of which suggest that the teenagers consummated their relationship … Shakespeare may not have written sexually explicit scenes for the Elizabethan audience, but were modern directors to adopt a less conventional approach, that fact alone would not compel the conclusion that the work was obscene.

"Contemporary movies pursue similar themes. Last year's Academy Awards featured the movie, Traffic, which was nominated for Best Picture … The film portrays a teenager, identified as a 16-year-old, who becomes addicted to drugs. The viewer sees the degradation of her addiction, which in the end leads her to a filthy room to trade sex for drugs. The year before, American Beauty won the Academy Award for Best Picture … In the course of the movie, a teenage girl engages in sexual relations with her teenage boyfriend, and another yields herself to the gratification of a middle-aged man. The film also contains a scene where, although the movie audience understands the act is not taking place, one character believes he is watching a teenage boy performing a sexual act on an older man.

"The Government cannot ban speech fit for adults simply because it may fall into the hands of children. The evil in question depends upon the actor's unlawful conduct, conduct defined as criminal quite apart from any link to the speech in question. This establishes that the speech ban is not narrowly drawn. The objective is to prohibit illegal conduct, but this restriction goes well beyond that interest by restricting the speech available to law-abiding adults."

In writing her dissent, Justice O'Connor writes:

"The Court concludes that the CPPA's ban on virtual-child pornography is over-broad. The basis for this holding is unclear. Although a content-based regulation may serve a compelling state interest, and be as narrowly tailored as possible while substantially serving that interest, the regulation may unintentionally ensnare speech that has serious literary, artistic, political, or scientific value or that does not threaten the harms sought to be combated by the Government. If so, litigants may challenge the regulation on its face as overbroad, but in doing so they bear the heavy burden of demonstrating that the regulation forbids a substantial amount of valuable or harmless speech … Respondents have not made such a demonstration. Respondents provide no examples of films or other materials that are wholly computer-generated and contain images that "appea[r] to be … of minors" engaging in indecent conduct, but that have serious value or do not facilitate child abuse. Their overbreadth challenge therefore fails.

"In sum, I would strike down the CPPA's ban on material that 'conveys the impression' that it contains actual-child pornography, but uphold the ban on pornographic depictions that 'appea[r] to be' of minors so long as it is not applied to youthful-adult pornography."

> **Living Laws**
>
> Computer-generated images that do not depict a recognizable child engaging in sexual acts are not a crime and do not have a victim. Therefore these images cannot be banned under the Child Pornography Protection Act. Freedom of speech takes precedent over prohibiting these images.

Preventing Children from Accessing Pornography on the Internet

Another major controversy that stirred a new law was access to pornography on the Internet. Congress, in an attempt to protect children from accessing this content at least at public libraries, passed a law that required libraries to install filtering programs if they wanted to receive federal funding that enables them to provide Internet services to the public. Funding comes from two sources: E-Rate discounts and Library Services and Technology Act (LSTA) grants.

Just the Facts

Libraries receive federal funding to enable them to offer Internet services through two programs— E-Rate and Library Services and Technology Act (LSTA) grants. E-Rate allows libraries to pay for Internet access at a discounted rate and LSTA grants provide money to buy equipment needed to start up or extend Internet access to patrons.

Living Laws

Libraries that receive federal funding for their Internet services to the public must filter their content to protect children from accessing pornography on the Internet.

The American Library Association (ALA) filed suit challenging Children's Internet Protection Act because it believed that access to information on the Internet was a First Amendment right and should not be controlled by the government. The ALA said that current technology is not advanced enough to achieve what the Congress intended when it passed the law because existing software would either "over-block" or "under-block" access to Internet information.

The ALA pointed out in its suit in district court that filtering is censorship and violates the First Amendment because patrons are not informed of what material is blocked. For example the ALA pointed out that filters block useful medical and political information that contains words such as "breast" (breast cancer information is blocked) and "dick" (information about politicians, such as "Congressman Dick Gephardt"). The same software often fails to block the pornographic images that the act intended to filter out. The ALA also quoted a test done by *Consumer Reports* in 2001 that found filters failed to block one of out five objectionable sites.

The district court agreed with the ALA because CIPA mandates a content-based restriction on access to a public forum for free speech. The district court said "strict scrutiny" is applied where a fundamental right, such as the First Amendment to free speech, is denied. In testing for "strict scrutiny," the district court found that there must be a compelling government interest to justify interference and the legislation must be narrowly tailored to further that interest. The court said that while government did have a compelling interest in preventing the dissemination of obscenity, child pornography and material harmful to minors, the requirement of filters does not meet the "narrowly tailored" test. The court ruled that Congress exceeded its power because "any library that complies with CIPA's conditions will necessarily violate the First Amendment."

The Supreme Court overturned the district court and found that since CIPA requires libraries to turn off filtering whenever an adult requests it, there really isn't a First Amendment problem. When questioned on this issue during oral arguments, the ALA said that some patrons would be embarrassed if forced to request that filtering be turned off.

In a 6 to 3 decision, the Court overturned the district court and found CIPA constitutional. Chief Justice Rehnquist wrote the opinion for the Court and was joined by Justices O'Connor, Scalia and Thomas. Justices Kennedy and Breyer wrote their own concurring opinions. Justice Stevens and Souter both wrote dissenting opinions and Justice Ginsburg joined Souter's dissent.

In writing the Supreme Court's opinion, Rehnquist said:

> "The E-Rate and LSTA programs were intended to help public libraries fulfill their traditional role of obtaining material of requisite and appropriate quality for educational and informational purposes. Congress may certainly insist that these 'public funds be spent for the purposes for which they were authorized.' Especially because public libraries have traditionally excluded pornographic material from their other collections, Congress could reasonably impose a parallel limitation on its Internet assistance programs."

In writing his dissent, Justice Souter had major questions regarding the rules relating to blocking and unblocking Internet content:

> "In any event, we are here to review a statute, and the unblocking provisions simply cannot be construed, even for constitutional avoidance purposes, to say that a library must unblock upon adult request, no conditions imposed and no questions asked. First, the statute says only that a library 'may' unblock, not that it must … In addition, it allows unblocking only for a 'bona fide research or other lawful purposes,' and if the 'lawful purposes' criterion means anything that would not subsume and render the 'bona fide research' criterion superfluous, it must impose some limit on eligibility for unblocking ….

> "We therefore have to take the statute on the understanding that adults will be denied access to a substantial amount of nonobscene material harmful to children but lawful for adult examination, and a substantial quantity of text and pictures harmful to no one. As the plurality concedes … this is the inevitable consequence of the indiscriminate behavior of current filtering mechanisms, which screen out material to an extent known only by the manufacturers of the blocking software …

> "We likewise have to examine the statute on the understanding that the restrictions on adult Internet access have no justification in the object of protecting children. Children could be restricted to blocked terminals, leaving other unblocked terminals in areas restricted to adults and screened from casual glances. And of course the statute could simply have provided for unblocking at adult request, with no questions asked. The statute could, in other words, have

protected children without blocking access for adults or subjecting adults to anything more than minimal inconvenience, just the way (the record shows) many librarians had been dealing with obscenity and indecency before imposition of the federal conditions. ... Instead, the Government's funding conditions engage in overkill to a degree illustrated by their refusal to trust even a library's staff with an unblocked terminal, one to which the adult public itself has no access.

"The question for me, then, is whether a local library could itself constitutionally impose these restrictions on the content otherwise available to an adult patron through an Internet connection, at a library terminal provided for public use. The answer is no. A library that chose to block an adult's Internet access to material harmful to children (and whatever else the undiscriminating filter might interrupt) would be imposing a content-based restriction on communication of material in the library's control that an adult could otherwise lawfully see. This would simply be censorship. True, the censorship would not necessarily extend to every adult, for an intending Internet user might convince a librarian that he was a true researcher or had a 'lawful purpose' to obtain everything the library's terminal could provide. But as to those who did not qualify for discretionary unblocking, the censorship would be complete and, like all censorship by an agency of the Government, presumptively invalid owing to strict scrutiny in implementing the Free Speech Clause of the First Amendment."

The next time you go to your public library, check out its Internet capabilities and see whether blocking software is in place and what you must do to have it turned off. Although you might agree that blocking children's access to Internet pornographic sites is a worthy goal, sometimes trying to attain that goal can deny access to sites that are not pornographic and do offer important information.

Allowing Cross Burning

No doubt when you think of cross burning, you think of people in white robes burning crosses to intimidate blacks. No matter how much you might disagree with someone who chooses to burn a cross, do they have a constitutional right to burn that cross?

You may think that issue was decided years ago, but a case that made it all the way to the Supreme Court involving the legality of a cross-burning law just made it to the Supreme Court in 2003. The Supreme Court ruled on April 7, 2003, that a state does have the right to ban cross burning carried out with the intent to intimidate, but it cannot write a law that stipulates that any cross burning is evidence of an intent to intimidate. The Supreme Court struck down a Virginia cross-burning law as unconstitutional because it was too broad.

The case started when Barry Black led a Ku Klux Klan (KKK) rally in Carroll County, Virginia on August 22, 1998. There were 25 to 30 people at the gathering that occurred on private property with the permission of the owner, who was in attendance. The sheriff of Carroll County learned about the KKK rally and observed the cross burning from the road.

After observing the burning, the sheriff asked who was in charge. Black admitted he led the rally, so he was charged with violating Virginia's ban on cross-burning. Black was convicted of violating a Virginia statute that makes it a felony "for any person … with the intent of intimidating any person or group … to burn … a cross on the property of another, a highway or other public place" and specifies that "any such burning … shall be *prima facie* evidence of an intent to intimidate a person or group."

> **Court Connotations**
>
> *Prima facie* in Latin means "first look." Prima facie evidence means that an act gives the appearance of guilt.

Black appealed the case to the Virginia Appeals Court at which his conviction was upheld, so he then appealed to the Virginia Supreme Court. The Virginia Supreme Court combined his appeal with the appeal of two others convicted on the same law in a separate incidence.

The second case started on May 2, 1998 when Richard Elliott and Jonathan O'Mara tried to burn a cross in the yard of James Jubilee, an African American who lived next door to Elliott and was married to a white woman. Elliott and O'Mara planted a cross on Jubilee's lawn to get back at him for firing a gun in his backyard. Elliott and O'Mara were not affiliated with the KKK. Their cross-burning attempt was not successful and when Jubilee got up the next morning he found a partially burned cross on his lawn.

Elliott and O'Mara were charged with a felony for violating Virginia's cross-burning law. O'Mara pleaded guilty, but reserved the right to challenge the law's constitutionality. Elliott pleaded not guilty, but was later convicted.

In a ruling that combined these two cases, the Virginia Supreme Court ruled that the cross-burning statute is unconstitutional and that the prima facie evidence provision renders the statute too broad because the "probability of prosecution under the statute chills the expression of protected speech." The state appealed the case to the U.S. Supreme Court.

Supreme Sayings

In questioning Virginia's state solicitor during oral arguments, the Justices seemed appalled at the state's position. Here are some examples:

"So, if you burn a cross on a hill outside the city, everyone in the city is intimidated?"

—Justice Kennedy

"So, even if a cross is burned in a desert somewhere, it's enough to sustain a conviction? Suppose he burned an O?"

—Justice Stevens

The U.S. Supreme Court did strike down the Virginia law. In writing the opinion for the Court, Justice O'Connor said:

> "The First Amendment permits Virginia to outlaw cross burnings done with the intent to intimidate because burning a cross is a particularly virulent form of intimidation. Instead of prohibiting all intimidating messages, Virginia may choose to regulate this subset of intimidating messages in light of cross burning's long and pernicious history as a signal of impending violence. Thus, just as a State may regulate only that obscenity which is the most obscene due to its prurient content, so too may a State choose to prohibit only those forms of intimidation that are most likely to inspire fear of bodily harm ... the prima facie provision strips away the very reason why a State may ban cross burning with the intent to intimidate. The prima facie evidence provision permits a jury to convict in every cross-burning case in which defendants exercise their constitutional right not to put on a defense. And even where a defendant like Black presents a defense, the prima facie evidence provision makes it more likely that the jury will find an intent to intimidate regardless of the particular facts of the case. The provision permits the Commonwealth to arrest, prosecute, and convict a person based solely on the fact of cross burning itself.

> "It is apparent that the provision as so interpreted 'would create an unacceptable risk of the suppression of ideas.' ... The act of burning a cross may mean that a person is engaging in constitutionally proscribable intimidation. But that same act may mean only that the person is engaged in core political speech. The prima facie evidence provision in this statute blurs the line between these two meanings of a burning cross. As interpreted by the jury instruction, the provision chills constitutionally protected political speech because of the possibility that a State will prosecute—and potentially convict—somebody engaging only in lawful political speech at the core of what the First Amendment is designed to protect."

Protecting freedom in the country does often mean that you must protect the right for someone to say or do something you strongly oppose and may even find offensive. You can see from these cases that protecting First Amendment rights can sometimes be in conflict with setting community norms.

In the next chapter, I'll review privacy laws, which as I have mentioned sometimes conflict with the public's right to know.

The Least You Need to Know

- The members of the press can use information collected through illegal wire-tapping provided they were not involved in the wiretapping.

- Computer-generated child pornography that does not clearly identify a child cannot be banned.

- Libraries that receive funds from the federal government for their Internet services must filter content for children.

- States can ban cross-burning, but the laws must not be too broad to overstep the bounds of free speech.

20

Protecting Our Privacy

In This Chapter

- ◆ Allowing media access to arrests
- ◆ Granting qualified immunity
- ◆ Testing politicians for drugs
- ◆ Balancing privacy with public's need to know about politicians

A person's right to privacy permeates many of the court cases that make it all the way to the Supreme Court. From issues involving the privacy of your bedroom to the privacy of school records, many court cases involve situations where exposure could hurt you or a family member for the rest of your lives.

As you read about cases throughout the book, you will see a privacy component in most of them. You may even be wondering whether you would have the courage to take a case all the way to the Supreme Court to challenge an issue, knowing that by doing so your case will become part of a very public record. In rare cases a pseudonym can be used if approved by the court, especially if there is a threat of physical harm or if intimate details are involved (such as Jane Roe in *Roe v. Wade*).

In this chapter, we'll focus on the types of cases where privacy and the government clash most often. These involve protections granted under the Fourth Amendment: "right of the people to be secure in their persons, houses, papers, and effects, against unreasonable searches and seizures." You may think protections relating to this amendment involve primarily criminal cases (which we'll explore in the next section) and they do, but in this chapter we'll concentrate on recent cases where the government abused its power and intruded on people's privacy.

Making Your House a Media Circus

In high profile cases, it's not unusual to see hordes of media waiting outside a house as a big name celebrity or well-known criminal is being arrested on a warrant. Usually by the time a warrant is issued for arrest in a case involving a well-known person, coverage already has been in the media for weeks. In these cases members of the media are probably already camped out at the person's house waiting for something to happen, or they've gotten a tip from a source inside the police department that an arrest is about to happen.

Most arrest warrants do not involve celebrities. More often they involve people you probably don't even know. Sometimes even though the person is not well known, the government wants to a make a public spectacle of the arrest to promote a certain type of crime fighting. If police take the press along to arrest someone, they could be charged with violating the privacy rights established by the Fourth Amendment. These rights were first clearly defined by the Supreme Court on May 24, 1999 in *Wilson* v. *Lane*, which involved a case where police officers invited media representatives into a private home while executing an arrest warrant.

The arrest in question was part of a major nationwide program called "Operation Gunsmoke" that involved both U.S. marshals and state and local policemen. One of the targets of this high profile operation was Dominic Wilson, son of Charles and Geraldine Wilson, whose arrest warrant indicated he had "violated his probation on previous felony charges of robbery, theft, and assault with intent to rob." His address in the official police files was the home of his parents in Rockville, Maryland.

Just the Facts _____

Operation Gunsmoke was a national fugitive apprehension program run by the attorney general of the United States in 1992. Its purpose was to arrest "armed individuals wanted on federal and/or state and local warrants for serious drug and other violent felonies." Ultimately the program resulted in over 3,000 arrests in 40 metropolitan areas.

In an attempt to get local publicity for the nationwide effort, police invited a reporter and photographer from the *Washington Post* to "ride along" during the early morning hours on April 16, 1992, to execute the Dominic Wilson warrants. Charles and Geraldine Wilson were still in bed when they heard the police enter the house. Some wake-up call!

Charles Wilson, dressed only in briefs, ran to his living room to investigate the noise and found five men in street clothes with guns. He angrily demanded an explanation, and according to police records repeatedly cursed at the officers. Since they believed him to be Dominic Wilson, they subdued him to the floor. Geraldine Wilson then entered the living room to investigate. She was in a nightgown and observed her husband being restrained by the armed officers.

After making a sweep of the house, the officers learned Dominic Wilson was not there and departed. The *Post* photographer took numerous photographs of the entire fiasco. The print reporter also observed the entire confrontation, but neither had any role in the actual execution of the arrest warrant. The *Post* never printed the photographs of the incident.

The Wilsons sued the law enforcement entities—U.S. Marshals Service and the Montgomery County Sheriff's Department—saying that by bringing members of the media to observe and record the attempted execution of the arrest warrant their Fourth Amendment rights had been violated.

The police defended themselves on the basis that they had a *qualified immunity* from being sued, which the district court denied. The 4th Circuit Court reversed the district court and ruled that the police did have a qualified immunity from being sued and did not even rule on the issue of the Fourth Amendment violation. The circuit court held that at the time of the search no court had found that police were violating Fourth Amendment rights by allowing media to "ride along" during police entry into a residence; therefore, it had not been clearly established that bringing media along on the execution of a warrant inside a home was a violation of constitutional rights.

> **Court Connotations**
>
> **Qualified immunity** protects government officials from being sued for liability on civil damages provided their conduct does not violate clearly established statutory or constitutional rights.

Circuit courts had ruled differently on this Fourth Amendment issue prior to this case making it to the Supreme Court, so the Court decided to take the case. In a unanimous ruling written by Chief Justice Rehnquist, the Court found that the Fourth Amendment rights of the homeowners had been violated. He wrote:

"Certainly the presence of reporters inside the home was not related to the objectives of the authorized intrusion. Respondents concede that the reporters did not engage in the execution of the warrant, and did not assist the police in their task. The reporters therefore were not present for any reason related to the justification for police entry into the home—the apprehension of Dominic Wilson.

"This is not a case in which the presence of the third parties directly aided in the execution of the warrant. Where the police enter a home under the authority of a warrant to search for stolen property, the presence of third parties for the purpose of identifying the stolen property has long been approved by this Court and our common-law tradition …

"Respondents argue that the presence of the *Washington Post* reporters in the Wilsons' home nonetheless served a number of legitimate law enforcement purposes … It may well be that media ride-alongs further the law enforcement objectives of the police in a general sense, but that is not the same as furthering the purposes of the search …

"Respondents next argue that the presence of third parties could serve the law enforcement purpose of publicizing the government's efforts to combat crime, and facilitate accurate reporting on law enforcement activities. There is certainly language in our opinions interpreting the First Amendment which points to the importance of "the press" in informing the general public about the administration of criminal justice … No one could gainsay the truth of these observations, or the importance of the First Amendment in protecting press freedom from abridgement by the government. But the Fourth Amendment also protects a very important right, and in the present case it is in terms of that right that the media ride-alongs must be judged.

"Surely the possibility of good public relations for the police is simply not enough, standing alone, to justify the ride-along intrusion into a private home. And even the need for accurate reporting on police issues in general bears no direct relation to the constitutional justification for the police intrusion into a home in order to execute a felony arrest warrant …

> **Living Laws**
>
> The police do violate your Fourth Amendment rights to privacy by bringing along the media to execute a warrant unless for some reason they are assisting with the execution of that warrant.

"The reasons advanced by respondents, taken in their entirety, fall short of justifying the presence of media inside a home. We hold that it is a violation of the Fourth Amendment for police to bring members of the media or other third parties into a home during the execution of a warrant when the presence of the third parties in the home was not in aid of the execution of the warrant."

The Court did grant the police officers qualified immunity from being sued for damages in this case because all but one of the justices believed the Fourth Amendment rights had not been clearly established by legal precedent. While the ruling regarding the Fourth Amendment rights was unanimous, Justice Stevens did dissent on the issue of qualified immunity. He believed there was clear precedent and the officers should have realized that it was a violation to bring along the press. Stevens wrote:

"In my view, however, the homeowner's right to protection against this type of trespass was clearly established long before April 16, 1992. My sincere respect for the competence of the typical member of the law enforcement profession precludes my assent to the suggestion that 'a reasonable officer could have believed that bringing members of the media into a home during the execution of an arrest warrant was lawful' … I therefore disagree with the Court's resolution of the conflict in the Circuits on the qualified immunity issue. The clarity of the constitutional rule, a federal statute, common-law decisions, and the testimony of the senior law enforcement officer all support my position that it has long been clearly established that officers may not bring third parties into private homes to witness the execution of a warrant … In its decision today the Court has not announced a new rule of constitutional law. Rather, it has refused to recognize an entirely unprecedented request for an exception to a well-established principle. Police action in the execution of a warrant must be strictly limited to the objectives of the authorized intrusion. That principle, like the broader protection provided by the Fourth Amendment itself, represents the confluence of two important sources: our English forefathers' traditional respect for the sanctity of the private home and the American colonists' hatred of the general warrant."

Whether or not your privacy was protected before this case may be in dispute, but one thing you can be sure of today is that if the police allow the media inside your home when executing a warrant, you do have the right to challenge that in court under the Fourth Amendment.

Testing Politicians for Drugs

Libertarians had their first win in the Supreme Court when they successfully sued to strike down a Georgia law that required all politicians be tested for drugs before being allowed on the ballot. The Supreme Court ruled this law unconstitutional on April 15, 1997.

Walker Chandler, who ran for lieutenant governor in Georgia in 1994, took and passed the required drug test, but filed suit questioning the validity of the law. The legal battle took three years to get to the Supreme Court. Chandler lost twice before making it to the Supreme Court, once in the district court and once in the 11th Circuit Court.

The Supreme Court finally agreed to hear his appeal on January 14, 1996. His argument was based on the Fourth Amendment's prohibition against "unreasonable" searches. Chandler believed there should be some limit to "suspicionless drug testing." The Supreme Court agreed with him voting 8 to 1 to declare Georgia's law unconstitutional.

Supreme Sayings

"[I]t is ... immaterial that the intrusion was in aid of law enforcement. Experience should teach us to be most on our guard to protect liberty when the Government's purposes are beneficent. Men born to freedom are naturally alert to repel invasion of their liberty by evil-minded rulers. The greatest dangers to liberty lurk in insidious encroachment by men of zeal, well-meaning but without understanding."

—Justice Louis Brandeis in *Olmstead* v. *United States* in 1928

Justice Ginsburg wrote the near unanimous decision for the Court, which was joined by all but Chief Justice Rehnquist, who dissented. In her opinion, she wrote:

> "By requiring candidates for public office to submit to drug testing, Georgia displays its commitment to the struggle against drug abuse. The suspicionless tests, according to respondents, signify that candidates, if elected, will be fit to serve their constituents free from the influence of illegal drugs. But Georgia asserts no evidence of a drug problem among the State's elected officials, those officials typically do not perform high risk, safety sensitive tasks, and the required certification immediately aids no interdiction effort. The need revealed, in short, is symbolic, not 'special,' as that term draws meaning from our case law ... where the risk to public safety is substantial and real, blanket suspicionless searches calibrated to the risk may rank as 'reasonable'—for example, searches now routine at airports and at entrances to courts and other official buildings ... But where, as in this case, public safety is not genuinely in jeopardy, the Fourth Amendment precludes the suspicionless search, no matter how conveniently arranged."

Chief Justice Rehnquist in his dissent called the near unanimous opinion a "strange holding," and wrote:

> "Under normal Fourth Amendment analysis, the individual's expectation of privacy is an important factor in the equation. But here, the Court perversely relies on the fact that a candidate for office *gives up* so much privacy—'[c]andidates for public office … are subject to relentless scrutiny—by their peers, the public and the press,' …—as a reason for *sustaining* a Fourth Amendment claim. The Court says, in effect, that the kind of drug test for candidates required by the Georgia law is unnecessary, because the scrutiny to which they are already subjected by reason of their candidacy will enable people to detect any drug use on their part … The privacy concerns ordinarily implicated by urinalysis drug testing are 'negligible,' … when the procedures used in collecting and analyzing the urine samples are set up 'to reduce the intrusiveness' of the process. Under the Georgia law, the candidate may produce the test specimen at his own doctor's office, which must be one of the least intrusive types of urinalysis drug tests conceivable. But although the Court concedes this, it nonetheless manages to count this factor against the State, because with this kind of test the person tested will have advance notice of its being given, and will therefore be able to abstain from drug use during the necessary period of time. But one may be sure that if the test were random—and therefore apt to ensnare more users—the Court would then fault it for its intrusiveness."

In both cases discussed in this chapter, suits were filed by people, who even though they were not charged with a crime, believed they were victims of an unreasonable invasion of their privacy in violation of their rights protected by the Fourth Amendment. In the next chapter, we'll explore the role the Fourth Amendment plays when evidence is being collected for the purpose of proving criminal activity.

The Least You Need to Know

- ◆ The police cannot invite media to join them inside a home when executing a warrant unless the media has a specific role in the execution of that warrant.

- ◆ You do have the right to sue government officials if they allow the media to enter your house and invade your privacy during the execution of a warrant.

- ◆ Politicians cannot be subjected to suspicionless drug testing unless there is clear proof of a drug problem among politicians.

Part 6

Dealing with Criminals

Sometimes you hear about a case that is thrown out of court on a technicality and the criminals are let go without punishment for their crimes. In this part, we'll discover the rules that police officers must follow to collect evidence and arrest people legally so a case doesn't get thrown out. Then we'll review cases that set the rules for the death penalty and other types of punishments.

Your honor, I'm not sure making my client sit in the corner for five years is such a good idea...

Chapter 21

Collecting Evidence

In This Chapter

◆ Searching the car after speeding

◆ Entering without knocking

◆ Seeking marijuana with thermal devices

◆ Getting searched as a bus passenger

Police must follow strict rules for collecting evidence in order to be certain not to overstep the bounds of a person's Fourth Amendment rights. Many recent challenges to evidence-collection methods derive from search and seizure techniques police used as part of the war on drugs.

Most commonly these questions arose when police were doing checks of all cars or on buses for illegal contraband, weapons, or drugs. Do you know when you are allowed to refuse a search and what rights you give up once agreeing to a search? I'll answer those questions in this chapter using some recent court cases.

Searching Your Car When You're Stopped for Speeding

Many of us have been stopped for speeding at least once in our lives. Do you know that if you are stopped for speeding and an officer asks to search your car, you have the right to say no? Most people don't.

Robert Robinette, who was stopped for speeding in 1992 on Interstate 70 in Ohio, did not know he had the right to refuse a search. After Sheriff's Deputy Roger Newsome saw he had no prior violations, he gave Robinette a verbal warning about speeding and asked if he was carrying any illegal contraband in the car. Robinette said no and then consented to a request by Newsome to search the car.

Newsome discovered a small amount of marijuana and one pill of the illegal drug "Ecstasy" in the car. Robinette was arrested and charged with possession of illegal drugs. The state trial court denied Robinette's request to suppress the drug evidence because he argued the search was not truly voluntary. He was convicted on the drug charge and appealed to the Ohio Supreme Court.

In 1995 the Ohio Supreme Court overturned the conviction, ruling that a driver's consent to a search is invalid unless the individual is informed that they are free to refuse the search and leave before consent to search is requested. The Ohio court said motorists must know when they are no longer obligated to cooperate with the police, so police cannot "turn a routine traffic stop into a fishing expedition for unrelated criminal activity."

> **Living Laws**
>
> When stopped for a speeding violation, you do have the right to refuse to allow your car to be searched for other reasons. You must know about that right. A police officer is not required to warn you of the right before asking for permission to search.

The state appealed the Ohio Supreme Court decision to the United States Supreme Court. The United States Supreme Court overturned the Ohio Supreme Court by a vote of 7 to 2 in a decision announced November 18, 1996, finding that evidence collected during the time Robinette was stopped for speeding could be used even if he wasn't told he was "free to go." The Court said that by granting permission to search the vehicle, Robinette had voluntary agreed to the search, so anything found during that search could be used against him.

Chief Justice Rehnquist wrote the opinion of the Court and was joined by Breyer, Kennedy, O'Connor, Scalia, Souter, and Thomas. Justice Ginsburg dissented and was joined by Stevens. In his opinion for the Court, Rehnquist wrote:

> "We have previously rejected a *per se* rule very similar to that adopted by the Supreme Court of Ohio in determining the validity of a consent to search.

In *Schneckloth* v. *Bustamonte* (1973), it was argued that such a consent could not be valid unless the defendant knew that he had a right to refuse the request. We rejected this argument: 'While knowledge of the right to refuse consent is one factor to be taken into account, the government need not establish such knowledge as the *sine qua non* of an effective consent' ... And just as it 'would be thoroughly impractical to impose on the normal consent search the detailed requirements of an effective warning,' ... so too would it be unrealistic to require police officers to always inform detainees that they are free to go before a consent to search may be deemed voluntary.

"The Fourth Amendment test for a valid consent to search is that the consent be voluntary, and '[v]oluntariness is a question of fact to be determined from all the circumstances.' ... The Supreme Court of Ohio having held otherwise, its judgment is reversed, and the case is remanded for further proceedings not inconsistent with this opinion."

Court Connotations

Per se is Latin for "by itself."

Sine qua non is Latin for "without which it could."

Justice Ginsburg disagreed and filed a dissent, which was joined by Justice Stevens. In her dissent, Ginsburg wrote:

"From their unique vantage point, Ohio's courts observed that traffic stops in the State were regularly giving way to contraband searches, characterized as consensual, even when officers had no reason to suspect illegal activity. One Ohio appellate court noted: '[H]undreds, and perhaps thousands of Ohio citizens are being routinely delayed in their travels and asked to relinquish to uniformed police officers their right to privacy in their automobiles and luggage, sometimes for no better reason than to provide an officer the opportunity to "practice" his drug interdiction technique' ...

"Against this background, the Ohio Supreme Court determined, and announced in Robinette's case, that the federal and state constitutional rights of Ohio citizens to be secure in their persons and property called for the protection of a clear-cut instruction to the State's police officers: An officer wishing to engage in consensual interrogation of a motorist at the conclusion of a traffic stop must first tell the motorist that he or she is free to go.

"The transition between detention and a consensual exchange can be so seamless that the untrained eye may not notice that it has occurred ....

"Most people believe that they are validly in a police officer's custody as long as the officer continues to interrogate them. The police officer retains the upper hand and the accouterments of authority. That the officer lacks legal license to continue to detain them is unknown to most citizens, and a reasonable person would not feel free to walk away as the officer continues to address him …

"While the legality of consensual encounters between police and citizens should be preserved, we do not believe that this legality should be used by police officers to turn a routine traffic stop into a fishing expedition for unrelated criminal activity. The Fourth Amendment to the federal Constitution and Section 14, Article I of the Ohio Constitution exist to protect citizens against such an unreasonable interference with their liberty."

Based on this ruling, police can ask to search your car before letting you know you do have the right to go.

Using the Right Not to Knock

Our next case deals with your rights regarding entry to your property without knocking. In a 1995 case, *Wilson* v. *Arkansas*, the Supreme Court ruled that the Fourth Amendment does require police officers to knock before entering your home and identify themselves before attempting forcible entry, but also ruled that the "flexible requirement of reasonableness should not be read to mandate a rigid rule of announcement that ignores countervailing law enforcement interests." The Supreme Court left it to the lower courts to determine the "circumstances under which an unannounced entry is reasonable under the Fourth Amendment."

One such test case for determining acceptable circumstances on the "no knock" law involved Steiney Richards, who was staying in a hotel in Madison, Wisconsin on December 31, 1991, when police executed a warrant in a drug felony investigation. While the judge had signed the warrant to allow police to search Richards' hotel room for drugs and related paraphernalia, he did not give police the right to enter without knocking and specifically deleted those portions of the warrant.

When police knocked on Richards hotel room door at 3:40 A.M., the lead officer was dressed as a maintenance man and stated he was from maintenance. With him were several plainclothes officers and at least one man in uniform. Richards cracked open the door, but left the chain attached. When he saw the officer in uniform, he quickly slammed the door. The officers waited a few seconds then starting kicking and ramming the door to gain entry to the locked room.

At trial, the officers testified they had identified themselves as police while they were kicking in the door. When they finally did break into the room, Richards tried to escape through the window and was caught. In the room they found cash and cocaine hidden in plastic bags above the bathroom ceiling tiles.

Richards tried to have the evidence that was collected in his hotel room suppressed at trial on the grounds that the officers failed to knock and announce their presence prior to forcing entry into the room. The trial court denied the motion and concluded the officers acted reasonably because he knew they were police officers and, if they hadn't acted the way they did, Richards might have tried to destroy evidence or escape. The judge emphasized the easily disposable nature of drug evidence in ruling in favor of the police.

Richards then appealed to the Wisconsin Supreme Court, which affirmed the lower court position. In reaching this conclusion, the Wisconsin court found it reasonable—after considering criminal conduct surveys, newspaper articles, and other judicial opinions—to assume that all felony drug crimes will involve "an extremely high risk of serious if not deadly injury to the police as well as the potential for the disposal of drugs by the occupants prior to entry by the police." Therefore, the court concluded the possibility of a no knock entry exists with all felony drug cases. The Wisconsin Supreme Court also found that the violation of privacy that occurs when officers who have a search warrant forcibly enter a residence without first announcing their presence is minimal, given that the residents would ultimately be without authority to refuse the police entry.

Richards then had only one option left—appeal the case all the way to the United States Supreme Court, which he did. The case was argued on March 24, 1997. The United States Supreme Court did not take long to issue a unanimous ruling on April 28, 1997, affirming the lower courts. Justice Stevens wrote the opinion for the court and said:

> "In order to justify a 'no knock' entry, the police must have a reasonable suspicion that knocking and announcing their presence, under the particular

circumstances, would be dangerous or futile, or that it would inhibit the effective investigation of the crime by, for example, allowing the destruction of evidence. This standard—as opposed to a probable cause requirement—strikes the appropriate balance between the legitimate law enforcement concerns at issue in the execution of search warrants and the individual privacy interests affected by no knock entries …

"Although we reject the Wisconsin court's blanket exception to the knock and announce requirement, we conclude that the officers' no knock entry into Richards' hotel room did not violate the Fourth Amendment. We agree with the trial court, and with Justice Abrahamson, that the circumstances in this case show that the officers had a reasonable suspicion that Richards might destroy evidence if given further opportunity to do so."

So, while the United States Supreme Court is not ready to give a blanket exception for "no knock" entry for search warrants involving drug charges, the Court did hold that in circumstances when police have a good reason to suspect that announcing their presence and intentions may be dangerous, futile, or result in destruction of evidence, a "no knock" entry is justified. The Court also said that Richards' action to immediately shut the door after seeing the officers outside gave police sufficient justification for breaking into this room, especially considering the disposable nature of the drugs.

Finding Marijuana with Thermal-Imaging Devices

A much more controversial drug case ruling decided by a 5 to 4 split on February 20, 2001, was *Kyllo* v. *United States*. The controversy surrounded the use of a thermal-imaging device to scan a residence for heat emissions.

Just the Facts

Federal agent William Elliot used a device that is widely available to the general public—an Agema Thermovision 210. Thermal-imaging devices detect infrared radiation, which is emitted by almost all objects, but is not visible to the naked eye.

Federal agent William Elliot suspected Danny Kyllo was growing marijuana in his home. Many people growing marijuana use high intensity heat generating lamps to facilitate its growth. Elliot parked his car across from Kyllo's home and aimed a thermal imager at the house to see if the heat emanating from Kyllo's home was consistent with readings that would be expected if these high intensity lamps were being used.

Elliot conducted the scan at 3:20 A.M. and took just a few minutes to find out that the garage roof and one wall of the house were hotter than the rest of the house as well as the houses of his neighbors.

Using this information, as well as the information from an informant and Kyllo's subpoenaed utility, Elliot got a search warrant to search Kyllo's home. The search revealed over 100 marijuana plants under the cultivation of high-intensity lamps as the imager showed. Kyllo tried to suppress the evidence, which was denied by the district court. Kyllo entered a conditional guilty plea and appealed his case to the 9th Circuit Court.

The 9th Circuit Court ruled that the district court should hold a hearing on whether the use of the thermal imager was intrusive and violated Kyllo's Fourth Amendment rights. The district court found the imager was non-intrusive, gave a crude visual image of heat being radiated from the outside of the house, did not show any people or activity in the house, and could not penetrate the walls or windows. Therefore no intimate details had been revealed by the scan. The 9th Circuit Court affirmed that Kyllo's rights had not been denied because of an unconstitutional search and seizure.

Kyllo then appealed the case to the United States Supreme Court. In a 5 to 4 decision, the Supreme Court found that to "explore the details of the home that would previously have been unknowable without physical intrusion, the surveillance is a 'search' and is presumptively unreasonable without a warrant." Justice Scalia wrote the opinion for the Court and was joined by Breyer, Ginsburg, Souter and Thomas. Justice Stevens dissented and was joined by Rehnquist, Kennedy, and O'Connor.

> **Living Laws**
>
> Police cannot use an electronic device that would explore the details of your home without first getting a search warrant.

In writing the opinion for the court, Justice Scalia said:

> "The present case involves officers on a public street engaged in more than naked-eye surveillance of a home. We have previously reserved judgment as to how much technological enhancement of ordinary perception from such a vantage point, if any, is too much. While we upheld enhanced aerial photography of an industrial complex in *Dow Chemical*, we noted that we found 'it important that this is *not* an area immediately adjacent to a private home, where privacy expectations are most heightened.' ...

> "We have said that the Fourth Amendment draws 'a firm line at the entrance to the house' ... That line, we think, must be not only firm but also bright—which requires clear specification of those methods of surveillance that require a warrant. While it is certainly possible to conclude from the videotape of the thermal imaging that occurred in this case that no 'significant' compromise of the homeowner's privacy has occurred, we must take the long view, from the original meaning of the Fourth Amendment forward ...

"Where, as here, the Government uses a device that is not in general public use, to explore details of the home that would previously have been unknowable without physical intrusion, the surveillance is a 'search' and is presumptively unreasonable without a warrant.

"Since we hold the Thermovision imaging to have been an unlawful search, it will remain for the district court to determine whether, without the evidence it provided, the search warrant issued in this case was supported by probable cause—and if not, whether there is any other basis for supporting admission of the evidence that the search pursuant to the warrant produced."

The case was sent back to the district court for a ruling on whether the other information used to attain the search warrant was sufficient to try Kyllo. Justice Paul Stevens dissented from this ruling and was joined by Chief Justice Rehnquist, Kennedy and O'Connor. In his dissent, Stevens said:

"Thus, the notion that heat emissions from the outside of a dwelling is a private matter implicating the protections of the Fourth Amendment … is not only unprecedented but also quite difficult to take seriously. Heat waves, like aromas that are generated in a kitchen, or in a laboratory or opium den, enter the public domain if and when they leave a building. A subjective expectation that they would remain private is not only implausible but also surely not 'one that society is prepared to recognize as "reasonable"…'

"To be sure, the homeowner has a reasonable expectation of privacy concerning what takes place within the home, and the Fourth Amendment's protection against physical invasions of the home should apply to their functional equivalent. But the equipment in this case did not penetrate the walls of petitioner's home, and while it did pick up 'details of the home' that were exposed to the public … it did not obtain 'any information regarding the *interior* of the home' … In the Court's own words, based on what the thermal imager 'showed' regarding the outside of petitioner's home, the officers 'concluded' that petitioner was engaging in illegal activity inside the home … It would be quite absurd to characterize their thought processes as 'searches,' regardless of whether they inferred (rightly) that petitioner was growing marijuana in his house, or (wrongly) that 'the lady of the house [was taking] her daily sauna and bath' … In either case, the only conclusions the officers reached concerning the interior of the home were at least as indirect as those that might have been inferred from the contents of discarded garbage, … or, as in this case, subpoenaed utility records … For the first time in its history, the Court assumes that an inference can amount to a Fourth Amendment violation …

"Notwithstanding the implications of today's decision, there is a strong public interest in avoiding constitutional litigation over the monitoring of emissions from homes, and over the inferences drawn from such monitoring. Just as 'the police cannot reasonably be expected to avert their eyes from evidence of criminal activity that could have been observed by any member of the public' ... so too public officials should not have to avert their senses or their equipment from detecting emissions in the public domain such as excessive heat, traces of smoke, suspicious odors, odorless gases, airborne particulates, or radioactive emissions, any of which could identify hazards to the community. In my judgment, monitoring such emissions with 'sense-enhancing technology' ... and drawing useful conclusions from such monitoring, is an entirely reasonable public service."

At least for now, use of new technology to scan your home is not constitutional, but given the closeness of this ruling this could change in a future Court.

Getting Searched on a Bus

Christopher Drayton and Clifton Brown were traveling on a Greyhound bus, which was stopped and boarded in Tallahassee, Florida as part of a routine drug and weapons search effort. Three officers entered the bus. One officer stationed himself at the front, another went to the back and the third questioned the passengers. Officers explained they were looking for drugs and weapons. The passengers were never informed that they had the right *not* to cooperate.

When the officer asked Drayton and Brown whether they were carrying drugs or weapons, they answered no. The officer asked permission to search their bags and their person. The officer testified that he was suspicious of the pair because they were wearing heavy jackets and baggy pants even though the weather was warm, which in his experience indicated possible drug traffickers because they often wore baggy clothing to conceal weapons or narcotics. During a pat-down search the officer found cocaine taped to their legs. Drayton and Brown were charged with federal drug crimes.

At trial, their attorneys asked that the searches be declared invalid because their consent to the search was coercive and therefore not voluntary. The district court disagreed and denied the motion. The 11th Circuit Court reversed the lower court, holding that bus passengers do not

> **Living Laws**
>
> If you are a passenger on a bus and the bus is stopped as part of a routine check, you do have the right not to cooperate with the police if they ask to search you or your bags. You must know about that right because police are not required to tell you.

feel free to disregard officers' requests to search unless they get some indication that consent may be refused.

The U.S. government then appealed the case to the Supreme Court to get a definitive ruling on whether police conducting random searches must advise bus passengers they have the right not to cooperate. The Supreme Court ruled 6 to 3 that the Fourth Amendment does not require police officers to advise bus passengers of their right not to cooperate and refuse consent to be searched.

Justice Kennedy wrote the opinion for the Court and was joined by Chief Justice Rehnquist and Justices Breyer, O'Connor, Scalia, and Thomas. Justice Souter dissented and was joined by Justices Ginsburg and Stevens. In writing the opinion for the Court, Justice Kennedy said:

> "… we conclude that the police did not seize respondents when they boarded the bus and began questioning passengers. The officers gave the passengers no reason to believe that they were required to answer the officers' questions. When Officer Lang approached respondents, he did not brandish a weapon or make any intimidating movements. He left the aisle free so that respondents could exit. He spoke to passengers one by one and in a polite, quiet voice. Nothing he said would suggest to a reasonable person that he or she was barred from leaving the bus or otherwise terminating the encounter … It is beyond question that had this encounter occurred on the street, it would be constitutional. The fact that an encounter takes place on a bus does not on its own transform standard police questioning of citizens into an illegal seizure … Indeed, because many fellow passengers are present to witness officers' conduct, a reasonable person may feel even more secure in his or her decision not to cooperate with police on a bus than in other circumstances …

> "In a society based on law, the concept of agreement and consent should be given a weight and dignity of its own. Police officers act in full accord with the law when they ask citizens for consent. It reinforces the rule of law for the citizen to advise the police of his or her wishes and for the police to act in reliance on that understanding. When this exchange takes place, it dispels inferences of coercion."

In writing his dissent, Justice Souter questioned whether this was a suspicionless search and therefore protected under the Fourth Amendment:

> "The issue we took to review is whether the police's examination of the bus passengers, including respondents, amounted to a suspicionless seizure under the Fourth Amendment. If it did, any consent to search was plainly invalid as a product of the illegal seizure … It is very hard to imagine that either Brown or

Drayton would have believed that he stood to lose nothing if he refused to cooperate with the police, or that he had any free choice to ignore the police altogether. No reasonable passenger could have believed that, only an uncomprehending one. It is neither here nor there that the interdiction was conducted by three officers, not one, as a safety precaution … The fact was that there were three, and when Brown and Drayton were called upon to respond, each one was presumably conscious of an officer in front watching, one at his side questioning him, and one behind for cover, in case he became unruly, perhaps, or 'cooperation' was not forthcoming. The situation is much like the one in the alley, with civilians in close quarters, unable to move effectively, being told their cooperation is expected. While I am not prepared to say that no bus interrogation and search can pass the *Bostick* test without a warning that passengers are free to say no, the facts here surely required more from the officers than a quiet tone of voice. A police officer who is certain to get his way has no need to shout."

As you can see, searches and seizures to collect evidence must be done by carefully following rules or the evidence cannot be used at trial. It is as important for you to understand the rules as the police. You need to know when you must cooperate and when you can refuse to cooperate with police to protect your own Fourth Amendment rights. In the next chapter, we will look at rules regarding arrests.

> **Just the Facts**
>
> The **Bostick** test was established in 1991 in the landmark case *Florida* v. *Bostick*, which determined that police questioning bus passengers was not a per se seizure. The issue of seizure is to be resolved instead based on the individual circumstances. A reasonable passenger must feel "free to decline the officers' requests or otherwise terminate the encounter" to pass the Bostick test.

The Least You Need to Know

- If you are stopped for speeding, you can refuse to allow a search of your car. Police do not have to tell you about that right.

- Police can execute a search warrant and enter your home without knocking if they have good reason to suspect announcing their presence could be dangerous, futile or result in evidence destruction.

- High-tech detection devices cannot be used to scan your house (essentially conducting a search) without a search warrant.

- If you are riding on a bus that is stopped for a routine search, you do have the right to refuse the search, but police do not have to tell you about that right.

Chapter 22

Arresting Rules

In This Chapter

- Reaffirming Miranda
- Striking down part of the crime bill
- Forcing medication
- Arresting illegally

When arresting people and getting them ready to stand trial, police must carefully follow rules set by Court precedent or the people arrested could be freed on a technicality—even if they are guilty. You've probably heard police read Miranda rights on many of the cop shows on television or in the movies. Reading those rights at the proper time is critical if police hope to use whatever is said when the case later goes to trial.

In addition to the 2000 landmark case upholding Miranda, I'll review rules related to forcing medication to make someone competent to stand trial, and those related to making a legal arrest so any confession obtained can be used at trial.

Upholding Miranda

When the Supreme Court decided to take the case *Dickerson* v. *United States*, many thought that Chief Justice Rehnquist would finally get his chance to overturn the 1966 case *Miranda* v. *Arizona*. The key question to be decided in *Dickerson* was whether Section 3501 of the Omnibus Crime Control Act of 1968, which Congress passed to overrule Miranda, should stand.

Just the Facts

In 1968, outraged by the Miranda ruling, Congress tried to overrule the ruling by passing the Omnibus Crime Control Act of 1968, which included a provision in Section 3501 to allow a confession—if given voluntarily—before Miranda rights are read. Even though this was written into the law, the provision was ignored by law enforcement people because they believed the Supreme Court Miranda ruling to be paramount.

Rehnquist, as an official in the Justice Department in the 1970s, was a vocal opponent of Miranda. Most expected he would use *Dickerson* to finally overturn the 1966 precedent set by the Supreme Court. In a surprise to most court observers, he not only voted to affirm Miranda rights, he wrote the opinion in support of them.

Now let's look at the case that netted this surprising result. Charles Dickerson's car, an Oldsmobile Ciera, was seen by eyewitnesses in January 1997 at the scene of a bank robbery that netted $876. When first questioned by FBI agents, Dickerson said he was in the vicinity of the bank at the time of the robbery, but was not involved. In a second statement he said that a relative named "Jimmy" may have robbed the bank while hitching a ride with him. The point of contention that took this case all the way to the Supreme Court was whether he was read his rights before the second statement was made.

Court Connotations

An **interlocutory appeal** is one that asks an appellate court to decide a legal issue that cannot be resolved on the facts of the case, but whose resolution is essential to a final decision in the case. This type of appeal prevents a trial from going forward until the appeal process is completed.

Dickerson was indicted for bank robbery, conspiracy to commit bank robbery and using a firearm in the course of committing a crime of violence. Before being tried, Dickerson's attorney filed a motion to suppress the confession on the grounds that he had not received Miranda warnings before being interrogated.

The district court agreed and granted the motion to suppress his confession. The government appealed this ruling to the 4th Circuit Court as an *interlocutory appeal*.

The 4th Circuit Court reversed the district court's suppression order. While it agreed Dickerson had not received his Miranda warnings, the circuit court invoked Section 3501 of the Omnibus Crime Control Act of 1968, which it said made Dickerson's voluntary confession admissible. The circuit court decided that Miranda was not a constitutional holding and therefore Congress could by statute have the final word on the question of admissibility.

Interestingly, neither Dickerson's legal team nor the government focused on the 1968 crime bill in arguing their appeals cases. The issue was raised in a friend-of-the-court brief submitted by the conservative Washington Legal Foundation. Experts writing about the case said courts normally base their rulings on what both sides argue in court or mention in later filings. In this case the 4th Circuit Court looked outside of this basic information to make its ruling.

In a 7 to 2 decision, the Supreme Court made it clear to the circuit court they had overstepped their bounds and upheld the district court's decision to suppress the confession. Chief Justice Rehnquist wrote the decision and was joined by Justices Breyer, Ginsburg, Kennedy, O'Connor, Souter, and Stevens. Justice Scalia filed a dissenting opinion and was joined by Justice Thomas. In writing the Court's opinion, Rehnquist said:

> "In *Miranda* v. *Arizona* … we held that certain warnings must be given before a suspect's statement made during custodial interrogation could be admitted in evidence. In the wake of that decision, Congress enacted [the Omnibus Crime bill with Section 3501] which in essence laid down a rule that the admissibility of such statements should turn only on whether or not they were voluntarily made. We hold that *Miranda*, being a constitutional decision of this Court, may not be in effect overruled by an Act of Congress, and we decline to overrule *Miranda* ourselves. We therefore hold that *Miranda* and its progeny in this Court govern the admissibility of statements made during custodial interrogation in both state and federal courts."

Living Laws

The requirement that you must receive a *Miranda* warning still stands. Police must warn you that you have the right to remain silent and that you have the right to have an attorney present during questioning if they want to use any confession they obtain during questioning as evidence.

Justice Scalia believes the Supreme Court went too far in its ruling. In his dissent, he wrote:

> "Those to whom judicial decisions are an unconnected series of judgments that produce either favored or disfavored results will doubtless greet today's decision as a paragon of moderation, since it declines to overrule *Miranda* v. *Arizona*, (1966). Those who understand the judicial process will appreciate that today's decision is not a reaffirmation of *Miranda*, but a radical revision of the most significant element of *Miranda* (as of all cases): the rationale that gives it a permanent place in our jurisprudence … As the Court chooses to describe that principle, statutes of Congress can be disregarded, not only when what they prescribe violates the Constitution, but when what they prescribe contradicts a decision of this Court that 'announced a constitutional rule' … the only thing that can possibly mean in the context of this case is that this Court has the power, not merely to apply the Constitution but to expand it, imposing what it regards as useful 'prophylactic' restrictions upon Congress and the States. That is an immense and frightening antidemocratic power, and it does not exist."

Scalia promised he would not follow the majority in future rulings related to Miranda and he would continue to apply his dissent in "all cases where there was a sustainable finding that the defendant's confession was voluntary."

Limiting Forced Medication

Can the government force psychotic defendants to take drugs? The Supreme Court limited the government's right to do that with the next case I'll review—*Sell* v. *United States*.

Dr. Charles Sell was a dentist, who in 1997 was charged with fraudulently billing Medicaid and private insurers, as well as with money laundering. He had a history of psychiatric hospitalizations for psychosis. Initially, he was considered competent to stand trial, but as his condition deteriorated over time his competency was questioned. During a bail revocation hearing, he yelled and spit at a magistrate. He also faced additional charges of conspiring to kill a witness and an FBI agent.

Following the incident at the bail hearing, Dr. Sell was sent for another evaluation and was found incompetent to stand trail. He was diagnosed with delusional disorder, persecutory type. He was then sent to a federal medical facility to determine if his competence could be restored. The evaluating physician said he could, but only if he was treated with antipsychotic medication. Dr. Sell refused treatment and remained confined to a federal prison hospital, where he still remained as of 2003.

In 1999 the federal magistrate judge held a competency hearing, and based on testimony from the physicians at the United States Medical Center for Federal Prisoners, which said Sell was a danger to himself and others but medication could render him less dangerous, ordered him to be forcibly medicated. The doctor testified that any serious side effects could be eased and that the benefits outweighed the risks. Additionally, the doctor said the drugs would return him to competency.

Dr. Sell appealed the magistrate's decision to district court. The district court found the dangerous claim erroneous, but concluded that medication was the only viable hope to render Sell competent to stand trial, which was necessary to serve the government's interest in deciding his guilt or innocence. The 8th Circuit Court affirmed the district court. Dr. Sell then appealed to the Supreme Court.

In a 6 to 3 ruling on June 16, 2003, the Supreme Court affirmed the government's authority to administer psychotic drugs to a criminal defendant solely for the purposes of rending him or her competent to stand trial, provided these four criteria are met:

1. There must be an important governmental interest at stake. Prosecution of serious crimes is an important interest, but it still must be reviewed on a case by case basis. Sell's attorney argued that Sell was already confined for a longer period than would be required from any eventual sentence.

2. Medication must be substantially likely to render the defendant competent to stand trial without offsetting side effects.

3. Medication must be necessary to achieve this result, and less intrusive procedures must be unlikely to produce substantially the same result.

4. Medication must be medically appropriate.

The Supreme Court vacated the lower court rulings and remanded the case back to the district court to consider these criteria.

Justice Breyer wrote the opinion for the Court and was joined by Chief Justice Rehnquist and Justices Ginsburg, Kennedy, Souter and Stevens. Justice Scalia wrote the dissenting opinion and was joined by O'Connor and Thomas. In writing for the Court, Breyer said:

> "We emphasize that the court applying these standards is seeking to determine whether involuntary administration of drugs is necessary significantly to further a particular governmental interest, namely, the interest in rendering the defendant *competent to stand trial*. A court need not consider whether to allow forced medication for that kind of purpose, if forced medication is warranted for a *different* purpose, such as the purposes set out in *Harper* related to the individual's

dangerousness, or purposes related to the individual's own interests where refusal to take drugs puts his health gravely at risk ... There are often strong reasons for a court to determine whether forced administration of drugs can be justified on these alternative grounds *before* turning to the trial competence question."

Just the Facts

In the 1990 landmark case, *Washington* v. *Harper*, the Supreme Court ruled that an individual does have the right to avoid the "unwanted administration of antipsychotic drugs." In that case, the Court set two criteria that must be met before forcing an inmate to take drugs against his or her will:

1. Prisoner must be a danger to himself or others; and

2. Prisoner is seriously disruptive to his or her environment and the treatment is in his or her "medical interests."

In writing the dissent, Justice Scalia did not question the criteria set by the Court, but instead questioned the necessity for an interlocutory appeal, which prevented the trial from going forward. Scalia wrote:

"Today's narrow holding will allow criminal defendants in petitioner's position to engage in opportunistic behavior. They can, for example, voluntarily take their medication until halfway through trial, then abruptly refuse and demand an interlocutory appeal from the order that medication continue on a compulsory basis .... But the adverse effects of today's narrow holding are as nothing compared to the adverse effects of the new rule of law that underlies the holding. The Court's opinion announces that appellate jurisdiction is proper because review after conviction and sentence will come only after 'Sell will have undergone forced medication—the very harm that he seeks to avoid' ... This analysis effects a breathtaking expansion of appellate jurisdiction over interlocutory orders. If it is applied faithfully (and some appellate panels will be eager to apply it faithfully), any criminal defendant who asserts that a trial court order will, if implemented, cause an immediate violation of his constitutional (or perhaps even statutory?) rights may immediately appeal. He is empowered to hold up the trial for months by claiming that review after final judgment 'would come too late' to prevent the violation."

Since the ruling just came down in June 2003, we won't know its full effects for years to come, but you can be certain it will be used for future appeals and likely make it back to a future Supreme Court.

Confessing Illegally

Tossing out a confession at trial can frequently result in the loss of a conviction, so police officials must be especially careful when someone is arrested that they have the right to arrest that person. In a landmark case, *Brown* v. *Illinois* (1975), the Supreme Court ruled that a confession "obtained by exploitation of an illegal arrest" may not be used against a criminal defendant.

The Court reaffirmed the rights of defendants if the confession was obtained through an illegal arrest in a recent test case—*Kaupp* v. *Texas*—with a *per curiam* decision by the court on May 5, 2003. The Court vacated the lower court ruling and sent it back to the Texas court for further consideration. Let's look at the facts of the case.

Court Connotations

Per curiam is a Latin phrase for "by the court." A per curiam decision means it is a decision by the entire court, with no judge identified as the specific author.

Robert Justin Kaupp was suspected of participating in the murder of a 14-year-old girl, who was the sister of his close friend. The friend confessed to the murder and implicated Kaupp.

The Texas police were unable to get approval for a warrant to question Kaupp, and they didn't have enough evidence against him. Instead, police woke Kaupp from his bed at 3 A.M., took him from his bed clad only in his underwear to the location of the crime scene, and then took him to the police station for questioning. The police never told him he was free to decline to go with them.

Once they got Kaupp to the interrogation room, they read him his rights. At first he denied involvement, but after learning about the brother's confession he admitted being involved in the crime. He did not admit to causing the fatal wound or confessing to the murder, for which he was later indicted.

Kaupp's attorney tried unsuccessfully to suppress the confession during trial as fruit of an illegal arrest. Kaupp was convicted and sentenced to 55 years in prison. The Texas State Court of Appeals affirmed the lower court decision to admit the confession. Kaupp then appealed to the United States Supreme Court on the basis that his seizure from his bedroom violated his Fourth and Fourteenth Amendment rights, so therefore the confession should not have been admitted.

The United States Supreme Court vacated the lower courts and found the seizure of Kaupp was in essence an illegal arrest. In the per curiam decision, the Court wrote:

"Such involuntary transport to a police station for questioning is 'sufficiently like arres[t] to invoke the traditional rule that arrests may constitutionally be made only on probable cause' ... The state does not claim to have had probable cause here, and a straightforward application of the test just mentioned shows beyond cavil that Kaupp was arrested within the meaning of the Fourth Amendment ... A 17-year-old boy was awakened in his bedroom at three in the morning by at least three police officers, one of whom stated 'we need to go and talk.' He was taken out in handcuffs, without shoes, dressed only in his under-wear in January, placed in a patrol car, driven to the scene of a crime and then to the sheriff's offices, where he was taken into an interrogation room and ques-tioned ... Kaupp's 'Okay' in response to Pinkins's [the police officer] statement is no showing of consent under the circumstances. Pinkins offered Kaupp no choice, and a group of police officers rousing an adolescent out of bed in the middle of the night with the words 'we need to go and talk' presents no option but 'to go.' There is no reason to think Kaupp's answer was anything more than 'a mere submission to a claim of lawful authority.'"

Living Laws

If the police come to your home and want to take you in for questioning, you do have the right to refuse if they do not have an arrest warrant, which is issued by the court and which you can ask to see before allowing the police to take you in. If they do have a warrant, they must read you your Miranda rights before starting to question you. You can refuse to answer questions and seek legal advice before answering questions.

Cases can be won and lost on a technicality. Knowing the technicalities and avoiding overstepping the rules set to protect people's Fourth and Fourteenth Amendment are critical in all arrest situations. Next we'll explore the rights of prisoners being pun-ished for their crimes.

The Least You Need to Know

- Even though overturning Miranda was a goal set by Chief Justice Rehnquist before he took a seat on the Supreme Court, he wrote the 2000 decision upholding it.

- The government must meet a four-criteria test before forcing someone to take antipsychotic drugs.

- The police can't just come into your bedroom and take you in for questioning without an arrest warrant.

Punishing the Criminals

In This Chapter

- ◆ Getting to the penalty phase
- ◆ When the death penalty is too cruel
- ◆ Jury input needed in death penalty decisions
- ◆ Facing a "third strike" sentence

Even after the evidence is collected properly and the arrests are made according to the rules, government officials must still be careful not to overstep the rights set in the Constitution when punishing convicted criminals. Criminals are protected from being unfairly convicted or punished by rights stated in two amendments—the Sixth Amendment (which requires a jury trial) and the Eighth Amendment (which prohibits "cruel and unusual punishment").

Over the years the question of whether the death penalty is "cruel and unusual" punishment has been raised many times in cases that made it all the way to the Supreme Court. This question was even raised as recently as 2002 in *Atkins* v. *Virginia* in which the Court ruled the death penalty was "cruel and unusual" punishment for the mentally retarded.

In addition to discussing *Atkins* in this chapter, I'll explore the issues in the 2002 landmark case, *Ring* v. *Arizona*, which declared the death penalty sentencing schemes in five states unconstitutional (Arizona, Colorado, Montana, Nebraska, and Ohio). Over 150 death penalty cases will need to be reviewed because of this ruling. This decision will likely affect an additional four states (Alabama, Delaware, Florida, and Indiana) with similar sentencing schemes where there are over 500 prisoners waiting on death row.

The issue of "cruel and unusual" punishment is not only raised in death penalty cases. For example, the third case I'll review in this chapter is *Lockyer* v. *Andrade* decided in 2003, which questioned whether penalties required in "third strike" cases were "cruel and unusual."

Is the Death Penalty Cruel and Unusual Punishment?

You may think the death penalty is too cruel in any case, but the United States does permit the death penalty in certain cases. Whether the death penalty will be imposed is dependent on the state in which you live, because most criminal cases are tried based on state laws. For the few cases that make it to the federal level, there are rare instances where the death penalty can be imposed.

> **Just the Facts**
>
> The imposition of the death penalty is rare. Between 1967 and 1996 there was one execution for every 1,600 murders. The total number of murders in the United States during that time was 560,000, with 358 murderers executed according to the FBI's Uniform Crime Report and the Bureau of Justice Statistics. About 5,900 persons were sentenced to death between 1973 and 1996. The average time a murderer spends on death row is 11 years and 2 months, according to a 1995 article, "Capital Punishment," published by the Bureau of Justice Statistics.

Daryl Renard Atkins started on the path to death row on August 16, 1996, when he and his friend William Jones abducted and robbed Eric Nesbitt with a semiautomatic handgun. The pair took all the money Nesbitt had on his person, then drove him to an automated teller machine (ATM). While there, they were caught on camera forcing him to withdraw more money. After getting the additional money, they drove Nesbitt to an isolated location and killed him by shooting him eight times.

Atkins was convicted of abduction, armed robbery, and capital murder and sentenced to death. Both Jones and Atkins testified in the guilt phase of the Atkins' trial. They each confirmed the incident, but differed on who actually shot and killed Nesbitt.

Jones, whose testimony was more coherent and credible to the jury than the mentally retarded Atkins, led the jury to convict Atkins and blame him for the shooting.

During the penalty phase of the trial, the state introduced victim-impact evidence and proved two aggravating circumstances to push for the death penalty. The state proved to the jury that Atkins posed a future danger because of his prior felony convictions. In addition, the state called four victims of earlier robberies and assaults to testify against Atkins. Also, the state proved the "vileness of the offense" by pointing to the pictures of the deceased's body and the autopsy report, which were part of the initial trial record.

Dr. Evan Nelson, a *forensic psychologist*, testified in the penalty phase that based on his evaluation of Atkins, he was "mildly mentally retarded." He testified that after reviewing Atkins school and court records plus administering a standard intelligence test, Atkins had a full scale IQ of 59 and was functioning somewhere between the ages of 9 and 12.

Court Connotations

A forensic psychologist is an expert who gives his psychological opinion in the courts to assist with fact finding in a criminal or civil case. A forensic psychologist must have a doctorate degree in psychology. After completing his doctorate, a psychologist will usually work under an experienced forensic psychologist to gain further expertise before being called on as an expert witness.

Based on this testimony, the jury sentenced Atkins to death, but the Virginia Supreme Court ordered a second sentencing hearing because the trial court used a misleading verdict form. At the second sentencing hearing, the same forensic psychologist testified, but additional testimony was added for the state by expert witness Dr. Stanton Samenow, who said that Atkins was not mentally retarded, but was of "average intelligence, at least" and diagnosable as having antisocial personality disorder. The jury again sentenced Atkins to death.

After the second sentencing hearing, the Virginia Supreme Court affirmed the imposition of the death penalty. Atkins did not argue before the Virginia Supreme Court that his sentence was disproportionate to penalties imposed for similar crimes in Virginia, but he did contend "that he is mentally retarded and thus cannot be sentenced to death."

The Virginia Supreme Court rejected his appeal, saying it was "not willing to commute Atkins' sentence of death to life imprisonment merely because of his IQ score." Two Virginia justices dissented, saying that they rejected Dr. Samenow's opinion that Atkins possesses average intelligence as "incredulous as a matter of law," and concluded that "the imposition of the sentence of death upon a criminal defendant who has the mental age of a child between the ages of 9 and 12 is excessive." In their dissent, they said "it is indefensible to conclude that individuals who are mentally retarded are not to some degree less culpable for their criminal acts. By definition, such individuals have substantial limitations not shared by the general population. A moral and civilized society diminishes itself if its system of justice does not afford recognition and consideration of those limitations in a meaningful way."

While in a 1989 case, *Penry* v. *Lynaugh*, the United States Supreme Court did rule that people with mental retardation could be put to death, many states have since changed their laws on this issue. The United States Supreme Court decided to hear Atkins' appeal in 2002 because of the dramatic shift in the position of state legislatures during the previous 13 years.

Just the Facts

Based on the 1910 landmark case, *Weems* v. *United States,* the Eighth Amendment prohibits the infliction of excessive bail, excessive fines, and unusual punishments. In that case the court ruled that a punishment of 12 years jailed in irons at hard and painful labor for the crime of falsifying records was excessive. The court said, "that it is a precept of justice that punishment for crime should be graduated and proportioned to the offense."

Over the years, the United States Supreme Court has held that judging whether punishment is excessive is not based on standards that prevailed when the Bill of Rights was adopted, but rather by those that currently prevail. Therefore, in determining whether punishments are "cruel and unusual" the Supreme Court looks to current-day standards set by recent legislatures.

In 1989, when the Supreme Court last looked at the issue of sentencing mentally retarded people to death, most states did allow that. In 2002, when the Supreme Court decided to revisit the issue, the political winds had changed and state legislatures were deciding against the death penalty in cases involving people with mental retardation. So the justices overturned *Penry* and ruled in favor of Atkins, reversed the Virginia Supreme Court, and remanded the case back to the lower courts for further decision.

The 6 to 3 ruling that the death penalty for Atkins was "cruel and unusual punishment," was written by Justice John Paul Stevens, who was joined by Justices Breyer, Ginsburg, Kennedy, O'Connor, and Souter. Chief Justice Rehnquist wrote a dissenting opinion and was joined by Justices Scalia and Thomas. Scalia also wrote a dissenting opinion and was joined by Rehnquist and Thomas. In writing for the Court, Stevens said:

"Those mentally retarded persons who meet the law's requirements for criminal responsibility should be tried and punished when they commit crimes. Because of their disabilities in areas of reasoning, judgment, and control of their impulses, however, they do not act with the level of moral culpability that characterizes the most serious adult criminal conduct. Moreover, their impairments can jeopardize the reliability and fairness of capital proceedings against mentally retarded defendants. Presumably for these reasons, in the 13 years since we decided *Penry* v. *Lynaugh*, (1989), the American public, legislators, scholars, and judges have deliberated over the question whether the death penalty should ever be imposed on a mentally retarded criminal. The consensus reflected in those deliberations informs our answer to the question presented by this case: whether such executions are "cruel and unusual punishments" prohibited by the Eighth Amendment to the Federal Constitution."

> **Living Laws**
>
> People who are found to be mentally retarded cannot be sentenced to death as of 2002, after the ban imposed by the United States Supreme Court in *Atkins* v. *Virginia*.

In writing his dissent, Chief Justice Rehnquist said:

"There are strong reasons for limiting our inquiry into what constitutes an evolving standard of decency under the Eighth Amendment to the laws passed by legislatures and the practices of sentencing juries in America. Here, the Court goes beyond these well-established objective indicators of contemporary values. It finds 'further support to [its] conclusion' that a national consensus has developed against imposing the death penalty on all mentally retarded defendants in international opinion, the views of professional and religious organizations, and opinion polls not demonstrated to be reliable … Believing this view to be seriously mistaken, I dissent."

Justice Scalia added in his dissent, "This newest innovation promises to be more effective than any of the others in turning the process of capital trial into a game." How this game will be played out will be seen in future death penalty cases that find their way to the Supreme Court.

Must a Jury Decide the Death Penalty?

Timothy Ring's road to death row started on November 28, 1994, when he and some friends decided to rob and murder a Wells Fargo driver, John Magoch, in Maricopa County, Arizona. Wells Fargo reported $800,000 in cash and checks missing after its courier Dave Morris finished a drop off at a Dillard's Department store and returned to find his Wells Fargo van missing.

There were no witnesses to the robbery or murder, but a bicyclist reported to police that he saw a white van followed by a red pickup truck that ran a stop sign on that afternoon. The police then got a lucky break in the case when an informant led the police to a girlfriend of James Greenham, who was a friend of Timothy Ring, who owned a red pickup truck.

Police got permission from the courts to listen in on phone calls between Greenham and Ring. During these conversations police heard the two scheme to disappear "up north" and negotiate payments. It became apparent during these conversations that Ring was holding Greenham's share of the money.

Police panicked Greenham when a detective left his card at Greenham's door. Greenham then made a call to Ring to warn him. Ring called a third man in the group, William Ferguson, and said cryptically, "I don't know what to think of it. Um, [Greenham's] house is clean. Mine, on the other hand, contains a very large bag." Police continued to use various tactics over the next two days to panic the three, including issuing press releases with phony witness reports hoping to get one of the three to crack.

Finally after two days of playing these tricks, police showed up with a search warrant at Ring's home where they found a rifle outfitted with a homemade sound suppressor and a duffel bag with Ring's name on it and $271,681 cash inside. Police also found a note on Ring's headboard with the number $575,995.

When adding the money found in the bag to the $575,995, it was about the same amount of cash Wells Fargo reported missing. Below that figure was the word "splits" and the letters "F," "Y" and "T." Police guessed that "F" was for "Ferguson," "Y" for "Yoda," Greenham's nickname, and "T," for "Tim."

Court Connotations

Circumstantial evidence is evidence given at a trial that is not directly from an eyewitness or participant. Circumstantial evidence is commonly perceived as weak by the public, but can include testimony about prior threats to a victim, fingerprints found at the crime scene, ownership of the murder weapon or being seen by a witness near the crime scene at the time the crime took place.

All the information gathered accumulated to a lot of *circumstantial evidence*, but not hard evidence. No bullet was found, so Ring's rifle couldn't be tied to the crime. A jury found Ring guilty of murder, a capital offense in Arizona. Under Arizona law, a judge must decide whether someone convicted of murder gets death or life imprisonment. A jury alone cannot decide.

Ring never confessed to the crime and none of his accomplices did either. So there was no evidence directly connecting Ring to the murder. By the time of Ring's sentencing hearing, James Greenham made a deal with prosecutors and pleaded guilty to second-degree murder and armed robbery. Greenham testified at Ring's special sentencing hearing that Ring was the shooter and that Ring asked to be congratulated for his shot the day after the killing. He also named Ring as the one who organized the robbery and murder. This testimony was only heard by the judge. There was no jury present.

At Ring's sentencing hearing, the judge used Greenham's testimony to rule that Ring "is the one who killed Mr. Magoch" and that Ring showed "reckless disregard for human life." Arizona law requires the judge to find beyond a reasonable doubt at least one aggravating factor in order to sentence a defendant to die. Thanks to Greenham's testimony, the judge found two:

1. the murder was committed for money, and

2. the crime was committed "in an especially heinous, cruel or depraved manner."

Death penalty cases are granted an automatic direct appeal to the Arizona Supreme Court. The state's highest court affirmed the sentence, rejecting arguments for a new trial. One argument did raise questions for one of Arizona Supreme Court justices. Justice Stanley Feldman, who wrote the opinion for the Arizona Court, asked whether two U.S. Supreme Court Cases—*Jones* v. *United States* in 1999 and *Apprendi* v. *New Jersey* in 2000 made Arizona's sentencing procedure for capital cases unconstitutional. While the sentencing scheme had been ruled constitutional in a 1990 case *Walton* v. *Arizona*, the more recent rulings in *Jones* and *Apprendi* appeared to conflict with the older 1990 ruling allowing a judge to sentence a convicted criminal to death.

Just the Facts

Jones v. *United States* set the precedent that removing a jury's control over the facts determining the "statutory sentencing range" would violate the Sixth Amendment. In *Apprendi* v. *New Jersey*, the United States Supreme Court held that "any fact that increases the penalty for a crime beyond the prescribed statutory maximum must be submitted to a jury, and proved beyond a reasonable doubt." Both rulings seemed to indicate that all evidence must be heard by the jury before the death penalty can be imposed or the sentence would not meet the requirements of the Sixth Amendment.

While the United States Supreme Court did say in its decision written in the *Apprendi* case that the *Walton* opinion stood because Arizona juries find defendants guilty of capital offenses before judges determine aggravating factors and apply the death penalty, Justice Sandra Day O'Connor questioned that stance and wrote in her dissent to *Apprendi*:

> "A defendant convicted of first-degree murder in Arizona cannot receive a death sentence unless a judge makes the factual determination that a statutory aggravating factor exists …. If the court does not intend to overrule *Walton*, one would be hard pressed to tell from the opinion it issues today."

Feldman agreed with O'Connor because the trial judge's determination of aggravating factors in Arizona death penalty cases was based solely on evidence presented at the sentencing hearing and never heard by the jury. Even given these facts, the United States Supreme Court justices who supported the majority opinion in the *Apprendi* case explicitly said that the Court did not mean to overturn *Walton*. Given that strong statement, Arizona's Supreme Court regarded its death penalty sentence scheme as constitutional and affirmed Ring's sentence.

The United States Supreme Court decided to hear the Ring case on January 11, 2002 and stayed the execution of a death-row inmate in Florida on January 23 because Florida's sentencing scheme was similar to Arizona's. Clearly the United States Supreme Court was ready to review the issue of Arizona's death penalty scheme and whether the 1999 and 2000 cases did overturn the *Walton* case on the issue of death penalty sentencing.

On June 24, 2002, the Court sided with Ring, and by a 7-2 vote, held that the sentences of those who were sentenced to die by judges, not juries, cannot stand. Justice Ruth Bader Ginsburg wrote the lead majority opinion and was joined by Kennedy, Souter, Scalia, Stevens, and Thomas. Breyer filed a concurring opinion. Justice O'Connor wrote the dissent and was joined by Chief Justice William Rehnquist. In writing her opinion for the Court, Justice Ginsburg said:

> "We overrule *Walton* to the extent that it allows a sentencing judge, sitting without a jury, to find an aggravating circumstance necessary for imposition of the death penalty."

Ginsburg went on to say that the Court also found that Arizona's enumerated aggravating factors operate as "the functional equivalent of a greater offense," and that the Sixth Amendment required that the jury be aware of these factors in order to determine appropriate sentencing. She added:

> "Capital defendants, no less than non-capital defendants, we conclude are entitled to a jury determination of any fact on which the legislature conditions an increase in their maximum punishment."

Since the jury during Ring's trial never heard the evidence used to determine a death sentence, the United States Supreme Court found that the judge imposed a stiffer penalty, the death penalty, based on evidence the jury never heard and therefore sentenced him beyond what the jury could consider. This was unconstitutional because the Sixth Amendment requires a jury trial.

The Court decided in *Apprendi* that the "Sixth Amendment does not permit a defendant to be 'expose[d] … to a penalty exceeding the maximum he would receive if punished according to the facts reflected in the jury alone.'" This decision came 10 years after the decision in *Walton* that held Arizona's sentencing scheme to be compatible with the Sixth Amendment.

> **Living Laws**
>
> A judge can only sentence you for crimes for which a jury has heard the evidence. If further evidence is offered at a sentencing hearing, you still cannot be sentenced to a stiffer penalty than would have been possible based on what the jury heard and decided.

The *Apprendi* ruling won out, to the dismay of Justice O'Connor, who wrote in a brief but pointed dissent that she would rather overrule *Apprendi* than *Walton*:

> "*Apprendi's* rule that any fact that increases the maximum penalty must be treated as an element of the crime, is not required by the Constitution, by history, or by our prior cases. And it ignores the 'significant history in this country of … discretionary sentencing by judges.'"

O'Connor believes the decision in *Ring* v. *Arizona* will open the floodgates to convicted defendants wanting to overturn their sentences. She added:

> "I fear that the prisoners on death row in Alabama, Delaware, Florida and Indiana, which the Court identified as having hybrid sentencing schemes in which the jury renders an advisory verdict but the judge makes the ultimate sentencing determination, may also seize on today's decision to challenge their sentences."

While the final determination has not been made in these hybrid cases at the time this book was written, it is probably only a matter of time before someone appeals his or her death row sentence in one of the affected states and gets it reversed along with other death row sentences based on the *Ring* ruling.

Are Penalties Required in "Third Strike" Laws Too Cruel?

Not all cruel and unusual punishment cases involve the death penalty. In the 2002 case of *Lockyer* v. *Andrade*, the Supreme Court looked at the question of whether two consecutive terms of 25 years to life was cruel and unusual punishment for a crime of petty theft involving the theft of about $150 worth of videotapes.

Leandro Andrade received that long sentence after being caught stealing for the third and fourth times in California. California has a "third strike" law that mandates the stiff penalty.

In November 1995, Andrade attempted to steal five videotapes from a Kmart. He was arrested upon leaving the store. Two weeks later, before trial on the first videotape theft offense, he was arrested outside another Kmart for trying to steal five more tapes. Andrade, who was a long-time heroin addict, had a 15-year criminal history with five felonies and two misdemeanors on his record. All previous crimes were nonviolent.

Based on his record, prosecutors determined that he already had two strikes under the California law when his prosecution started for the petty theft in the Kmart stores. Petty theft is a so-called "wobbler," which means it can be tried as a misde-meanor or felony depending on circumstances. Andrade, who was 37, was convicted and sentenced to 25 years for each of the videotape petty theft counts (strikes three and four). According to Cali-fornia's three strikes law, these sentences had to be served consecutively (not at the same time), so Andrade would become eligible for parole in 50 years at age 87.

> **Living Laws**
>
> You can be sentenced to 25 years to life for petty theft if it's your third strike and you are con-victed in a state that has a "three strikes" law.

Andrade appealed the case to the California State Court of Appeals, which affirmed the lower court sentence. Next he appealed it to the 9th Circuit Court, which over-turned the sentence as being "grossly disproportionate" to the crime committed. The state of California then appealed to the United States Supreme Court. The issue to be decided by the United States Supreme Court was whether the California "three strikes" law violates the Eighth Amendment protection against "cruel and unusual" punishment.

In a closely divided 5 to 4 decision, the United States Supreme Court ruled in favor of the state and overturned the circuit court. Justice Sandra Day O'Connor wrote the decision for the Court and was joined by Chief Justice Rehnquist and Justices

Kennedy, Scalia and Thomas. Justice Souter wrote the dissenting opinion and was joined by Justices Breyer, Ginsburg, and Stevens. In writing the opinion for the court, O'Connor ruled that the California court did not err, but instead the 9th Circuit Court erred in overturning the California court on the principle of "gross disproportionality". O'Connor wrote:

> "The gross disproportionality principle reserves a constitutional violation for only the extraordinary case. In applying this principle ... it was not an unreasonable application of our clearly established law for the California Court of Appeal to affirm Andrade's sentence of two consecutive terms of 25 years to life in prison."

In writing the dissent, Justice Souter disagreed:

> "The State, in other words has not chosen 25 to life because of the inherent moral or social reprehensibility of the triggering offense in isolation; the triggering offense is treated so seriously, rather, because of its confirmation of the defendant's danger to society and the need to counter his threat with incapacitation. As to the length of incapacitation, the State has made a second helpful determination, that the public risk or danger posed by someone with the specified predicate record is generally addressed by incapacitation for 25 years before parole eligibility ... The three-strikes law, in sum, responds to a condition of the defendant shown by his prior felony record, his danger to society, and it reflects a judgment that 25 years of incapacitation prior to parole eligibility is appropriate when a defendant exhibiting such a condition commits another felony.

> "Whether or not one accepts the State's choice of penalogical policy as constitutionally sound, that policy cannot reasonably justify the imposition of a consecutive 25-year minimum for a second minor felony committed soon after the first triggering offense. Andrade did not somehow become twice as dangerous to society when he stole the second handful of videotapes; his dangerousness may justify treating one minor felony as serious and warranting long incapacitation, but a second such felony does not disclose greater danger warranting substantially longer incapacitation. Since the defendant's condition has not changed between the two closely related thefts, the incapacitation penalty is not open to the simple arithmetic of multiplying the punishment by two, without resulting in gross disproportion even under the State's chosen benchmark ... I know of no jurisdiction that would add 25 years of imprisonment simply to reflect the fact that the two temporally related thefts took place on two separate occasions, and I am not surprised that California has found no such case, not even under its three-strikes law ... In sum, the argument that repeating a trivial crime justifies doubling a 25-year minimum incapacitation sentence based on a threat to the public does not raise a

seriously debatable point on which judgments might reasonably differ … This is the rare sentence of demonstrable gross disproportionality, as the California Legislature may well have recognized when it specifically provided that a prosecutor may move to dismiss or strike a prior felony conviction 'in the furtherance of justice.'"

At least for now, petty theft can lead to a 50-year sentence given circumstances similar to those that Andrade faced. Whether this ruling will stand for a long time depends on the future makeup of the Court when the next case winds its way to the Supreme Court's doorstep.

Now that we've explored criminal cases, we'll turn our sights on cases that impact the business environment.

The Least You Need to Know

- ◆ The Supreme Court has ruled that the death penalty is cruel and unusual punishment for someone who is mentally retarded.

- ◆ The death penalty cannot be imposed by a judge based on evidence that was not presented during the jury trial.

- ◆ If a state has a "three strikes" law, it is not a sentence of "gross disproportionality" to sentence a man to 50 years to life for petty theft on his third and fourth strikes.

Part 7

Taking Care of Business

Reading the fine print on contracts and finding out how that fine print can impinge on your future rights are just some of the key issues you'll find in this business section. You'll also discover whether corporate public relations is entitled to free speech protections, how to handle a hostile work environment, and what to do if you are exposed to a deadly disease.

Chapter 24

Keeping Things Moving

In This Chapter

- ◆ Trading with Burma
- ◆ Who controls foreign trade—feds or states?
- ◆ Public relations—free speech or commercial speech?
- ◆ Bankruptcy protects licenses

Keeping things moving across state lines without undue interference by states has long been a purview of the Supreme Court. Anyone who operates a business in the United States knows how difficult it can be to sort out state regulations versus federal regulations, as well as varying regulations among the states. The Supreme Court's role is to be certain no state law unfairly impacts interstate commerce or foreign trade. One such case I'll review in this chapter involves trade restrictions imposed by the state of Massachusetts on companies that do business with Burma.

Because corporations are treated like a person in the courts, appeals to the Supreme Court can also include such questions as free speech and bankruptcy rights. Two recent controversial cases I'll review involving these rights are Nike's battle for free speech protections and NextWave's battle to keep its licenses under bankruptcy protection laws.

Placing Restrictions on Foreign Trade

Human rights activists successfully used selective purchasing laws to protest apartheid in South Africa in the 1970s and 1980s by forcing major corporations to choose between lucrative state contracts and doing business in South Africa. Activists found it easier to get these laws passed at the state or local level than to push restrictions through at the federal level. Many credit these *selective purchasing laws* with forcing U.S. corporations to divest their interests in South Africa, which ultimately led to the end of apartheid there and forced majority rule.

> **Court Connotations**
>
> **Selective purchasing laws** restrict state entities from purchasing goods or services from corporations that do business with repressive governments outside the United States. The purpose of these laws is to force companies to choose between lucrative state or local contracts and doing business with certain foreign countries.

Finding success with this strategy, human rights groups then sought similar selective purchasing laws against other repressive regimes such as Cuba, Nigeria, and Burma. As these laws became more popular, the National Foreign Trade Council (NFTC) with the help of the European Union decided it was time to question their constitutionality. The NFTC, which represents about 600 corporations, chose the Massachusetts Burma Law as a good test case and filed suit in 1998 to strike down that law.

The Massachusetts Burma Law was passed in 1996. It required companies that did business in Burma to add 10 percent to all of their bids for procurement contracts with the state. Massachusetts was not the only one with such a law. In fact more than 20 states and local governments, including New York, Los Angeles, Minneapolis, and San Francisco, had similar selective purchasing laws against doing business with Burma. These laws protested the military junta that suppressed democratic opposition in Burma.

Massachusetts, in defending its law, told the courts that states "should be free … to apply a moral standard to their spending decisions … Nothing in the federal Constitution … requires the states to trade with dictators." On November 4, 1998, federal district court Judge Joseph Tauro ruled the Burma law unconstitutional because it encroached upon the exclusive power of the federal government to manage foreign affairs.

The 1st Circuit Court not only upheld the decision, but broadened the ruling. The 1st Circuit Court found that not only did the Massachusetts law burden foreign commerce, but it also preempted federal sanctions against the military government of Burma. Congress authorized federal sanctions in September, 1996, just several months after the Massachusetts law was enacted. Congress passed a statute imposing a set of mandatory and conditional sanctions on Burma as part of the Foreign Operations, Export Financing, and Related Programs Appropriations Act of 1997.

The state then appealed the decision to the Supreme Court, *Crosby* v. *National Foreign Trade Council*, and the Supreme Court accepted it. Oral arguments were heard on March 22, 2000. In a unanimous ruling, the Supreme Court struck down the Massachusetts Burma Law, but on much narrower grounds than the lower courts. Instead of ruling on the constitutionality of selective purchasing laws, Justice Souter, who wrote the opinion for the court, found that the Congressionally enacted law directed at Burma trade sanctions preempted any action taken by local or state governments. Souter wrote:

> "Because the state Act's provisions conflict with Congress's specific delegation to the President of flexible discretion … with direction to develop a comprehensive, multilateral strategy under the federal Act, it is preempted, and its application is unconstitutional, under the Supremacy Clause."

Souter specified four aspects of the Massachusetts law that undermined the discretion given the president:

♦ The state law undermined the discretion expressly given the president by Congress to devise a Burma policy.

♦ The state law differed from the federal approach because the state law banned both new and pre-existing business with Burma while the federal law only banned new investment in Burma.

♦ The federal law only targeted U.S. companies, while the Massachusetts law included foreign companies as well.

♦ The state law undermined Congress' instruction that the president undertake multilateral efforts because it proved to be a distraction to the international efforts being led by the president on the Burma front.

Supreme Sayings

"It's a yellow light, not a red light (for selective-purchasing laws). Yes, it's a red light when Congress has specifically delegated power to the President. This was not decided by a sweeping constitutional theory that says states have no role in adopting standards of public morality in determining purchasing."

—Georgetown University Law Professor Robert Strumberg, who helped prepare the case for Massachusetts, in a interview with Inter Press News Service on June 20, 2000

The Supreme Court chose not to rule on the constitutionality of all selective purchasing laws, only this specific law that targeted a country that was the subject of Congressional sanctions. This leaves open the possibility that a state law directed at a country not under federal sanctions could be constitutional.

Both human rights activists and the NFTC have vowed to continue their fights. Human rights groups vowed they would find alternative ways to involve state governments in their struggle against repressive regimes and NFTC vowed to continue fighting state or local laws that delve into foreign trade issues. No doubt future cases will make it to the Supreme Court that may finally settle this issue.

Seeking Free Speech Rights for Corporate Public Relations

When defending your company using advertising and public relations statements, do you have the Constitutional protection of free speech? At least for now that depends upon whether you sell your products in the state of California. Let's take a look at the case that brought this question into the limelight.

In the late 1990s, environmental and labor activists charged that U.S. apparel and shoe manufacturers, such as Nike, failed to meet core labor standards in their overseas factories and assembly plants set forth by the International Labor Organization. Nike hired Goodworks International, a consultancy firm owned by former U.N. Ambassador Andrew Young, to audit its factories. Goodworks gave Nike a favorable review, which it touted in full-page newspaper ads in 1997. In addition to the ads, Nike sent out press releases and letters to newspaper editors to deny that it was mistreating or underpaying workers at its foreign plants.

Activists charged these claims and the Goodworks audit were not only misleading, but untrue. So in 1998, environmentalist Marc Kasky filed suit in California state court claiming that Nike engaged in unfair business practices because it was making false statements regarding conditions in its Asian factories. California has tough consumer-protection laws that allow people to file lawsuits to enforce the law even if they can't prove that they have personally suffered as a result of the misleading statements.

Nike defended its position and said that its efforts to defend itself were "free speech" rather than "commercial speech" because the subject of the ads and press releases related to a topic of public interest rather than an attempt to sell a product. Free speech is protected by the First Amendment to the Constitution while commercial speech is not. Nike asked that the case be dismissed and the lower courts in California agreed with Nike.

The California Supreme Court disagreed with the lower courts and ruled in the activists' favor in May 2002 when it said that if a corporation makes "factual representations about its own products or its operations, it must speak truthfully." The California Supreme Court, in a 4 to 3 split decision, said the case could not be dismissed and remanded the case for further action in the lower courts. In writing for the California Supreme Court, Justice Joyce Kennard set a three-prong test for determining whether speech should be considered commercial:

- Speaker must be engaged in commerce.

- Intended audience should be the actual or potential customers.

- Content of the message must be commercial in character.

Two of the three dissenters on the California Supreme Court wrote in response to the Court's decision, "If Nike utters a factual misstatement, unlike its critics, it may be sued for restitution, civil penalties and injunctive (relief). When Nike tries to defend itself from these attacks, the majority denies it the same First Amendment protection Nike's critics enjoy."

Environmental and labor activists hailed the California Supreme Court decision and called it a major breakthrough for countering sophisticated public relations campaigns that corporations use to defend themselves on issues such as environmental protection or labor relations. But free speech activists joined the corporate side of the argument.

Nike appealed the California Supreme Court decision to the U.S. Supreme Court, still hoping to get the case dismissed. The U.S. Supreme Court agreed to hear the case in 2003, but on June 26, 2003 ruled the writ of certiorari was "improvidently granted." The U.S. Supreme Court decided it would not get involved during these pretrial maneuvers.

> **Supreme Sayings**
>
> "It essentially shuts business speakers out of the public debate on any issue that affects them. That kind of analysis is antithetical to the basic First Amendment principle that we let the people, not the government, decide who's right and who's wrong on an issue of public dispute." — Ann Brick of the American Civil Liberties Union, which supports Nike's position

Justice Breyer dissented with this decision and was joined by Justice O'Connor. He wrote in dissent:

> "If permitted to stand, the state court's decision may well 'chill' the exercise of free speech rights ... Continuation of this lawsuit itself means increased expense,

and, if Nike loses, the results may include monetary liability (for 'restitution') and injunctive relief (including possible corrective 'counterspeech') … The range of communications subject to such liability is broad; in this case, it includes a letter to the editor of *The New York Times*. The upshot is that commercial speakers doing business in California may hesitate to issue significant communications relevant to public debate because they fear potential lawsuits and legal liability … This concern is not purely theoretical. Nike says without contradiction that because of this lawsuit it has decided 'to restrict severely all of its communications on social issues that could reach California consumers, including speech in national and international media.'"

This case now goes back to the California courts for further pretrial maneuvers and ultimately a court trail. Until this free speech versus commercial speech issue is finally decided by the courts, corporations will have to be very careful about what they say to California consumers.

Protecting Licenses Under Bankruptcy Laws

If a company files for bankruptcy protection, are licenses that have been awarded by the Federal Communications Commission protected property if that property is secured by a promissory note? The answer the Supreme Court gave to this question in 2003 was a near unanimous yes, with only one justice dissenting.

The case started in the late 1990s when the FCC auctioned off licenses for personal broadband communications services. NextWave, which planned to provide high-speed wireless Internet access and voice communication services, successfully bid on a number of licenses. After making a down payment of $500 million for the licenses, NextWave signed promissory notes for the balance, giving the FCC a security interest in the licenses.

During the period of 1999 to 2001, NextWave filed for bankruptcy. As part of its reorganization plans, NextWave said it would pay all government fees to keep the licenses. Court challenges to its bankruptcy reorganization plans delayed the payments, but using private funds NextWave started its initial network of wireless facilities during 2001 and 2002.

Because the FCC's promissory notes were conditioned upon "full and timely payment of all monies due" and "failure to comply with this condition would result in their automatic cancellation," the FCC challenged the payment delay caused by the bankruptcy. The FCC objected to the bankruptcy plan and decided instead to cancel NextWave's licenses automatically when NextWave missed its first payment deadline.

Instead of waiting for the money, the FCC announced that NextWave's licenses were available for auction.

The Bankruptcy Court invalidated the FCC's cancellation and said it was a violation of the bankruptcy code. The 2nd Circuit Court disagreed with the Bankruptcy Court and said that only the Court of Appeals could review FCC's regulatory action. NextWave then asked the FCC for reconsideration of the license cancellation. When the FCC denied NextWave reconsideration, NextWave appealed the decision to the District of Columbia Circuit Court, which held that the cancellation violated section 525 of the bankruptcy code. This section states, a "governmental unit may not ... revoke ... a license ... to ... a debtor ... solely because such ... debtor ... has not paid a debt that is dischargeable in the case."

> **Living Laws**
>
> Debts to the federal government do have the full protection offered by the bankruptcy code. A federal regulatory agency cannot choose to ignore bankruptcy protections.

In an 8 to 1 decision, the U.S. Supreme Court agreed with the lower courts that the FCC's cancellations of NextWave's licenses violated section 525 of the bankruptcy code. In writing the opinion for the Court, Justice Scalia said:

> "Petitioners contend that NextWave's license obligations to the Commission are not 'debt[s] that [are] dischargeable' in bankruptcy ... First, the FCC argues that 'regulatory conditions like the full and timely payment condition are not properly classified as "debts"' under the Bankruptcy Code ... In its view, the 'financial nature of a condition' on a license 'does not convert that condition into a debt.' ... Under the Bankruptcy Code, 'debt' means 'liability on a claim,' and 'claim,' in turn, includes any 'right to payment.' ... In short, a debt is a debt, even when the obligation to pay it is also a regulatory condition."

NextWave finally got its go-ahead to use the licenses and begin its reorganization plans after the Supreme Court ruled on January 27, 2003.

Now that we've taken a quick look at state and federal regulations and how they impact business operations, in the next chapter we'll look at cases involving contract disputes that made it to the Supreme Court.

The Least You Need to Know

- ◆ State or local laws restricting foreign trade are unconstitutional if Congress has passed a bill giving the president discretionary powers involving trade restrictions for the same foreign country.

◆ The Supreme Court put off making a controversial decision about whether advertising and public relations is protected by the free speech provisions of the First Amendment or is considered unprotected commercial speech.

◆ U.S. regulatory agencies are subject to the bankruptcy code and must allow its protections for promissory notes granted by the agency.

Chapter 25

Writing It Down

In This Chapter

- Testing the faith
- Excessive punitive damage awards
- Reopening Agent Orange claims
- Arbitrating claims

Reading the fine print of any contract is an important task that many of us fail to do, especially when it relates to insurance policies and financial loans. We assume these are standard contracts and there is little we can do to amend them, which is probably true in most cases. Our only alternative, most times, if we don't like one of these standard contracts is to walk away and make a deal with a different company.

In this chapter I'll review cases relating to contracts that made it all the way to the Supreme Court. One involves excessive punitive damages awarded to a couple after they won a suit against State Farm. Two others involve whether arbitration can be required in contract disputes.

I'll also review the rare nondecision by the Supreme Court related to Agent Orange disputes. Since the Supreme Court could not make a decision, the circuit court ruling stood.

Suing Your Insurance Company

You may think insurance companies are all powerful and you don't have a chance in winning a claim against them, but that was not the case for the Campbells. In fact they won an award of $2.6 million in *compensatory damages* and $145 million in *punitive damages* because of their suffering caused by State Farm.

Court Connotations

Compensatory damages are monetary awards that are intended to make you whole. For example, if your car is destroyed in an accident, you would receive the amount of money that is equal to the fair market value of the car. If the car was used for business, such as a taxi, you might also be entitled to receive monetary damages for loss of profits during the time you were without a vehicle.

Punitive damages are awarded if the defendant's conduct is found to be intentional, willful, or malicious to punish the defendant for his or her conduct and discourage similar future conduct. Punitive damages are awarded in addition to compensatory damages and are usually some multiple of the compensatory damages.

Let's look at how all this started. Curtis Campbell was driving with his wife, Inez Preece Campbell, in Utah in 1981. He passed six vans traveling ahead of them on a two-lane highway. Todd Ospital was driving a small car in the opposite direction. To avoid hitting Campbell head-on (Campbell was on the wrong side of the highway), Ospital swerved onto the shoulder, lost control of his car and hit a third vehicle driven by Robert G. Slusher. Ospital was killed and Slusher was permanently disabled. The Campbells were not hurt.

Ospital's family filed a wrongful death suit against Campbell and Campbell insisted he was not at fault. Early investigations were not conclusive, but in the end investigators and witnesses concluded that Campbell's unsafe pass had caused the crash. Campbell was insured by State Farm, which decided to contest the liability and declined settlement offers by Slusher and Ospital's estate to settle the claims for the policy limit of $50,000 or $25,000 per claimant.

State Farm ignored the advice of its own investigators and took the case to trial, assuring the Campbells that according to trial records, "their assets were safe, that they had no liability for the accident, that [State Farm] would represent their interests, and that they did not need to procure separate counsel."

State Farm's gamble was incorrect and the jury determined that Campbell was 100 percent at fault, awarding $185,849 to Slusher and the estate of Ospital, which was $135,849 in excess of State Farm's contracted liability of $50,000. State Farm's attorney told the Campbells after the verdict, "You may want to put for sale signs on your property to get things moving," and refused to post bond to allow the Campbells to appeal the judgment.

Finally, Campbell realized he did need his own counsel and sought advice to appeal the verdict. During the appeal process in 1984, the Campbells reached an agreement with Slusher and the Ospital estate. In this agreement the Slushers and Ospitals agreed not to pursue their claims against the Campbells in exchange for the Campbells pursuing a bad faith action against State Farm. The Campbells also agreed to be represented by Slusher's and Ospital's attorneys. The Campbells also agreed to give the Slushers and Ospitals the right to play a part in all major decisions on the bad faith action, including any settlement approvals. Slusher and Ospital would receive 90 percent of the verdict against State Farm.

In 1989, the Utah Supreme Court denied Campbell's appeal in the wrongful death action. State Farm paid the entire judgment, including the amount in excess of policy limits. The Campbells then filed a complaint against State Farm alleging bad faith, fraud, and intentional infliction of emotional distress.

State Farm filed a motion for summary judgment since it had paid the excess verdict and the trial court agreed. Campbell appealed this verdict and won on appeal so the trial had to go forward.

Next, State Farm made a motion to prevent the Campbells from including evidence about the Performance, Planning and Review (PP&R) program collected in states outside Utah. The court refused the motion, but did separate the case into two parts—one to hear evidence related to State Farm's decision not to settle and the second related to State Farm's liability for fraud and intentional infliction of emotional distress, as well as compensatory and punitive damages.

The two phases were heard by two different juries. The first phase with the first jury did find State Farm's decision not to settle unreasonable because of the likelihood of an excess

Just the Facts

In 1979, State Farm established a program called Performance, Planning and Review (PP&R) that was implemented by top management to use the claims-adjustment process as a profit center. Evidence at the Campbell trial showed that employees were encouraged to "deny benefits owed to consumers by paying out less than fair value in order to meet preset, arbitrary payout targets designed to enhance corporate profits."

verdict. Before the second phase of the trial could start, the United States Supreme Court decided a case limiting punitive damages—*BMW of North America* v. *Gore* (1996). In that case the Supreme Court refused to sustain a verdict of $2 million punitive damage award based on only $4,000 in compensatory damages. *Gore* established guidelines for punitive damages that included a three step test:

1. the degree of reprehensibility of the defendant's misconduct,

2. the disparity between the actual or potential harm suffered by the plaintiff and the punitive damages award, and

3. the difference between the punitive damages awarded by the jury and the civil penalties authorized or imposed in comparable cases.

The *Gore* decision was partially based on the use of out-of-state damages to prove the case, which the Supreme Court did not allow. Therefore, based on this decision, State Farm asked that evidence of out-of-state damages not be used in this case. The motion was denied because the trial court ruled that such evidence was admissible to determine "whether State Farm's conduct in the Campbell case was indeed intentional and sufficiently egregious to warrant punitive damages."

During the second phase of the trial, State Farm argued that its decision to take the case to trial was an "honest mistake" and did not warrant punitive damages. The Campbells introduced evidence to show that the company's decision to take the case to trial was part of a national scheme called PP&R to meet fiscal goals by capping payouts on claims company-wide.

The PP&R evidence presented referred to business practices by State Farm over a 20-year period of implementing the PP&R policy. The jury awarded the Campbells $2.6 million in compensatory damages and $145 million in punitive damages, which the trail court reduced to $1 million and $25 million respectively. Both parties appealed.

Living Laws

The State Farm case teaches us several things. One, be sure to read the fine print of any contract. Two, be certain that your rights are being protected and don't necessarily believe that an insurance company will protect you. And, three, don't be afraid to appeal a ruling you believe is unfair.

The Utah Supreme Court, using the guidelines set in *Gore*, reinstated the $145 punitive damages by relying in large part on the extensive evidence concerning the PP&R policy. The Utah Supreme Court concluded that State Farm's conduct was reprehensible, as the first critical test in *Gore* required. The court relied on evidence outside of Utah to make this decision. The Utah Supreme Court also ruled that State Farm's "massive wealth" and the fact that its "clandestine" actions would result in punishment in one out of every 50,000 cases justified the large difference between punitive and compensatory damages to satisfy *Gore* test number two. The third test was justified according to the Utah Supreme Court because State Farm could have been faced with fines of $10,000 for each act of fraud and suspension of its license to conduct business in Utah, as well as the surrendering of its profits and imprisonment.

State Farm then appealed the awards to the United States Supreme Court, which overturned the Utah Supreme Court on April 7, 2003. The United States Supreme Court in a 6 to 3 decision found the punitive damages excessive and in violation of the due process clause of the Fourteenth Amendment. The damage award was overturned and sent back to the state of Utah for a review of the award. Justice Kennedy wrote the opinion for the Court and was joined by Chief Justice Rehnquist and Justices Breyer, O'Connor, Stevens, and Souter. Justices Ginsburg, Scalia and Thomas each wrote dissenting opinions. Kennedy wrote for the Court:

> "We must acknowledge that State Farm's handling of the claims against the Campbells merits no praise. The trial court found that State Farm's employees altered the company's records to make Campbell appear less culpable. State Farm disregarded the overwhelming likelihood of liability and the near-certain probability that, by taking the case to trial, a judgment in excess of the policy limits would be awarded. State Farm amplified the harm by at first assuring the Campbells their assets would be safe from any verdict and by later telling them, postjudgment, to put a for-sale sign on their house. While we do not suggest there was error in awarding punitive damages based upon State Farm's conduct toward the Campbells, a more modest punishment for this reprehensible conduct could have satisfied the State's legitimate objectives, and the Utah courts should have gone no further.

> "This case, instead, was used as a platform to expose, and punish, the perceived deficiencies of State Farm's operations throughout the country. The Utah Supreme Court's opinion makes explicit that State Farm was being condemned for its nationwide policies rather than for the conduct directed toward the Campbells …

> "The courts awarded punitive damages to punish and deter conduct that bore no relation to the Campbells' harm. A defendant's dissimilar acts, independent from the acts upon which liability was premised, may not serve as the basis for punitive damages. A defendant should be punished for the conduct that harmed the plaintiff, not for being an unsavory individual or business. Due process does not permit courts, in the calculation of punitive damages, to adjudicate the merits of other parties' hypothetical claims against a defendant under the guise of the reprehensibility analysis, but we have no doubt the Utah Supreme Court did that here…"

The three dissenting justices all believed the United States Supreme Court should not be ruling on the size of punitive awards. Justice Thomas does not believe that the Constitution sets any restraint on the size of punitive awards. Justice Scalia dissented even in *Gore*, which set a new precedent that the due process clause protects against "excessive" or "unreasonable" awards of punitive damages. Scalia does not believe this protection is embodied in the due process clause. Justice Ginsburg added in dissent specifics about the State Farm case:

> "There was ample basis for the jury to find that everything that had happened to the Campbells—when State Farm repeatedly refused in bad-faith to settle for the $50,000 policy limits and went to trial, and then failed to pay the 'excess' verdict, or at least post a bond, after trial—was a direct application of State Farm's overall profit scheme, operating through Brown and others ... State Farm's 'policies and practices,' the trial evidence thus bore out, were 'responsible for the injuries suffered by the Campbells,' and the means used to implement those policies could be found 'callous, clandestine, fraudulent, and dishonest.' ... (finding 'ample evidence' that State Farm's reprehensible corporate policies were responsible for injuring 'many other Utah consumers during the past two decades'). The Utah Supreme Court, relying on the trial court's record-based recitations, understandably characterized State Farm's behavior as 'egregious and malicious.'"

Ginsburg also went on to warn about the long-term effects of the ruling in the State Farm case:

> "When the Court first ventured to override state-court punitive damages awards, it did so moderately. The Court recalled that '[i]n our federal system, States necessarily have considerable flexibility in determining the level of punitive damages that they will allow in different classes of cases and in any particular case. ... Today's decision exhibits no such respect and restraint. No longer content to accord state-court judgments 'a strong presumption of validity,' ... the Court announces that 'few awards exceeding a single-digit ratio between punitive and compensatory damages, to a significant degree, will satisfy due process.' ... Moreover, the Court adds, when compensatory damages are substantial, doubling those damages 'can reach the outermost limit of the due process guarantee.' ... In a legislative scheme or a state high court's design to cap punitive damages, the handiwork in setting single-digit and 1-to-1 benchmarks could hardly be questioned; in a judicial decree imposed on the States by this Court under the banner of substantive due process, the numerical controls today's decision installs seem to me boldly out of order."

How this ruling will be played out in the courts in unknown. The Utah courts will reconsider the damages based on this April 7, 2003 ruling and, after they do, the case could land back at the U.S. Supreme Court's doorstep. If not, a similar case from another state could review this newly forming precedent, especially now that the issue of excessive damage awards is making the newspapers almost every month.

Revisiting Agent Orange Claims

The chemical companies thought they were in the clear when an *Agent Orange* settlement was reached in 1985 that created a $180 million fund financed by the companies to pay veterans who had developed diseases because of Agent Orange exposure. This settlement estimated a 50,000 member class of the 2.6 million Vietnam veterans that were disabled because of Agent Orange exposure between 1971 and 1994. These estimates did not include veterans who later developed conditions after 1994 because many of the related diseases do not appear for 20 to 30 years after exposure.

About 2.4 million U.S. Vietnam veterans and their families have been exposed to Agent Orange. Many of these people did not realize until recently that Agent Orange exposure could result in serious and potentially deadly side effects including cancer, neurological disorders, and diabetes. The 1985 fund was totally depleted in 1994, leaving anyone diagnosed after 1994 with no compensation from the settlement.

> **Court Connotations**
>
> **Agent Orange** was a herbicide developed for military use to clear dense jungles and destroy lush Vietnamese terrains to expose the enemy hiding in those terrains.

Two Vietnam veterans filed suit, claiming that they were not adequately represented by the 1985 class-action lawsuit. Both were diagnosed with deadly cancers. Joe Isaacson was diagnosed with non-Hodgkin's lymphoma in 1996 and Dan Stephenson was diagnosed with multiple myeloma (a primary tumor of the bone marrow) in 1998. The federal district court dismissed both liability suits against the manufacturers of Agent Orange, which include Dow Chemical, Monsanto, and other chemical companies, because the judge ruled they were bound by the 1985 settlement.

The 2nd Circuit Court reversed the lower court ruling, holding that future victims were not adequately represented by the class action. Two questions were appealed to the Supreme Court:

1. whether people who are unaware of their involvement in a class action suit are allowed to argue later that they were not properly represented; and

2. what standard should be used if those lawsuits are allowed.

In a rare ruling, the United States Supreme Court tied in its decision. A two-paragraph per curiam decision was announced on June 9, 2003. In the Isaacson case, the 2nd Circuit Court verdict was vacated and remanded for further consideration. *Dow Chemical* v. *Stephenson* was affirmed by an equally divided court, letting the 2nd Circuit Court verdict stand and allowing the litigation to go forward in the lower court.

Four justices agreed with the district court and believed the plaintiffs were bound by the settlement and four agreed with the circuit court and believed they were not adequately represented, so litigation could proceed in the lower court. The ninth justice who could have broken the tie, Justice John Paul Stevens, whose son served in Vietnam and died of cancer in 1996, *recused* himself from the case.

Since this Supreme Court decision was announced on June 9, 2003, none of the Agent Orange cases have made it to trial at the time of this writing. If you or someone in your family may be impacted by these decisions be sure to watch the cases carefully as they make it through the courts. A good website for this information is www.agent-orange-lawsuit.com. There is no way of knowing what levels of compensation may be available for veterans suffering from diseases related to Agent Orange that have been discovered since the Agent Orange settlement funds ran out in 1994.

> **Just the Facts** _____
>
> If you are a Vietnam veteran and think you may be suffering from diseases relating to exposure to Agent Orange, you can find out more information about these cases and your rights at the Agent Orange Lawsuit site (www.agent-orange-lawsuit.com).

> **Just the Facts** _____
>
> To **recuse** yourself from a case means to refuse to be involved. A judge usually does this when there is a conflict of interest or other good reason, such as acquaintanceship with one of the parties.

An even greater impact of this case could be that future litigants, who were not fairly represented during a class action lawsuit, could revisit the settlements. A reopening of class action settlements could have a huge impact on costs for businesses that thought a case was already settled and their damages determined.

Setting Rules for Arbitration

Many contracts that you'll sign over your lifetime include an *arbitration* clause, which stipulates that any claim must be settled by arbitration rather than court trial. Businesses prefer arbitration because they want to avoid the staggering costs of litigation. You'll find arbitration clauses in many financial contracts and car purchase contracts, as well as many others with lots of fine print.

Court Connotations

Arbitration involves a hearing led by a person or persons chosen by the parties involved in a dispute. The facts are heard and a determination is made setting an award based on these facts. Sometimes one person serves as arbiter and other times each party chooses an arbiter and then agrees on a third person who serves as an umpire. Read the arbitration clause in any contract before signing. This is where any future arbitration process is stipulated.

The U.S. Supreme Court historically has shown great support for arbitration over trial in many cases that have made it to its doorstep. That belief was reaffirmed in two cases in 2003. One was brought by doctors called *PacifiCare Inc.* v. *Book* and the second was brought by borrowers in *Green Tree Financial* v. *Bazzle*. Each of these cases is covered in the sections that follow.

Seeking Trial Instead of Arbitration

A group of physicians filed suit against several managed health care organizations (HMOs) including PacifiCare Health Systems, Inc., and PacifiCare Operations, Inc. (collectively, PacifiCare), and UnitedHealthcare, Inc. and UnitedHealth Group Inc. (collectively, United). The physicians claimed the HMOs unlawfully failed to reimburse them for health-care services that they had provided to patients covered by their health plans. They based their cases under Racketeer Influenced Corrupt Organizations Act (RICO), the Employee Retirement Income Security Act of 1974 (ERISA), and federal and state prompt-pay statutes, as well as claims for breach of contract and unjust enrichment.

Provisions in their contracts stipulated that arbitration would be used to settle claims rather than court trial. The doctors believed that arbitration was not appropriate because if they proved their RICO claims, punitive damages could not be awarded in arbitration. Under the RICO statute treble (triple) damages could be authorized in a court ruling, but not as part of arbitration.

Just the Facts

Racketeer Influenced Corrupt Organizations Act (RICO) was passed for the purpose of convicting organized-crime families. The crime was not that a person belonged to a crime family, but instead the person or people were found to collectively engage in extortion or to commit usury or other crimes. Private persons injured by these criminal activities can sue for damages, pain, suffering and loss of property.

The district court agreed with the doctors and refused to compel arbitration because they could not obtain "meaningful relief for allegations of statutory violations in an arbitration forum." It found the arbitration agreements were unenforceable with respect to the RICO claims. The 11th Circuit Court affirmed the district court opinion, so the HMOs appealed the case to the Supreme Court in *PacificCare* v. *Book*.

The Supreme Court in an 8 to 0 decision reversed the 11th Circuit Court and ruled that arbitration should be compelled since the facts were not yet known in the case. Justice Scalia wrote the decision for the Court and was joined by all but Justice Thomas, who did not participate in this case. Scalia wrote:

> "… since we do not know how the arbitrator will construe the remedial limitations, the questions whether they render the parties' agreements unenforceable and whether it is for courts or arbitrators to decide enforceability in the first instance are unusually abstract … the proper course is to compel arbitration. The judgment of the Court of Appeals is reversed, and the case is remanded for further proceedings consistent with this opinion."

The physicians will have to accept arbitration and could later appeal if the arbiters determine there are RICO claims that require litigation to determine punitive damages outside the purview of the arbitrator.

Denying Class Action Arbitration

When you borrow money from a financial institution, you will frequently find an arbitration clause in that agreement. That was true for Lynn and Burt Bazzle when they borrowed money for a home-improvement loan from Green Tree Financial in 1995. The contract included this relatively common arbitration clause:

> "ARBITRATION—All disputes, claims, or controversies arising from or relating to this contract or the relationships which result from this contract … shall be resolved by binding arbitration by one arbitrator selected by us with consent of you. This arbitration contract is made pursuant to a transaction in interstate commerce, and shall be governed by the Federal Arbitration Act at 9 U.S.C. section 1 …. THE PARTIES VOLUNTARILY AND KNOWINGLY WAIVE ANY RIGHT THEY HAVE TO A JURY TRIAL, EITHER PURSUANT TO ARBITRATION UNDER THIS CLAUSE OR PURSUANT TO COURT ACTION BY US (AS PROVIDED HEREIN) …. The parties agree and understand that the arbitrator shall have all powers provided by the law and the contract. These powers shall include all legal and equitable remedies, including, but not limited to, money damages, declaratory relief, and injunctive relief."

When closing the loan, Green Tree Financial failed to provide them with a form that would have told them of their right to name their own lawyers and insurance agents in violation of South Carolina law, so they filed suit seeking damages. The Bazzles filed the case in court in 1997 in order to establish a class action. Green Tree tried to stop the court proceedings and compel arbitration.

After the court established a class action suit in 1998, it compelled arbitration. Green Tree selected an arbitrator with the Bazzles' consent. The arbitrator awarded $10,935,000 in statutory damages to the class plus attorney's fees. The trial court confirmed the award. Green Tree appealed the decision, claiming that the arbitration clause did not permit class arbitration. The trial court denied the motion and Green Tree appealed the decision to the state appeals court, which sided with Green Tree.

The State Supreme Court then took control of the Bazzle case, as well as a similar case filed by Daniel Lackey and George and Florine Buggs and consolidated the cases. In its ruling, the South Carolina Supreme Court found that the arbitration clause was silent on the issue of class action and authorized the class arbitration. Green Tree then appealed to the United States Supreme Court in a case entitled *Green Tree* v. *Bazzle*.

In a 5 to 4 decision, the United States Supreme Court vacated the judgment of the State Supreme Court and remanded the case back to the state. Justice Breyer wrote the opinion for the Court and was joined by Ginsburg, Scalia, and Souter. Justice Stevens filed a separate concurring opinion. Chief Justice Rehnquist filed a dissenting opinion and was joined by Kennedy and O'Connor. Justice Thomas filed a separate dissent. In writing for the Court, Justice Breyer said:

> "The question here—whether the contracts forbid class arbitration ... concerns neither the validity of the arbitration clause nor its applicability to the underlying dispute between the parties. ... It concerns contract interpretation and arbitration procedures. Arbitrators are well situated to answer that question. Given these considerations, along with the arbitration contracts' sweeping language concerning the scope of the questions committed to arbitration, this matter of contract interpretation should be for the arbitrator, not the courts, to decide."

Again, the Supreme Court decided that the question should be left in the laps of the arbitrator and not the courts. In the dissent, Chief Justice Rehnquist wrote:

> "While the observation of the Supreme Court of South Carolina that the agreement of the parties was silent as to the availability of class-wide arbitration is literally true, the imposition of class-wide arbitration contravenes ... the provision about the selection of an arbitrator. To be sure, the arbitrator that administered the proceedings was 'selected by [petitioner] with consent of' the Bazzles, Lackey, and the Buggses ... But petitioner had the contractual right to choose

an arbitrator for each dispute with the other 3,734 individual class members, and this right was denied when the same arbitrator was foisted upon petitioner to resolve those claims as well. Petitioner may well have chosen different arbitrators for some or all of these other disputes; indeed, it would have been reasonable for petitioner to do so, in order to avoid concentrating all of the risk of substantial damages awards in the hands of a single arbitrator. As petitioner correctly concedes … the FAA does not prohibit parties from choosing to proceed on a class-wide basis. Here, however, the parties simply did not so choose."

So in dissenting, Chief Justice Rehnquist believed that since Green Tree Financial did not choose to accept the class arbitration, it had the final word in that decision—not the courts or the arbitrator. Either way an arbitrator will be the one to decide any cases brought against Green Tree Financial based on this arbitration clause.

Now that you have a better idea what to watch out for to protect your contract rights, I'll now move on to the legal issues surrounding your protections as an employee or employer.

The Least You Need to Know

- Insurers may tell you that you don't need your own attorney, but you cannot always be sure they will represent your best interest if a case goes to court.

- If a class-action suit determines your award and you were not aware you were a part of the class at the time the award was determined, you might have a right to revisit the issues of that class action.

- Many contracts include arbitration clauses. Be sure you understand how that clause is worded and what your rights will be under that clause before you sign a contract.

Chapter 26

Getting to Work

In This Chapter

- ◆ Hostile work environments
- ◆ Proving sexual harassment
- ◆ Small businesses and discrimination
- ◆ Fearing cancer

As we discussed in Chapter 2, the majority of employment-related cases that found their way to the Supreme Court in recent years raise questions about discrimination and harassment. In this chapter, I'll review cases involving discrimination relating to disability in a small business environment and employer responsibility in a hostile work environment.

Another frequent issue that makes its way through the courts is related to disease exposure. One recent case I'll explore decides the issue of asbestos exposure and the fear of cancer.

Liability for a Hostile Work Environment

Is an employer responsible if a worker finds himself or herself in a hostile work environment because of sexual harassment by supervisors? If sexual harassment occurs, what type of notification must the employer receive? These critical issues were decided in the 1998 case, *Faragher* v. *City of Boca Raton*.

Beth Ann Faragher worked as a lifeguard for the city of Boca Raton in Florida. Her supervisor was Bill Terry, who was Chief of Marine Safety. David Silverman, a marine safety lieutenant, supervised daily lifeguard duties. Because Terry and Silverman were located at a worksite removed from the rest of city government, their authority was virtually unchecked by higher-level managers.

Faragher claimed that she and another female lifeguard, Nancy Ewanchew, were the subjects of uninvited and offensive touching by Terry. Silverman reportedly made offensive comments and gestures to both women. Both women complained to a supervisor, to a marine safety lieutenant and to the training captain, Robert Gordon. Although Gordon received complaints about Silverman's language and conduct from other lifeguards as well, he never reported the complaints to Terry or to another city official.

Ewanchew and Faragher resigned their lifeguard positions with the city in 1989 and 1990. In April of 1990, Ewanchew wrote a letter to the city's director of personnel complaining that while employed with the city, she and other female lifeguards were sexually harassed by Terry and Silverman. The city, after investigating the complaint, concluded that Terry and Silverman engaged in inappropriate conduct. Both were reprimanded and disciplined.

In 1992, Faragher sued the city of Boca Raton for sexual harassment under *Title VII of the Civil Rights Act*. The U.S. district court ruled in favor of Faragher, saying she was subjected to sufficiently severe and pervasive offensive conduct in a hostile work environment. The district court held the city directly liable for Terry's and Silverman's conduct because of the severity. The court also found the city had constructive knowledge of the sexual harassment.

Court Connotations

Title VII of the Civil Rights Act prohibits discriminatory employment practices on the basis of sex, race, religion, color, and national origin. Sexual harassment is seen by the courts to be particularly offensive because it negatively impacts work performance and opportunities for advancement in the same way sex discrimination impacts hiring.

The 11th Circuit Court overturned the lower court and found that the court did not find a factual basis to conclude that the harassment was so pervasive or that the city had constructive knowledge. The 11th Circuit Court thus concluded that the city was neither indirectly or directly liable for the harassment. Faragher appealed the decision to the Supreme Court.

Arguments were heard by the Supreme Court on March 25, 1998 and in a 7 to 2 ruling on June 26,

1998, the Supreme Court found that an employer is liable to a sexual harassment plaintiff when a hostile work environment is created by a supervisor or a successively higher authority over the employee. The court ruled that to successfully defend against a sexual harassment suit involving a "tangible employment action":

♦ An employer must exercise reasonable care to prevent and correct promptly any sexually harassing behavior, and

♦ An employer must prove that an employee failed to take advantage of any preventive or corrective opportunities provided by the employer or to avoid harm otherwise.

The court defined a "tangible employment action" as including discharge, demotion, or undesirable reassignment. In the Boca Raton case, the court ruled that the city had not met the elements of an affirmative defense.

Justice Souter wrote the opinion for the Court and was joined by Chief Justice Rehnquist and Justices Breyer, Ginsburg, Kennedy, O'Connor, and Stevens. Justice Thomas dissented and was joined by Scalia. In writing for the court, Justice Souter said:

"The District Court found that the City had entirely failed to disseminate its policy against sexual harassment among the beach employees and that its officials made no attempt to keep track of the conduct of supervisors like Terry and Silverman. The record also makes clear that the City's policy did not include any assurance that the harassing supervisors could be bypassed in registering complaints …. Under such circumstances, we hold as a matter of law that the City could not be found to have exercised reasonable care to prevent the supervisors' harassing conduct. Unlike the employer of a small workforce, who might expect that sufficient care to prevent *tortious* behavior could be exercised informally, those responsible for city operations could not reasonably have thought that precautions against hostile environments in any one of many

> **Living Laws**
>
> Women who experience sexual harassment in a work environment must find out about their employer's sexual harassment policy or other grievance procedures. If a woman does not make use of the established procedures and take advantage of their protections, she must be prepared to show evidence that she made a reasonable decision not to make use of established procedures.

Court Connotations

Tortious refers to an act which is a tort or a civil wrong.

departments in far-flung locations could be effective without communicating some formal policy against harassment, with a sensible complaint procedure."

The Supreme Court reversed the decision of the 11th Circuit Court and reinstated the district court's ruling.

Setting Standards for Small Businesses and Discrimination

Small businesses with fewer than 15 employees are exempt from many of the discrimination laws. In 2003, the Supreme Court decided whether a small business qualifies as a small business if some of the people working in that business are also owners and shareholders. The case involved was *Clackamas Gastroentrology* v. *Wells*.

Deborah Wells worked as a bookkeeper for Clackamas Gastroenterology Associates, a medical clinic in Oregon, from 1986 to 1997. She was fired in 1997 and claimed Clackamas terminated her employment in violation of the Americans with Disabilities Act (ADA).

Wells filed suit in district court. Clackamas asked for summary judgment because it said it had only 14 employees plus the four physicians, who should not be considered employees but instead be counted as partners even though they were corporate shareholders. ADA protection requires that a business have 15 or more employees for 20 or more weeks. The district court agreed that the physicians were more analogous to partners than to shareholders in a corporation, so therefore were not employees, and dismissed the case.

The 9th Circuit Court disagreed and found that the professional corporation had no reason to argue it was a partnership, so it could not avoid counting the physicians as employees to avoid the ADA suit. The 9th Circuit Court ruled since Clackamas reaped the tax and other advantages of being a corporation it could not at the same time argue it was like a partnership to avoid liability for unlawful discrimination.

Clackamas then appealed to the Supreme Court, which settled the matter and found in a 7 to 2 decision that the common-law element of control is the principal guidepost to be followed in deciding whether the four director-shareholder physicians in this case were to be counted as employees or not.

Court Connotations

The **Equal Employment Opportunity Commission** is the federal agency responsible for the special enforcement responsibilities under the ADA and other federal statutes relating to equal employment issues.

The Court picked the six factor test used by the *Equal Employment Opportunity Commission* (EEOC) to determine whether the physicians were employees.

The six factors taken from the EEOC compliance manual include:

1. whether the organization can hire or fire an individual or set rules and regulations of an individual's work;

2. whether, and if so, to what extent the organization supervises the individual's work;

3. whether the individual reports to someone higher in the organization (for example, even a partnership has lower level partners who report to managing partners);

4. whether, and if so to what extent, the individual is able to influence the organization;

5. whether the parties intended that individual to be an employee as expressed in written agreements or contract; and

6. whether the individual shares in the profits, losses and liabilities of the organization.

The Supreme Court decided the district court needed to find out the facts related to these six factors and remanded the case back to the lower court. Justice Stevens wrote the opinion for the Court and was joined by Chief Justice Rehnquist and Justices Kennedy, O'Connor, Scalia, Souter, and Thomas. Justice Ginsburg filed a dissenting opinion and was joined by Justice Breyer. In writing for the Court, Justice Stevens said:

> "As the EEOC's standard reflects, an employer is the person, or group of persons, who owns and manages the enterprise. The employer can hire and fire employees, can assign tasks to employees and supervise their performance, and can decide how the profits and losses of the business are to be distributed. The mere fact that a person has a particular title—such as partner, director, or vice president—should not necessarily be used to determine whether he or she is an employee or a proprietor ... 'An individual's title ... does not determine whether the individual is a partner, officer, member of a board of directors, or major shareholder, as opposed to an employee' .... Nor should the mere existence of a document styled 'employment agreement' lead inexorably to the conclusion that either party is an employee ... the answer to whether a shareholder-director is an employee depends on 'all of the incidents of the relationship ... with no one factor being decisive.'"

Justice Ginsburg in her dissent saw no reason for the complicated test. She wrote:

> "The physician-shareholders, it bears emphasis, invite the designation 'employee' for various purposes under federal and state law. The Employee Retirement Income Security Act of 1974 (ERISA), much like the ADA, defines 'employee' as 'any individual employed by an employer' … Clackamas readily acknowledges that the physician-shareholders are 'employees' for ERISA purposes … Indeed, gaining qualification as 'employees' under ERISA was the prime reason the physician-shareholders chose the corporate form instead of a partnership … Further, Clackamas agrees, the physician-shareholders are covered by Oregon's workers' compensation law … a statute applicable to 'person[s] … who … furnish services for a remuneration, subject to the direction and control of an employer,' … Finally, by electing to organize their practice as a corporation, the physician-shareholders created an entity separate and distinct from themselves, one that would afford them limited liability for the debts of the enterprise … I see no reason to allow the doctors to escape from their choice of corporate form when the question becomes whether they are employees for purposes of federal antidiscrimination statutes."

Since this case was decided on April 22, 2003, there was no final ruling on the physicians' employee status at the time of this writing. The case will likely add another twist to the decision when a small business is trying to determine whether to form as a partnership or a corporation.

Fearing Cancer After Asbestos Exposure

Can an employer be required to pay damages for pain and suffering for a disease not yet contracted? That was what the Supreme Court had to decide in the case *Norfolk & Western Railway Co.* The case involved six former railroad employees who sued the railroad under the Federal Employers Liability Act (FELA), which was passed by Congress to protect and compensate railroad employees injured on the job, because they were diagnosed with *asbestosis*.

Court Connotations

Asbestosis is a common and usually nonmalignant disease caused by exposure to asbestos. When asbestos fibers enter the lung they cause tissue to harden and scar around them. In extreme cases a person can experience difficulty breathing. Varying degrees of impairment in mobility and lifestyle can occur. Cancer is a possibility.

The workers brought the FELA action because they believed their former employer, Norfolk, negligently exposed them to asbestos, which caused them to contract the occupational disease asbestosis. They sought damages for mental anguish based on their fear of developing cancer.

Norfolk moved to exclude all evidence referring to cancer as irrelevant and prejudicial. The district court denied the motion, and evidence relating to cancer was heard by the jury, including expert testimony that asbestosis sufferers with smoking histories have a significantly increased risk of developing lung cancer. Of the six asbestosis workers, five had smoking histories and two continued to smoke even after being diagnosed. This increased their risk of dying of mesothelioma, a fatal cancer of the lining of the lung or abdominal cavity.

Because none of the six workers could show he was reasonably certain to develop cancer, the district court instructed the jury that damages could not be awarded to any claimant "for cancer or any increased risk of cancer." The testimony about cancer, the court explained, was relevant "only to judge the genuineness of plaintiffs' claims of fear of developing cancer." The district court specifically said, "[A]ny plaintiff who has demonstrated that he has developed a reasonable fear of cancer that is related to proven physical injury from asbestos is entitled to be compensated for that fear as a part of the damages you may award for pain and suffering."

The jury awarded damages for each of the six asbestosis claimants, ranging from $770,000 to $1.2 million. After reduction for three claimants' comparative negligence from smoking and for settlements with non-FELA entities, the final judgments amounted to approximately $4.9 million. The district court denied Norfolk's motion for a new trial and the Supreme Court of Appeals of West Virginia denied Norfolk's request for a discretionary review, so Norfolk appealed the case to the United States Supreme Court.

The United States Supreme Court in a unanimous ruling found that an employee who has developed asbestosis as a result of actions or negligence of his employer does have a reasonable fear of cancer and may collect damages for emotional distress caused by this fear. The Court also found that under FELA, the railroad is liable for damages caused "in whole or in part" by its negligence. The railroad has the responsibility to seek contribution from other parties that may be involved in causing the damage.

In writing the opinion for the Court, Justice Ginsburg said:

> "Under the FELA, an employee who suffers an 'injury' caused 'in whole or in part' by a railroad's negligence may recover his or her full damages from the railroad, regardless of whether the injury was also caused 'in part' by the actions of a third party … The 'elephantine mass of asbestos cases' lodged in state and

federal courts, we again recognize, 'defies customary judicial administration and calls for national legislation.' … Courts, however, must resist pleas of the kind Norfolk has made, essentially to reconfigure established liability rules because they do not serve to abate today's asbestos litigation crisis. "

In its opinion the Court cited the administrative procedures in place for black lung disease as a reasonable legislative response to asbestos cases. Black lung disease is the common name for coal workers' pneumoconiosis (CWP), a lung disease of older workers in the coal industry that is caused by inhalation, over many years, of small amounts of coal dust. The 1969 Black Lung Law set up a black lung disability benefits program to compensate coal miners who have been disabled by on-the-job dust exposure in addition to setting up regulations for dust levels in mines.

Be a Court Watcher

Our tour of Supreme Court cases is completed. As you've learned during our trip through recent Court decisions, almost every aspect of our lives seems to find its way to the Supreme Court in one way or another. Even though only about 100 cases make it to the Court each year, the justices carefully select those cases most likely to have the greatest impact on issues facing us each day, whether in the workplace, in our towns and cities, or in our homes.

You can see why it is important to be a Court watcher and pay attention to who gets appointed to the Court each time there is an opening. Hopefully this book helped you to better understand the power of the Court and how its decisions are made.

The Least You Need to Know

- If you are faced with a hostile work environment filled with sexual harassment, find out your company's policies and follow procedures indicated in those policies. Without taking those first steps, you can't take your claim to court if your complaint is not satisfied inside your company.

- Small businesses with fewer than 15 employees are not obligated to follow the Americans with Disability Act (ADA). The number of employees can be questionable in small businesses depending on whether all partners or owners are counted as employees.

- Asbestosis sufferers can sue for damages based on their fear of getting cancer.

Glossary

Agent Orange   A herbicide developed for military use to clear dense jungles and destroy lush Vietnamese terrains, which exposed the enemy hiding in those terrains.

Appeals process   This involves filing briefs (written legal arguments) and then arguing these legal issues before judges after the initial trial in a courtroom. How many levels of appeals will depend upon where the case started. If a case started in a state court, then it must first be appealed in the state to the highest court there before being taken to the federal court level.

Appellate jurisdiction   This limits the role of the Supreme Court to one of hearing appeals from lower courts. The Supreme Court cannot just pick out a controversial issue and make a decision. It must act on cases brought to the court based on actual disputes raised in actual court cases.

Asbestosis   A common and usually nonmalignant disease caused by exposure to asbestos. When asbestos fibers enter the lung they cause tissue to harden and scar around them. In extreme cases a person can experience difficulty breathing. Varying degrees of impairment in mobility and lifestyle can occur. Cancer is a possibility.

Bench trial   This is a trial without a jury. The judge determines all question of law and tries the defendant.

Brethren   Or "brother," is a self-referential term used by the justices, who were an exclusively male club until 1981 when the first female justice, Sandra Day O'Connor, was appointed during Burger's term. Some wondered if her appointment would end the tradition. Today even with two women on the court, the tradition holds.

Briefs   Written legal arguments.

Capital offenses   These are the most serious crimes, usually related to murder or other crimes in which the death penalty could be imposed. Whether a crime is a misdemeanor, felony, or capital offense is determined by each state. Federal law also has similar designations for crimes against the government.

Child Pornography Prevention Act of 1996 (CPPA)   This prohibits "any visual depiction, including any photograph, film, video, picture, or computer or computer-generated image" that appears to show a minor engaging in "sexually explicit conduct."

Children's Internet Protection Act (CIPA)   This addresses problems associated with the availability of Internet pornography in public libraries. In order for a library to receive federal assistance it must install software that blocks images that show obscenity or child pornography and must prevent minors from accessing this material.

Circumstantial evidence   This is evidence given at a trial that is not directly from an eyewitness or participant. Circumstantial evidence is commonly perceived as weak by the public, but can include testimony about prior threats to a victim, fingerprints found at the crime scene, ownership of the murder weapon, or being seen by a witness near the crime scene at the time the crime took place.

Commerce clause   This is in Article I of the Constitution and gives the federal government the right "To regulate commerce with foreign Nations, and among the several States, and with the Indian Tribes."

Concurring opinions   These are opinions that agree with the position of the Court, but vary on the legal reasons for deciding that way.

Constitutional amendments   These alter the language of the original draft of the Constitution. The Constitution can be changed either through an amendment proposed by two-thirds of both houses of Congress or by a call for a constitutional convention by two-thirds of the state legislatures.

Copyrights   These are legal rights granted to an author, composer, playwright, publisher, or distributor to exclusive publication, production, sale, or distribution of a literary, musical, dramatic, or artistic work.

Dane Professor of Law This was established at Harvard College in 1829 with a donation from Nathan Dane, who gave a total of $15,000 over his lifetime to Harvard Law School. These donations paid for the Dane professorship and the founding of Dane Hall. Nathan Dane served in positions for both the Massachusetts and U.S. government. His service included being a delegate from Massachusetts for the Continental Congress from 1785 to 1787.

De minimis This is the Latin word for "of minimum importance" or "trifling." In law it refers to something or a difference that is so small or tiny that the law does not refer to it or consider it. For example in a contract deal, a $1 million error could be questioned legally, while a $10 error is de minimis.

Dissenting opinions These are opinions that disagree with the opinion of the Court.

Equal Employment Opportunity Commission This is the federal agency responsible for the special enforcement responsibilities under the Americans with Disabilities Act and other federal statutes relating to equal employment issues.

Equal protection This clause of the Constitution states, "No state shall make or enforce any law which shall abridge the privileges or immunities of citizens of the United States; nor shall any state deprive any person of life, liberty, or property, without due process of law; nor deny to any person within its jurisdiction the equal protection of the laws." This is most commonly used in cases involving the death penalty. To use this clause, there must be proof that someone is being harmed by not receiving equal protection under law.

Executive privilege This is a claim not mentioned in the Constitution, but one in which presidents invoke on the constitutional principle of separation of powers. Presidents believe that this privilege permits them to resist requests for information by the Congressional and judicial branches and keep certain activity within the executive branch secret.

Family and Medical Leave Act of 1993 (FMLA) This entitles an eligible employee to take up to 12 work weeks of unpaid leave annually for the onset of a "serious health condition" by the employee's spouse or other family-related medical needs. The act is most frequently used by women after giving birth to a child or to care for elderly parents or children.

Federal Election Commission This commission administers and enforces the Federal Election Campaign Act (FECA)—the statute that governs the financing of federal elections. Its duties include the disclosure of campaign finance information and the enforcement of FECA related to limits and prohibitions on contributions. It also oversees the public funding of presidential elections.

Federal Judicial Center   This is the research and education agency for the federal judicial system. It conducts and promotes education and training for judges and court employees, develops recommendations about court operations, and conducts or promotes research on federal judicial procedures, court operations, and history.

Felonies   These are more serious crimes than misdemeanors, with stronger penalties, usually larger fines and longer jail terms. Whether a crime is a misdemeanor, felony, or capital offense is determined by each state. Federal law also has similar designations for crimes against the government.

Fifteenth Amendment   This amendment to the Constitution prohibits denying the right to vote on the grounds of race, color, or previous conditions of servitude.

Filibuster   This is a tactic that can be used by senators to extend debate on an issue indefinitely and prevent a vote. There is no Senate rule that can force a vote. Debate must first be cut off and that requires a 60-vote majority. When the Senate is closely divided, it can be very difficult to get those 60 votes. The practice dates back to the 1800s. The term comes from "filibusteros" used by early nineteenth century Spanish pirates who held ships hostage for ransom.

Forensic psychologist   This is an expert who gives his psychological opinion in the courts to assist with fact-finding in a criminal or civil case. A forensic psychologist must have a doctorate degree in psychology. After completing his doctorate, a psychologist will usually work under an experienced forensic psychologist to gain further expertise before being called on as an expert witness.

Fourth Amendment   This amendment to the Constitution states, "The right of the people to be secure in their persons, houses, papers, and effects, against unreasonable searches and seizures, shall not be violated, and no warrants shall issue, but upon probable cause, supported by oath or affirmation, and particularly describing the place to be searched, and the persons or things to be seized." This is the amendment that is used to protect you against illegal search and seizure in your own home, on your person, or in your vehicle.

Good behavior   This grants a person the position of chief justice or associate justice for life. A justice can be impeached if he or she commits a crime or is found guilty of serious judicial misconduct, but only one Supreme Court justice in the history of the nation ever faced an impeachment trial—Samuel Chase (in 1805).

Interlocutory appeal   This is an appeal that asks an appellate court to decide a legal issue that cannot be resolved on the facts of the case, but whose resolution is essential to a final decision in the case. This type of appeal prevents a trial from going forward until the appeal process is completed.

Internments camps   These were set up by President Franklin D. Roosevelt in 1942 when he signed an executive order to establish the War Relocation Authority, which had the responsibility to remove Japanese Americans from their homes and place them in camps. These camps housed more than 110,000 Japanese Americans who lived along the Pacific Coast. Some of these Japanese Americans lived in the country since the early 1900s and some were second-generation Japanese born in America.

Judicial Conference of the United States   This makes policy with regard to the administration of the United States courts and supervises the director of the Administrative Office of the United States Courts.

Laissez faire   This is an economic principle on which capitalism is based that opposes governmental regulation of or interference in commerce unless necessary to enable the operation of a free enterprise system based solely on its own economic laws.

Lame-duck Congress   This is a Congress that meets after the election in November and before the new Congress takes over.

Law clerks   These are selected each year to serve each of the Supreme Court justices for one year and assist him or her with research. Law clerks who serve at the Supreme Court are the cream-of-the-crop of recent law school graduates and usually have at least one year clerking for a lower court justice. In addition to top grades, recommendations from former professors and judges play an important part in the selection process.

Misdemeanors   These are minor crimes with the least severe level of penalty, usually small fines and sometimes a short jail sentence.

Missouri Compromise   This was the brainchild of Henry Clay. Missouri was admitted as a slave state, while at the same time Maine was admitted as a free state. This kept the balance of 12 free states and 12 slaves states. As future states were added over the next 30 years, the balance had to be kept with one free state and one slave state admitted at the same time. States north of the 36 degree 30 latitude, which was the southern boundary of Missouri, were free states. States south of that line could decide for themselves.

New Deal   This was a series of legislative initiatives proposed by President Franklin D. Roosevelt to get people back to work by establishing various federal works projects. Roosevelt also formed the Federal Emergency Relief Administration to provide federal monetary assistance to the most desperate people. Social Security also became law during this period of time.

Ninth Amendment   This amendment to the Constitution states, "The enumeration in the Constitution, of certain rights, shall not be construed to deny or disparage others retained by the people." This amendment was used in previous cases to grant individuals fundamental rights to be protected from governmental infringement.

Oyez   This is actually an Anglo-Norman word derived from "oyer" or "to hear." It literally means "hear ye" and was used during the Middle English period beginning about 1425.

Patents   These are legal rights granted to the creator of an invention for the sole right to make, use, and sell that invention for a set period of time.

Per curiam   This is a Latin phrase for "by the court." A per curiam decision means it is a decision by the entire court with no judge identified as the specific author.

Per se rule   This is a rule set by judges after long experience with certain practices that are common in a given market condition. Once set, the per se rule helps to avoid expensive litigation in areas that a clear rule of law has been set. Before this per se rule is set, cases are determined on a rule of reason that looks at the specific issues of the case before the judge.

Petitions for certiorari   These are documents filed by the losing party in a law suit asking the Supreme Court to review a decision of a lower court. Certiorari is a Latin word that means "to be informed of, or to be made certain in regard to."

Prima facie   In Latin, this means "first look." Prima facie evidence means that an act gives the appearance of guilt.

Qualified immunity   This protects government officials from being sued for liability on civil damages provided their conduct does not violate clearly established statutory or constitutional rights.

Regulatory taking   Or "inverse condemnation," means the government has regulated the use of a property to so great an extent that it no longer has an economically beneficial use for the owner—essentially condemning the land. When this happens the property may be considered "taken" without just compensation. Court cases filed on this issue generally involve denied wetlands permits, denied coastal development permits, denied zoning variances, and other denied development applications.

Selective purchasing laws   This restricts state entities from purchasing goods or services from corporations that do business with repressive governments outside the United States. The purpose of these laws is to force companies to choose between lucrative state or local contracts and doing business with certain foreign countries.

Sine qua non   This is Latin for "without which it could."

Sixteenth Amendment   This amendment to the Constitution states, "The Congress shall have power to lay and collect taxes on incomes, from whatever source derived, without apportionment among the several states, and without regard to any census or enumeration." The amendment was in direct response to the 1895 case *Pollock* v. *Farmer's Loan and Trust Co.* and established that the federal government could tax without having to apportion the tax among the states.

Smithsonian Institution   It is best known for its museums in Washington, D.C., and New York. In addition to running its 16 museums and the National Zoo, the institution does extensive behind-the-scenes research through its institutes.

Title I of the Americans with Disabilities Act of 1990   The Americans with Disabilities Act (ADA) prohibits employers from "discriminat[ing] against a qualified individual with a disability because of th[at] disability … in regard to … terms, conditions, and privileges of employment." Employers must make reasonable accommodations for the employee with a disability.

Title VII of the Civil Rights Act   This prohibits discriminatory employment practices on the basis of sex, race, religion, color, and national origin. Sexual harassment is seen by the courts to be particularly offensive because it negatively impacts work performance and opportunities for advancement in the same way sex discrimination impacts hiring.

Title IX of the Educational Amendments of 1972   This is the landmark legislation that bans sex discrimination in schools, whether it be in academics or athletics. Title IX states: "No person in the U.S. shall, on the basis of sex, be excluded from participation in, or denied the benefits of, or be subjected to discrimination under any educational program or activity receiving federal aid."

Trademarks   These are legal rights granted to a company for a name, symbol, or other device identifying a product, officially registered and legally restricted to the use of the owner or manufacturer.

Writ of mandamus   This is a common law practice that dates back to English law. A judge can force an official to carry out his or her official duties if the writ is granted.

Resources

Websites

The United States Supreme Court official website:
www.supremecourtus.gov
At this site you will be able to find an overview of the Supreme Court, its
traditions and procedures, biographies of the current members of the
Supreme Court, members of the Supreme Court from 1789 to present,
case scheduling, case handling guides, schedule of oral arguments, case
rules, and opinions.

The Supreme Court Historical Society:
www.supremecourthistory.org
This site preserves and disseminates the history of the Supreme Court of
the United States. The society is a not-for-profit organization founded by
the late Chief Justice Warren E. Burger who served as its first honorary
chairman. The society conducts public and educational programs, publishes books and other materials, supports historical research, and collects
antiques and artifacts related to the Court's history. At this site you will be
able to find the history of the Supreme Court and how the court works, as
well as society publications, a learning center, and how to research the
Court.

United States Courts:

www.uscourts.gov

The official site of the United States courts serves as a clearinghouse for information about the judicial branch of the U.S. government. You can find links to the Supreme Court, the U.S. Court of Appeals, the U.S. district courts, and the U.S. bankruptcy courts. You can also find educational information and information on federal rule-making.

Findlaw:

http://supreme.lp.findlaw.com/supreme_court/resources.html

This is an excellent source for searching not only Supreme Court opinions, but also the briefs that were filed before the cases were heard. The Supreme Court Center at Findlaw includes:

♦ Supreme Court cases by oral argument date plus links to lower court decisions, docket sheets, oral argument transcripts and Supreme Court briefs, as available, starting with the October 1999 term and going up to 2004 scheduled cases.

♦ Topic index of current term Supreme Court cases that have been granted certiorari (or accepted to be heard by the Court).

♦ Decisions since 1893.

♦ Supreme Court orders on pending cases, grants, and denials of certiorari.

♦ Briefs indexed by cases granted certiorari.

♦ Rules of the Supreme Court and Court filing guidelines.

♦ Supreme Court calendar including argument days, conference days, nonargument sessions and court holidays.

Legal Information Institute (LII):

http://supct.law.cornell.edu/supct

This site is run by Cornell University Law School and is also an excellent resource for finding information about the Supreme Court, its decisions and orders. Its archives are organized by case topic, author of the opinion, and parties filing the cases. LLI also publishes a bulletin and a CD-ROM of historic court decisions. You can also find a useful glossary of legalese on the site, as well as Supreme Court rules.

OYEZ:

www.oyez.org/oyez/frontpage

If you'd like to hear Supreme Court decisions and oral arguments you can do that at OYEZ. The OYEZ Project began at a baseball game in Wrigley Field in the late 1980s. During one of the Chicago Cubs games, the idea of creating a multimedia-based Supreme Court experience took root. The first iteration was a series of complex HyperCard stacks built on a baseball-card metaphor. The "Hitchhiker's Guide to the U.S. Supreme Court" demonstrated the power of multimedia integration with serious academic content. Dozens of students worked on various versions before the development of a web-based version.

Richard Barone of Northwestern's Learning Technologies Group developed the web-based version of the project with a hardware support grant from the National Science Foundation, followed by a major "Teaching with Technology" grant from the National Endowment for the Humanities. Additional support from the National Science Foundation, under its Digital Libraries 2 Initiative, enabled enhancement of the audio collection effort. Additional and substantial support also came from Northwestern University Libraries, Northwestern's Weinberg College of Art and Sciences, the M. R. Bauer Foundation, Findlaw, and the law firm of Mayer, Brown, Rowe & Maw.

Today, The OYEZ Project provides access to more than 2,000 hours of Supreme Court audio. All audio in the Court recorded since 1995 is included in the project. Before 1995, the audio collection is selective. It remains the OVEZ aim to create a complete and authoritative archive of Supreme Court audio covering the entire span from October 1955 through the most recent release.

Fedworld:
www.fedworld.gov/supcourt
Another useful research tool for searching Supreme Court cases is at Fedworld, where you can search for cases using keywords. Information is included on 7,407 cases from 1937 to 1975. Decisions are available as ASCII text files that can be read on your browser's screen or saved to your hard drive and accessed by using most word processor programs.

Federal Judicial Center:
www.fjc.gov
Includes helpful information about our Judicial system and all the key players in that system. Click on the "Federal judicial history" link to find the following informational links:

◆ **Judges of the United States Courts** provides access to the Federal Judges Biographical Database, which contains entries for more than 2,800 individuals who have served as district, circuit, and appellate federal judges, as well as Supreme Court justices. The record for each judge includes information on the nomination and confirmation process, service on the federal courts, and educational and professional experience. A detailed description of the compilation and use of the biographical database is available. This section also includes a description of bankruptcy and magistrate judgeships, a list of milestones of judicial service, and a list of judicial impeachments.

◆ **Courts of the Federal Judiciary** contains a legislative history for every district court, circuit court, and court of appeals, as well as the Supreme Court. You can also find a chronological list of judges who served on these courts. Information on the official records and published histories available for the courts provide access to further research sources. Other entries describe the history of the judiciary's courts of special jurisdiction.

◆ **Landmark Judicial Legislation** presents the texts of 21 statutes related to the organization and jurisdiction of the federal judiciary, from the Judiciary Act of 1789 to the establishment of the Federal Circuit in 1982. The entries include brief historical notes on each statute and, when available, suggestions for further reading.

◆ **Judicial Administration and Organization** describes the history of the federal judicial circuits, the administrative agencies or departments that have served the judiciary, and the court officers and staff positions. It includes lists of members of the Judicial Conference of the United States, the U.S. Sentencing Commission, the directors and board of the Federal Judicial Center, and the directors of the Administrative Office of the U.S. Courts.

◆ **Historic Courthouse Photograph Exhibit** is an expanded, online version of an exhibit on display at the Federal Judicial Center. It includes photographs of 35 courthouses constructed under the direction of the Office of the Supervising Architect of the Department of the Treasury between 1852 and 1939. The original photographs are now in the collection of the Still Pictures Branch of the National Archives and Records Administration. Each photograph is accompanied by a description of the building and its use by the United States courts.

◆ **Judicial History News** describes current activities of court historical programs in the federal judiciary and describes recent publications related to the history of the federal courts.

◆ *Amistad*: **The Federal Courts and the Challenge to Slavery** explores the Amistad case, which is one of the most famous slave cases.

There are also links to other Internet sites related to publications from the Federal Judicial Center and to the history of the federal judiciary. Users may also contact the Federal Judicial History Office at the FJC with any questions or comments related to the history of the federal courts.

Constitution Society:
www.constitution.org
The Constitution Society is a private non-profit organization dedicated to research and public education on the principles of constitutional republican government. It publishes documentation, engages in litigation, and organizes local citizens' groups to work for reform.

Washington Post:
www.washingtonpost.com/wp-dyn/nation/courts/supremecourt
You can keep up-to-date on Supreme Court activities by linking to this special page of the *Washington Post*. When the Court is in session, you can usually find new stories at this site.

Law.com:
http://dictionary.law.com
This site features an excellent legal dictionary.

Books

Nearly two thousand books have been written about the Supreme Court and its decisions. Most of them focus either on a particular justice or on a particular issue. Here are some of the top, more general books about the court.

Abraham, Henry J. *Justices, Presidents, and Senators: A History of the U.S. Supreme Court Appointments from Washington to Clinton.* Lanham, Maryland: Rowman and Littlefield Publishing, 1999.

Abraham is one of the nation's leading scholars of the judicial branch. In this book he gives a comprehensive history of the selection of the first 108 justices to serve on the Supreme Court. He also talks about why justices were nominated and discusses some of the nominees who never made it to the court.

Day O'Connor, Sandra. *The Majesty of the Law: Reflections of a Supreme Court Justice.* New York: Random House, 2003.

Presents her view of the U.S. legal system, starting with the Magna Carta and working up to today's system. She also discusses key cases related to states' rights and legal rights related to women's issues.

Hall, Kermit L. and James W. Ely with editors Joel B. Grossman and William M. Wiecek. *The Oxford Companion to the Supreme Court of the United States.* England: Oxford Press, 1992.

This book is one of the most thorough reference books published about the Supreme Court, with brief defining entries and longer essays by almost 300 contributors including lawyers, judges, scholars, and journalists. The book is arranged alphabetically with entries that cover the internal operations and history of the Court; biographical information on all of the justices plus other relevant historical figures; definitions of basic legal and constitutional terminology; and the process of selecting, nominating, and confirming justices. There are also brief writeups of key cases.

Irons, Peter H. *A People's History of the Supreme Court*. New York: Penguin USA, 2000.

This book focuses on the Court from the perspective of the people impacted by the cases.

Rehnquist, Chief Justice William H. *The Supreme Court*. New York: Vintage Books, 2002.

Rehnquist gives the reader a unique behind-the-scenes look at what happens at the Supreme Court. Rehnquist also reviews key Supreme Court landmark decisions.

Schwartz, Bernard. *A History of the Supreme Court*. England: Oxford University Press, 1995.

Schwartz does an excellent job of discussing the history of how the Supreme Court was built into the institution it is today. He starts with explaining the legal thinking of America's founding fathers in designing the Court and follows the Court through the term of Chief Justice Burger. Schwartz also has special chapters on four of the Court's most controversial cases: *Dred Scott* v. *Sandford*, *Lochner* v. *New York*, *Brown* v. *Board of Education*, and *Roe* v. *Wade*.

Supreme Court Justices and Circuit Courts

Here are the courts within each circuit and the Supreme Court justices assigned to that circuit.

1st Circuit—David H. Souter

Court of Appeals

Maine Bankruptcy Court

Maine District Court

Massachusetts Bankruptcy Court

Massachusetts District Court

New Hampshire Bankruptcy Court

New Hampshire District Court

Puerto Rico Bankruptcy Court

Puerto Rico District Court

Puerto Rico Pretrial Services Office

Puerto Rico Probation Office

Rhode Island Bankruptcy Court

Rhode Island District Court

2nd Circuit–Ruth Bader Ginsburg

Connecticut Bankruptcy Court

Connecticut District Court

Court of Appeals

New York Eastern Bankruptcy Court

New York Eastern District Court

New York Northern Bankruptcy Court

New York Northern District Court

New York Southern Bankruptcy Court

New York Southern District Court

New York Western Bankruptcy Court

New York Western District Court

Vermont Bankruptcy Court

Vermont District Court

3rd Circuit–David H. Souter

Court of Appeals

Delaware Bankruptcy Court

Delaware District Court

New Jersey Bankruptcy Court

New Jersey District Court

New Jersey Pretrial Services

Pennsylvania Eastern Bankruptcy Court

Pennsylvania Eastern District Court

Pennsylvania Middle Bankruptcy Court

Pennsylvania Middle District Court

Pennsylvania Western Bankruptcy Court

Pennsylvania Western District Court

Virgin Islands District Court

4th Circuit—William H. Rehnquist

Court of Appeals

Maryland Bankruptcy Court

Maryland District Court

North Carolina Eastern Bankruptcy Court

North Carolina Eastern District Court

North Carolina Middle Bankruptcy Court

North Carolina Middle District Court

North Carolina Western Bankruptcy Court

North Carolina Western District Court

South Carolina Bankruptcy Court

South Carolina District Court

Virginia Eastern Bankruptcy Court

Virginia Eastern District Court

Virginia Eastern Pretrial Services Office

Virginia Western Bankruptcy Court

Virginia Western District Court

West Virginia Northern Bankruptcy Court

West Virginia Northern District Court

West Virginia Southern Bankruptcy Court

West Virginia Southern District Court

West Virginia Southern Probation Office

5th Circuit–Antonin Scalia

Court of Appeals

Louisiana Eastern Bankruptcy Court

Louisiana Eastern District Court

Louisiana Eastern Pretrial Services Office

Louisiana Eastern Probation Office

Louisiana Middle Bankruptcy Court

Louisiana Middle District Court

Louisiana Western Bankruptcy Court

Louisiana Western District Court

Mississippi Northern Bankruptcy Court

Mississippi Northern District Court

Mississippi Southern Bankruptcy Court

Mississippi Southern District Court

Texas Eastern Bankruptcy Court

Texas Eastern District Court

Texas Eastern Probation Office

Texas Northern Bankruptcy Court

Texas Northern District Court

Texas Southern District/Bankruptcy Courts

Texas Western Bankruptcy Court

Texas Western District Court

6th Circuit–John Paul Stevens

Court of Appeals

Federal Magistrate Judges Secretaries Association

Kentucky Eastern Bankruptcy Court

Kentucky Eastern District Court

Kentucky Western Bankruptcy Court

Kentucky Western District Court

Kentucky Western Probation Office

Michigan Eastern Bankruptcy Court

Michigan Eastern District

Michigan Eastern Probation Office

Michigan Western Bankruptcy Court

Michigan Western District Court

Ohio Northern Bankruptcy Court

Ohio Northern District Court

Ohio Southern Bankruptcy Court

Ohio Southern District Court

Ohio Southern Probation Office

Tennessee Eastern Bankruptcy Court

Tennessee Eastern District Court

Tennessee Middle Bankruptcy Court

Tennessee Middle District Court

Tennessee Middle Probation and Pretrial Services Office

Tennessee Western Bankruptcy Court

Tennessee Western District Court

Tennessee Western Probation Office

7th Circuit–John Paul Stevens

Court of Appeals

Illinois Central Bankruptcy Court

Illinois Central District Court

Illinois Northern Bankruptcy Court

Illinois Northern District Court

Illinois Southern Bankruptcy Court

Illinois Southern District Court

Illinois Southern Probation Office

Indiana Northern Bankruptcy Court

Indiana Northern District Court

Indiana Northern Probation and Pretrial Services Office

Indiana Southern Bankruptcy Court

Indiana Southern District Court

Indiana Southern Probation Office

Wisconsin Eastern Bankruptcy Court

Wisconsin Eastern District Court

Wisconsin Western Bankruptcy Court

Wisconsin Western District Court

Wisconsin Western Probation Office

8th Circuit–Clarence Thomas

Arkansas Eastern District Court

Arkansas Eastern and Western Bankruptcy Court

Arkansas Western District Court

Court of Appeals

Iowa Northern Bankruptcy Court

Iowa Northern District Court

Iowa Southern Bankruptcy Court

Iowa Southern District Court

Minnesota Bankruptcy Court

Minnesota District Court

Missouri Eastern Bankruptcy Court

Missouri Eastern District Court

Missouri Eastern Pretrial Services

Missouri Eastern Probation Office

Missouri Western District and Bankruptcy Courts

Nebraska Bankruptcy Court

Nebraska District Court

North Dakota Bankruptcy Court

North Dakota District Court

South Dakota Bankruptcy Court

South Dakota District Court

9th Circuit—Sandra Day O'Connor

Alaska Bankruptcy Court

Alaska District Court

Arizona Bankruptcy Court

Arizona District Court

Bankruptcy Appellate Panel of the Ninth Circuit

California Central Bankruptcy Court

California Central District Court

California Eastern Bankruptcy Court

California Eastern District Court

California Eastern Probation Office

California Northern Bankruptcy Court

California Northern District Court

California Southern Bankruptcy Court

California Southern District Court

California Southern Pretrial Services

California Southern Probation Office

Court of Appeals

Guam District Court

Hawaii Bankruptcy Court

Hawaii District Court

Idaho Bankruptcy/District Court

Montana Bankruptcy Court

Montana District Court

Nevada Bankruptcy Court

Nevada District Court

Northern Mariana Islands District Court

Office of the Circuit Executive

Oregon Bankruptcy Court

Oregon District Court

Washington Eastern Bankruptcy Court

Washington Eastern District Court

Washington Western Bankruptcy Court

Washington Western District Court

10th Circuit–Stephen Breyer

Bankruptcy Appellate Panel of the Tenth Circuit

Colorado Bankruptcy Court

Colorado District Court

Colorado Federal Courts All Units

Court of Appeals

Kansas Bankruptcy Court

Kansas District Court

New Mexico Bankruptcy Court

New Mexico District Court

New Mexico Pretrial Services

New Mexico Probation Office

Oklahoma Eastern Bankruptcy Court

Oklahoma Eastern District Court

Oklahoma Northern Bankruptcy Court

Oklahoma Northern District Court

Oklahoma Western Bankruptcy Court

Oklahoma Western District Court

Utah Bankruptcy Court

Utah District Court

Wyoming Bankruptcy Court

Wyoming District Court

11th Circuit—Anthony Kennedy

Alabama Middle Bankruptcy Court

Alabama Middle District Court

Alabama Northern Bankruptcy Court

Alabama Northern District Court

Alabama Southern Bankruptcy Court

Alabama Southern District Court

Court of Appeals

Florida Middle Bankruptcy Court

Florida Middle District Court

Florida Middle Probation Office

Florida Northern Bankruptcy Court

Florida Northern District Court

Florida Southern Bankruptcy Court

Florida Southern District Court

Georgia Middle Bankruptcy Court

Georgia Middle District Court

Georgia Northern Bankruptcy Court

Georgia Northern District Court

Georgia Southern Bankruptcy Court

Georgia Southern District Court

D.C. Circuit–William Rehnquist

D.C. Bankruptcy Court

D.C. Circuit Court of Appeals

D.C. District Court

Federal Public Defender

Federal Circuit–William Rehnquist

U.S. Court of Appeals for the Federal Circuit

Association of Bankruptcy Judicial Assistants

Commission on Structural Alternatives for the Federal Courts

Court of Appeals for Veterans' Claims

Judicial Panel on Multi-District Litigation

Library of Congress

U.S. Court of Appeals for the Armed Forces

U.S. Court of Federal Claims

U.S. Court of International Trade

U.S. Supreme Court

U.S. Tax Court

United States Sentencing Commission

Index